Hiking the Adirondacks

HELP US KEEP THIS GUIDE UP TO DATE

Every effort has been made by the author and editors to make this guide as accurate and useful as possible. However, many things can change after a guide is published—trails are rerouted, regulations change, techniques evolve, facilities come under new management, and so on.

We would appreciate hearing from you concerning your experiences with this guide and how you feel it could be improved and kept up to date. While we may not be able to respond to all comments and suggestions, we'll take them to heart, and we'll also make certain to share them with the author. Please send your comments and suggestions to the following address:

Globe Pequot Press
Reader Response/Editorial Department
P.O. Box 480
Guilford, CT 06437

Or you may e-mail us at: editorial@GlobePequot.com

Thanks for your input, and happy trails!

Hiking the Adirondacks

A Guide to 42 of the Best Hiking Adventures
in New York's Adirondacks

Lisa Densmore

FALCONGUIDES

GUILFORD, CONNECTICUT
HELENA, MONTANA

AN IMPRINT OF GLOBE PEQUOT PRESS

For Jack, who makes even the muddiest slog a joy to hike and who makes me a better photographer and writer with every mountain we explore together

To buy books in quantity for corporate use or incentives, call **(800) 962–0973** or e-mail **premiums@GlobePequot.com.**

FALCONGUIDES®

Copyright © 2010 by Morris Book Publishing, LLC

ALL RIGHTS RESERVED. No part of this book may be reproduced or transmitted in any form by any means, electronic or mechanical, including photocopying and recording, or by any information storage and retrieval system, except as may be expressly permitted in writing from the publisher. Requests for permission should be addressed to Globe Pequot Press, Attn: Rights and Permissions Department, P.O. Box 480, Guilford CT 06437.

FalconGuides is an imprint of Globe Pequot Press.
Falcon, FalconGuides, and Outfit Your Mind are registered trademarks of Morris Book Publishing, LLC.

Interior photos by Lisa Densmore
Maps by Hartdale Maps © Morris Book Publishing LLC
Project editor: Julie Marsh
Layout artist: Kevin Mak

Library of Congress Cataloging-in-Publication Data
Densmore, Lisa Feinberg.
  Hiking the Adirondacks : a guide to 42 of the region's greatest hiking adventures / Lisa Densmore.
    p. cm.
  Includes index.
  ISBN 978-0-7627-4524-1
  1. Hiking–New York (State)–Adirondack Mountains–Guidebooks. 2. Trails–New York (State)–Adirondack Mountains–Guidebooks. 3. Adirondack Mountains (N.Y.)–Guidebooks. I. Title.
  GV199.42.N652D46 2010
  917.47'53–dc22
                              2010001423

Printed in the United States of America

10 9 8 7 6 5 4 3 2 1

Contents

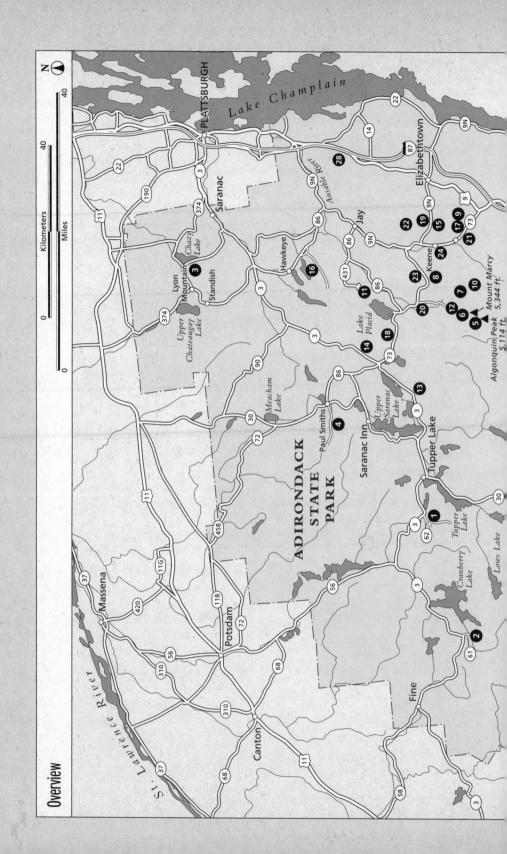

Overview

N

Kilometers

Miles

St. Lawrence River

Massena

Potsdam

Canton

Fine

ADIRONDACK STATE PARK

PLATTSBURGH

Lake Champlain

Saranac

Lyon Mountain

Standish

Upper Chateaugay Lake

Chazy Lake

Paul Smiths

Saranac Inn

Meacham Lake

Hawkeye

Lake Placid

Saranac

Upper Saranac Lake

Tupper Lake

Cranberry Lake

Lows Lake

Ausable River

Jay

Keene

Elizabethtown

Mount Marcy 5,344 ft.

Algonquin Peak 5,114 ft.

ACKNOWLEDGMENTS

Writing a guidebook is really an excuse for adventure—forty-two adventures in this case, from summer 2007 through fall 2008. But each step along the trail would have been much more challenging and only half as fulfilling without the valuable insights and opinions of the many people who helped me with this project.

I am often asked to name my favorite hikes in the Adirondacks. My favorites are not due to the nuances of the trail or the views—they are exceptional because of the friends and family who accompanied me on the trail: Jason Densmore; my son Parker Densmore, age eleven, who made it to the top of Mount Marcy, along with his cousin Hannah Feinberg; Hannah's brother Palmer Feinberg, who has an uncanny knack for spotting newts and frogs along the trail; Phil Brown, editor of *Adirondack Explorer,* who showed me Nun-da-ga-o, slid down Pitchoff with me, and gave me his valuable opinions on where *not* to hike; my brother Wayne, who miraculously agreed to hike up Mount Baker even though he's allergic to hiking; my dear friend Liz Venesky, who celebrated her newly minted nursing degree with her first-ever backpacking trip; my friend and colleague Peggy Shinn, who is now ready for bigger peaks in exotic places; Andrea Varano, a student from North Country Community College, who assisted me (for credit) one fine autumn day; Joseph Busch and Anthony Salomon, who I met at the trailhead for Pharaoh Mountain, my last hike for this book, and who made climbing Pharaoh one of the most entertaining and memorable hikes of all; and most specially Jack Ballard, who accompanied me on 30 percent of the hikes in this book, quite a feat considering he lives in Montana! Thank you to all of these special people who shared the mud, the bugs, the spectacular views, and many smiles with me.

There are others to whom I owe my sincerest gratitude, particularly Peter Sachs at Lowa (footwear and X Socks), Lindy Speizer at Leki (trekking poles), and Gary Fleming at Lowe Alpine (backpacks). Thank you for your moral support, sense of humor, and for helping to outfit me for my endless hours on the trail. You've made my life much more comfortable!

And last but certainly not least, I would like to thank the New York State Department of Environmental Conservation and the Adirondack Mountain Club for their maintenance of the many paths I followed and for reviewing portions of this book's text.

INTRODUCTION

Human History of the Adirondacks

The commonly accepted origin of the name "Adirondack" is from the Iroquois word "ha-de-*ron*-dah," which means "bark eater." The Iroquois who traveled into the Adirondacks in late prehistoric times to hunt, fish, and gather plants called the Algonquins "bark eaters" as an insult. The Mohawk, one of the six Iroquois nations, had a similar word, "ratirondacks," which also translated to "they eat trees." The Algonquins and the Mohawks were likely the first to live in the region shortly after the last ice age, about 10,000 years ago, on the west side of Lake Champlain.

The first European to see the Adirondacks was likely Samuel de Champlain, who in 1609 sailed up the Saint Lawrence River to the north of today's Adirondack Park and the "Riviere de Iroquois" near what would become the location of Ticonderoga on the northern tip of Lake George. By the mid-1700s Ticonderoga and the eastern edge of the Adirondacks were of strategic military importance. In 1758 the British captured "Carillon," a fort built by the French, and renamed it Fort Ticonderoga in an important battle during the French and Indian War. Seventeen years later the Americans claimed an early victory during the Revolutionary War, capturing Fort Ticonderoga and Crown Point. Cannons from here then were used to drive the British out of Boston.

By the late 1700s opportunities for iron ore and logging enticed people into the interior of the Adirondacks, though serious exploration of the region did not occur for another hundred years. In 1883 the state of New York commissioned Verplanck Colvin to survey and map the Adirondack wilderness. Around this same time, the public began to romanticize wilderness areas. Writers such as Henry David Thoreau and Ralph Waldo Emerson and painters such as Frederic Remington, who canoed the Oswegatchie River, and William James Stillman, who spent the summer of 1857 near Raquette Lake, portrayed the region as one of untouched beauty and serenity, which in turn triggered an influx of tourism. Over 200 hotels sprang up, and the wealthiest built many of the Adirondack "Great Camps" during this heyday. Also in the latter half of the nineteenth century, Dr. Edward Livingston Trudeau, ill with tuberculosis, moved to Saranac Lake. In 1884 he founded a sanatorium and laboratory for the study and treatment of the disease, which attracted tuberculosis patients from all over the world in need of "fresh air and complete bed rest." Today the "cure cottages" remain, though now as private homes in this part of the High Peaks region.

Dismayed by over-logging and intense human intrusion into the pristine Adirondacks, Colvin urged the state of New York to create a forest preserve to protect the area as a water source for the Erie Canal, which was an important part of the state's

◀ *Abandoned logging equipment on the High Falls Loop (Hike 2)*

economy at the time. In 1885 the state created the Adirondack Forest Preserve, followed in 1892 by the Adirondack Park, which was integrated into New York's constitution, which states:

The lands of the State . . . shall forever be kept as wild forest lands. They shall not be leased, sold or exchanged, nor shall timber thereon be sold, removed or destroyed.

The Adirondack Forest Preserve and Park were later used as a model for the National Wilderness Act of 1964.

Though there are expansive tracts of designated wilderness within the Adirondacks, it is really a patchwork of public and private lands. The economy of the Adirondacks remains dependent on tourism, logging, and mining. About 130,000 people reside within the park in 105 towns, villages, and hamlets. Another 100,000 visitors come to the area each year. About 52 percent of the land is privately owned, though the Adirondack Park Agency (APA) controls the extent to which humans can modify even private land within the park. Growth is allowed primarily within existing communities and where roads, utilities, and other services already exist, leaving wilderness areas forever wild.

Geology

There are over one hundred peaks in the Adirondack Mountains, forty-six of them over 4,000 feet, with Mount Marcy the highest, at 5,344 feet. Although the Adirondack Mountains have a reputation as one of the oldest mountain ranges in the world,

Exposed rock in the alpine zone on Mount Marcy (Hike 6)

they are neither a mountain range nor old. They are a geologic dome consisting of numerous groups of mountains and individual peaks, 160 miles wide and 1 mile high. They are considerably active, rising 1 to 3 millimeters per year, which exceeds their rate of erosion. You might think the Northeast is geologically stable, but earthquakes in the Adirondacks have exceeded 5 on the Richter scale, and tremors, though uncommon, can be felt on occasion.

While the rocks of the Adirondacks are indeed ancient, over 1,000 million years old, they pushed up into mountains a mere five million years ago, rather youthful in geologic terms. The High Peaks are mainly anorthosite, an igneous rock that intrudes through a broad shelf of metamorphic rock. Gneiss is the primary rock under the rest of the region. The Adirondacks are at the southernmost end of the Canadian Shield, which includes eastern and northern Canada and Greenland. Though geographers include the Adirondacks within the Appalachian chain, geologically they are really part of the Canadian Laurentians, which lie to the north across the Saint Lawrence River.

Wildlife

During the last ice age, glaciers covered all but the highest Adirondack summits. As the ice receded, it carved cirques and valleys and left behind the 1,300 lakes and ponds, 30,000 miles of streams and brooks, and 1,000 miles of rivers that have become intrinsic to the region's rugged appeal. The extensive waterways and accompanying wetlands are perhaps the greatest natural resource within the Adirondacks, providing not only superb hiking destinations but also supporting various species of fish and wildlife. In addition, there are distinct climate zones based on elevation, ranging from temperate to alpine, each supporting a variety of creatures unique to that zone.

The Adirondack Park is home to over fifty species of mammals. While it's uncommon to see animals on hiking trails, signs of them surround you. Hoofprints and scat of whitetail deer are common in the upland forests. Almost every hike outside of the High Peaks area and many within it pass by at least one beaver pond where surrounding trees have been gnawed off to pointed stumps. Black bears are also prevalent. Unfortunately, some have learned that humans carry food. Hanging food is no longer

Beaver lodge (Hike 41)

an accepted option. If you are planning a backpacking trip, you must store your food, toiletries, and trash in a bear canister. The rangers stationed at Adirondak Loj and at the interior outposts will check that you have one. If you don't, you can rent or buy one from the Adirondack Mountain Club and at local camping supply stores.

Over 200 species of birds breed in the Adirondacks. Don't be surprised if you flush a spruce grouse as you hike. You'll likely hear loons calling across a pond long after dark or see a great blue heron wading along a shoreline. Bald eagles and osprey nab small fish in their talons. Sparrows, flycatchers, and chickadees flit from branch to branch in the forest ahead of you. And rare Bicknell's thrush perch among the gnarled krummholz near the top of Whiteface Mountain and some of the other taller summits.

The Adirondacks also harbor a variety of amphibians and snakes. All but one, the timber rattlesnake, are benign. This downsized cousin of the diamondback is a threatened species and is found mainly in the Tongue Mountain Range by Lake George. More likely, your snake encounters will be limited to the occasional garter snake slithering quietly away from you in the grass. The odds are higher that you will step over a newt or see frogs and toads hop off the trail as you approach.

Seasons and Weather

Though locals claim there are two seasons in the Adirondacks, winter and July, the region really has a distinct summer, fall, winter, and spring. It's a humid climate with about 36 inches of precipitation per year.

Summers are short with a growing season less than one hundred days at lower elevations. While temperatures can hit the 90s on occasion, the average summer temperature is 68 degrees Fahrenheit. It's perfect hiking weather, though it's also perfect bug-hatching weather. The black flies from early June through mid-July can be relentless. Don't leave the car without bug spray.

Fall comes quickly after Labor Day with the first frost. It is a favorite season for hiking due to the vibrant foliage and lack of bugs. The wilderness landscape turns from green to a breathtaking red and yellow thanks to the maples, mountain ash, staghorn sumac, birch, and hobblebush in the forest mix. The leaves change first in the High Peaks and northern Adirondacks. Peak color in these two regions usually occurs during the last week of September. Other parts of the park hold their color a week or two longer. Expect ice on the northern side of the taller mountains and be prepared for snow any time after the first week in October.

Adirondack winters are harsh, with snow and ice storms periodically halting wilderness travel. The region is typically among the coldest places in the Lower 48, with temperatures dipping as low as minus 40 degrees Fahrenheit. If you plan a winter hike, be prepared with not only the right clothing but also snowshoes, crampons, and ski poles. Check the weather and avalanche conditions before venturing into the backcountry, particularly in the High Peaks region above tree line.

Mud season—April and May—is the only time of the year to avoid hiking in the

Adirondacks. Snow can linger in the mountains and sheltered valleys until early May. Stay off the trails during mud season for the trails' sake. Many routes climb directly up slopes rather than around switchbacks, making them more susceptible to erosion from foot traffic when conditions are muddy.

Backcountry Safety and Hazards

The Adirondack Mountains may be only a third the elevation of the Rockies, but they are rugged and, like all mountains, susceptible to a change in weather without warning and other hazards. But with a few basic precautions, your time in this expansive, beautiful wilderness area should be nothing but enjoyable.

Always sign in at the registration box by the trailhead. In addition, be sure to let a friend or relative in town know your route and when you plan to return. Then stick to your plan! That way, if you don't return to civilization within a reasonable period of time, others will know where to search for you. Cell phone service is sporadic at best, except around the biggest towns, so do not rely on your phone to call for help.

The maintained trails throughout the Adirondack Park, which are on public land or on public right-of-ways, are marked with circular plastic discs nailed to trees that say "New York State Department of Environmental Conservation (NYSDEC) Foot Trail." They are color-coded. The most obvious exception is in the Adirondack For-

est Preserve in the High Peaks region near St. Huberts. The trail marks within the preserve are similar to the NYSDEC discs but with "ADIS" on them. There are also a number of unmaintained trails throughout the Adirondacks and well-known herd paths up some of the 4,000-footers in the High Peaks, but none of these routes are in this book. If you follow the trail markers and stay on the trail, you are unlikely to get lost.

On broad expanses of rock slab where there are no trees for markers, the route is typically marked by either paint or with rock cairns. The cairns might be very small, only three rocks in an informal pile, so you need to be observant when the trail leaves the trees.

If you do get lost, don't panic. Try to retrace your steps as best you

Trailhead sign-in

can, consulting your map and compass for the right heading. If you have a GPS, retrace along the route it tracked for you. Most likely you only strayed a short distance from the trail before realizing you had left it. The region is heavily forested, so if you begin to bushwhack inadvertently, you'll know it due to the thick trees and undergrowth.

Lightning. Weather poses the biggest hazard in the Adirondacks, particularly lightning. If you hear thunder, assume there's lightning even if you cannot see it. Most of the destinations in this book are bare mountaintops, many with fire towers, which puts you at the high point and the most likely place for a lightning strike. At the slightest hint of a storm, head immediately below tree line to an area where the trees are at least twice as tall as you are. If this is impossible, try to find a low spot where you can hunker down. Even below tree line, avoid using the tallest trees for shelter, and have everyone in your party spread out. Then, if lightning strikes, it singes only one person.

Tree hit by lightning

Wind. It is a rare day when the wind is not blowing on a mountaintop in the Adirondacks. While it usually won't knock you over, it will pull heat out of your body very quickly, especially if you are wet from perspiration or rain. Always carry a fleece or wool sweater, a waterproof, breathable jacket, and a wool hat in your pack, even in July. It might be 75 degrees at the trailhead but only 50 degrees with the wind-chill at the summit. The trick to preventing hypothermia is staying warm and dry.

Rabid animals. Animal encounters are rare during daylight hours. If an animal approaches you, especially if it looks mangy, has foam around its mouth, or acts erratically, it might have rabies. Any animal can get rabies, but raccoons, skunks, bats, and foxes are among the more common carriers of this deadly disease. Grab a long sturdy stick if possible, then immediately depart the area, keeping an eye out for the animal. Rabies is transmitted through saliva and spinal fluid. If the animal follows, use the stick to keep it away. If it bites you and breaks the skin, seek medical attention immediately. If the animal touches you in any way, wash the area thoroughly with soap and water. The rule of thumb is to scrub for twenty minutes! Call the NYSDEC as soon as possible to report the animal.

Bears. There are about 4,000 black bears in the Adirondacks, one of the largest bear populations in the East. The average adult male weighs about 300 pounds. While bears are generally shy, they are omnivorous and opportunists when it comes to food. You might have a chance encounter with a bear, but more likely it will raid your campsite looking for food. Here's how to minimize the risk of a bear attack:

- Hike in a group.
- Hike during daylight hours.
- Make noise, talking or singing as you walk.
- Leave scented toiletries at home.
- Prepare and eat food away from your tent or lean-to.
- Do not clean fish within 100 feet of your campsite.
- Finish eating and clean up thoroughly before sunset.
- Store all food, trash, and scented items in a bear canister and place it overnight at least 100 feet from your campsite.
- Sleep in different clothes than what you wore for cooking and eating.

If you find yourself close to a bear, here are some guidelines:

- Remain calm.
- Do not run, as this might trigger a prey-chase reaction. You cannot outrun a bear, which can sprint at speeds up to 35 miles per hour, and it can climb a tree much more efficiently than you can.
- Talk calmly in a low voice, which tells the bear you are human.
- Hold your arms out to the side, or open your jacket and hold it out to appear larger.
- Do not make direct eye contact. Bears perceive eye contact as a threat or a challenge.
- Slowly move upwind of the bear if you can do so without crowding it. If the bear smells you as human, it might retreat.
- If the bear charges or bluffs a charge, which is usually a precursor to the real thing, fight back by kicking or punching. If it perceives you as difficult prey, it might depart in search of an easier meal.

Bear track in mud

- If a bear gets into your food or shelter, do not try to drive it away. Bears become aggressive when defending a food source.

Moose. After many mooseless decades, moose have begun to migrate into the Adirondacks from Canada and New England in recent years. The state estimates about 500 moose in the region as this book goes to print, though biologists believe the area is on the cusp of a moose explosion. They are the largest animals in the park, weighing up to 1,800 pounds. They can move surprisingly fast for their size, charging when provoked, protecting young (springtime), or during the rut (early fall). If a moose blocks the trail, shout loudly to shoo it away. If it does not move, or if it seems aggressive, take a detour around it. If it charges, put a large tree between you and the animal, and then run if you get an opening. A moose will not pursue you very far. It is not a predator, and once the threat (you) is gone, it will usually give up the fight and amble away.

Poison ivy. Poison ivy is the only poison plant in the Adirondacks. It grows below 4,000 feet along the edge of lakes and ponds and on the edge of trails and clearings where it can get sunlight without getting trampled. It can take the form of ground cover or a woody vine. An itchy rash appears on your skin anywhere from two hours to several days after contact with the plant, unless you clean the area thoroughly with soap and water or an alcohol-laden wipe to remove the urushiol oil that causes the rash. You've got a narrow window—from a half hour to two hours—to remove the oil, depending on how sensitive your skin is.

Poison ivy

Giardia lamblia. Although there are thousands of pristine-looking water sources in the Adirondacks, assume they all contain the waterborne parasite *Giardia lamblia,* even running water. This microscopic parasite causes giardiasis, or "beaver fever." The symptoms include nausea and severe diarrhea. To prevent contracting beaver fever, filter or boil all drinking water.

Ticks. Lyme disease has been another growing problem in the Adirondacks over the last ten years. While less of a risk in the High Peaks region, lower, milder areas in the eastern, southern, and western parts of the park harbor deer ticks, which carry the disease. Wear light-colored clothing and long pants and sleeves to see ticks more easily and to lessen the chance of a tick bite. It helps to use a bug spray with tick repellent in it.

Safe hiking practices. Despite this list of potential hazards, the Adirondacks are a relatively safe place to hike if you use common sense and follow three important principals of safe hiking:

1. Hike in a group and stay together. Always hike at the pace of the slowest person.
2. Be self-reliant. Learn about the terrain, the condition of the trail, the weather, and how to use your gear before you start.
3. Know when to turn back. Weather can change suddenly. A route may take longer than expected. You may become fatigued. You can always try again another time.

Backcountry Essentials

What you wear and what you bring in your pack will go a long way toward making your hiking experience in the Adirondacks more enjoyable. For clothing, dress in layers and avoid cotton, which retains moisture and can lead to hypothermia. Bring a waterproof, breathable jacket *every* time you head into the mountains, even if the sky is crystal clear. The weather could change without warning. The cotton rule goes for your socks, too. Socks made from wool or blended synthetic and wool fibers that wick moisture and help cushion and support your feet are not a luxury but a necessity, especially on a high-mileage day.

Your choice of footwear is perhaps most critical when it comes to comfort and stability on uneven, slippery terrain. Hiking boots come with low, mid-length, and high cuffs. The higher the sides and back of the boot, the more ankle support it provides. A mid-length *A hiker's best friends...*

Common water filter

or high boot is recommended if you are carrying over forty pounds, whether the weight is a pack filled with food, water, and gear, or a child carrier. The trails in the Adirondacks are muddy, dotted with wet mossy rocks, and turn into streambeds after a rainstorm. For this reason, no matter how "built" your boot, opt for a Gore-Tex version to keep your feet dry. You'll be glad you did!

With the abundance of water in the Adirondacks, you might think carrying a lot of water into the backcountry foolish, but it's not. Many of the smaller streams along hiking trails dry up by midsummer, and those that remain could carry water-borne illnesses. Carry at least two quarts of water per person per day, or plan to filter it as you go if you are sure of reliable water along the route.

Much of the trail system in the Adirondacks follows original paths blazed by early Native Americans and European settlers. They go directly uphill and directly downhill often rather steeply. Washouts, roots, rocks, and erosion down to bedrock are all common. Consider using hiking poles for more power going uphill, to lessen stress on your joints, for additional stability crossing flooded areas, and for balancing on uneven terrain.

With the exception of the trails that start at the Adirondak Loj, trailhead parking is free. Shelters and tent sites are available on a first-come, first-served basis and are also free. However, if you lay claim to a lean-to for a night, be prepared to share if your group doesn't fill it up.

You do not need a permit before going into the Adirondack Park to hike or camp on state land unless you are planning to stay in one place for more than three days or if your group has more than ten people. Multiday and large-group permits are available through the forest ranger responsible for that area.

Camping is prohibited within 150 feet of roads, trails, and water unless there is a "camp here" marker (a yellow disk with a red tent symbol in the middle). Camping is not allowed above 4,000 feet between December 15 and April 30, though it is generally not advisable to sleep above tree line at any time of the year for safety reasons and to protect the fragile alpine flora.

Most designated campsites and lean-tos have an outhouse and a fire ring. If you are primitive camping at a random place in the woods, bring a small trowel to bury human waste in a cat hole 6 to 8 inches deep, then cover the hole. The hole should be

Fire ring near Middle Settlement Lake (Hike 42)

at least 150 feet from a trail and water. The 150-foot rule goes for soap, too, whether washing your body or your dishes.

A portable camp stove is the preferred method and a more efficient way to cook while camping, but campfires are legal where fire rings exist. If you make a fire, use only dead or downed wood near your campsite, or use purchased firewood harvested in the Adirondacks, so that you don't accidentally bring wood-borne pests and tree diseases into the park. After an evening by a crackling fire, be sure that it is out before leaving it unattended. Only emergency fires are allowed above 4,000 feet.

Not all hiking routes in the Adirondacks are dog-friendly. And not all dogs are hike-ready. Before committing Fifi to a 10-miler, check that the terrain is smooth enough and your dog is fit enough for the route. Many trails in the Adirondacks are simply too rocky for all but the most mountain-savvy canines. Some have steep ladders that are impossible for a dog to negotiate. In this book the hike summary at the beginning of each route tells whether it is dog-friendly. If you bring your four-legged friend, he should be under control at all times and on a leash around other hikers. In the eastern High Peaks, dogs *must* be on a leash at all times. All of the principles of low-impact hiking that apply to people apply to dogs as well.

Zero Impact

While it is impossible to have zero impact as you pass through the Adirondack wilderness, here are some key ways to minimize your impact.

Carry out everything that you carry in. This includes items that you think are biodegradable, like apple cores and orange peels. While they might degrade over a period of time, it can take much longer than you think, depending where you drop them, and they are not native to the ecosystem, which makes them simply ugly litter.

Take only pictures, leave only footprints. Picking a flower may seem harmless, but it could be an endangered species. Likewise, leave wildlife alone both for your safety and their survival.

Stay on the trail. Walking around mud holes may keep your boots drier and cleaner, but it widens the trail over time. In addition, avoid taking shortcuts and cutting corners on switchbacks. It may save a few seconds here and there, but it increases erosion and leaves unsightly scars in the woods. Above tree line it is vital that you stay on the trail, walking on rock as much as possible. Fragile alpine plants grow very slowly, enduring the harsh mountaintop environment, but they cannot withstand trampling.

Camp on durable surfaces. Put your tent on bedrock or compacted dirt. If you must put your tent on live plant life, set it up late and take it down early to minimize the time the plants are compressed.

Diapensia, endangered alpine flower

Be considerate of others. Voices carry, particularly across bodies of water. Try to keep noise to a minimum so that all can enjoy the serenity of the wilderness.

Hiker's Checklist

Here is a basic list of things to put in your pack to ensure you are prepared for a day in the backcountry without weighing you down. This is a fair-weather list. Winter hikers will need additional items, such as a down jacket, gaiters, crampons, gloves, and goggles.

- ❑ Bug spray
- ❑ Rain gear
- ❑ Fleece or wool sweater
- ❑ Wool hat
- ❑ Ball cap
- ❑ Sunscreen
- ❑ Food
- ❑ Water
- ❑ Topographic map
- ❑ Compass
- ❑ First-aid kit
- ❑ Whistle
- ❑ Waterproof matches or a reliable lighter
- ❑ 10+ feet of rope
- ❑ Flashlight or headlamp
- ❑ Swiss Army knife or other multi-tool
- ❑ Bandana or other all-purpose rag
- ❑ Camera

How to Use This Guide

There are over 2,000 miles of trails in the Adirondack Park. It is a hiker's nirvana and too much to cover in one book. The Adirondack Mountain Club crams them into *seven* books. This book cherry-picks the best forty-two routes. Of course, this is subjective, but this guidebook includes many of the classic routes plus a few lesser-known but equally interesting and scenic ones.

This book is divided into the six regions commonly used by the Adirondack Mountain Club: High Peaks, eastern, northern, southern, central, and west-central. Within these regions you'll find hikes of varying lengths and ability levels. No matter where you are and no matter your backcountry experience, you have options. That said, there are many premier hikes that have been omitted in order to get geographic diversity and a selection of easy to challenging routes.

If you are unfamiliar with the Adirondack Park, go to the section of the book that covers the area where you would like to hike and then select the route that best fits your fitness level and hiking goals. Be honest about your fitness level. Bagging a peak over 4,000 feet can require at least half that in vertical gain and over 10 miles of rugged walking and rocky scrambling.

The "Nearest town" given for each hike is for the trailhead, which might be different than the summit. For example, the trailhead for Whiteface Mountain is closest to Lake Placid, though the summit is actually in Wilmington. Also, the word "town" in this context really means a population center that has a name and appears on most road maps. It might be a very small hamlet or a larger village, but in Adirondack vernacular, it is not a town per se. In the Adirondacks, townships are bigger than a village and smaller than a county and usually include more than one village or hamlet. For example, the village of Saranac Lake is in the town of Harrietstown, which also includes the smaller hamlets of Axton Landing, Coreys, Fish Creek, Lake Clear, Lake Colby, McMasters Landing, and Wawbeek.

Distance, elevation gain, and hiking time are given for the entire hike, start to finish, including multiday backpacking trips. In other words, on day two of a three-day trip, the mileage begins where it left off the night before, not at zero. After total mileage each route is listed as an "out-and-back," "loop," "point-to-point," or "lollipop" hike. A "lollipop" hike is a loop hike that retraces 0.5 mile or more from the point between where you close the loop and the trailhead.

Hiking time is a rough estimate that assumes a moderate pace with periodic rest stops and a half hour at the summit and other scenic destinations. The estimate is conservative but is consistent from hike to hike. As you try different routes, you will begin to see how fast or slow your average pace is compared to the estimate and plan accordingly. In addition to overall hiking time, you can gauge your progress by the mileage points given within the description of the route and highlighted separately at the end of the description.

One of the greatest gifts you can give your child is a day in the woods. To ensure that the experience is a positive one, wait for a nice day and then pick a route that matches your child's age and fitness level and that has a big reward, such as a fire tower to climb. The total distance of the hike should equal half your child's age. In other words, if she is six years old, keep the outing at less than 3 miles.

Each hike in this book is rated "easy," "moderate," "strenuous," or "experts only." The rating system takes into account three factors: distance, vertical gain, and terrain. While there is a basic formula for this rating system, e.g., a 10-mile hike would never be considered "easy," it can be a judgment call. A 6-miler might be rated "moderate" if the terrain is relatively smooth and flat. Likewise a 4-miler might be rated "experts only" if there are multiple steep rock chimneys or other difficult obstacles to negotiate. That said, here are the general guidelines for day hikes:

- Easy: Under 4.0 miles round-trip and under 500 vertical feet

- Moderate: 4.0 miles to 7.0 miles round-trip and 500 feet to 1,500 feet vertical gain
- Strenuous: More than 7.0 miles but under 10.0 miles round-trip, and more than 1,500 feet but less than 2,500 feet vertical gain
- Experts only: 10.0 miles or more round-trip, and more than 2,500 feet vertical gain

You will also find an original map for each hike created by GPS, the name of the USGS map that includes the hike, directions to and a GPS waypoint for the trailhead, and a photograph. Every step of every trail was tracked by GPS to ensure the most current portrayal of the route on the maps in this book and the most accurate mileage. In a number of cases, the mileage given in this book might not match a trail sign. Trust the book. Trail signs can be inconsistent and may have been measured years ago by less accurate means. In addition, trails are sometimes rerouted due to washouts, blowdowns, or general wear and tear.

Unlike other FalconGuides, a contact is not given in the specs at the start of each hike description. That's because it's the same two contacts for every hike, the Adirondack Mountain Club and the New York State Department of Environmental Conservation (NYSDEC). The contact information for both is in the appendix at the back of the book. Likewise, seasonality and fees are the same everywhere in the park. The trails are open year-round, although I do not recommend hiking during mud season (early April through mid-May). You will get muddy, the footing can be slick, and the trails are prone to more erosion that time of the year. There are no fees for use of the trails. The only parking fee is at the trailheads by Adirondak Loj.

The goal of this book is to give you all the details of a hike before you go and then guide you through it step by step. That said, every time you venture into the Adirondack Park, you will be treated to a unique adventure. Be safe and enjoy this vast wilderness!

Trail Finder

	Kid-Friendly	Dog-Friendly	Lean-To	Tentsites	Open Rock or Alpine Summit	Lake, Pond	Brook, River	Waterfall	Observatory, Fire Tower
Northern Adirondacks									
1. Mount Arab	•	•			•				•
2. High Falls Loop - Cat Mountain		•	•	•	•	•	•	•	
3. Lyon Mountain	Older kids	•			•				•
4. Saint Regis Mountain	Older kids	•			•				closed
High Peaks: A Sampling of 4,000-footers									
5. Algonquin Peak		Fit dogs	•	•	•	•	•	•	
6. Avalanche Lake - Mount Marcy Loop			•	•	•	•	•	•	
7. Big Slide - Yard Mountain Loop			•	•	•		•		
8. Cascade Mountain	•	•			•				
9. Giant Mountain				•	•	•			
10. Great Range Loop (Gothics, Armstrong, Upper Wolfjaw, Lower Wolfjaw)					•		•	•	
11. Whiteface Mountain		Fit dogs	•		•	•	•		•
12. Wright Peak		Fit dogs	•	•	•	•	•	•	

High Peaks: Lower Peaks with Big Rewards

	Kid-Friendly	Dog-Friendly	Lean-To	Tentsites	Open Rock or Alpine Summit	Lake, Pond	Brook, River	Waterfall	Observatory, Fire Tower
13. Ampersand Mountain	Older kids	•			•				
14. Baker Mountain	•	•			•	•			
15. Baxter Mountain	•	•			•				
16. Catamount Mountain	Older kids				•				
17. Giant's Nubble	Older kids	•		•	•	•			
18. Haystack Mountain (Ray Brook)	Older kids	•			•		•		
19. Hurricane Mountain	Older kids	•			•				closed
20. Mount Jo	•	•			•	•			
21. Noonmark Mountain-Round Mountain Loop					•				
22. Nun-da-ga-o Ridge-Weston Mountain-Lost Pond Loop	Older kids	•	•		•	•			
23. Pitchoff Mountain	Older kids	•			•				
24. Rooster Comb-Snow Mountain Loop	Older kids	•			•				

	Kid-Friendly	Dog-Friendly	Lean-To	Tentsites	Open Rock or Alpine Summit	Lake, Pond	Brook, River	Waterfall	Observatory, Fire Tower
Eastern Adirondacks									
25. Black Mountain	Older kids	•			•				
26. Buck Mountain	Older kids	•			•				
27. Pharaoh Mountain	Older kids	•			•	•			
28. Poke-O-Moonshine	•	•		•	•				•
29. Tongue Mountain Loop				•		•			
Southern Adirondacks									
30. Crane Mountain-Crane Pond Loop	•			•	•	•			
31. Echo Cliff	•	•			•				
32. Hadley Mountain	•	•			•				•
33. Kane Mountain	•	•			•				•
Central Adirondacks									
34. Blue Mountain	•	•			•				•
35. Goodnow Mountain	•	•			•		•		•
36. Snowy Mountain		•							•

	Kid-Friendly	Dog-Friendly	Lean-To	Tentsites	Open Rock or Alpine Summit	Lake, Pond	Brook, River	Waterfall	Observatory, Fire Tower
37. Vanderwhacker Mountain	Older kids	•			•	•			•
38. Wakely Mountain	Older kids	•							•
Western Central Adirondacks									
39. Bald Mountain - Rondaxe	•	•			•				•
40. Black Bear Mountain	•				•				
41. Gleasman's Falls	Older kids	•		•	•		•	•	
42. Middle Settlement Lake	Older kids	•	•	•	•	•			

Map Legend

Transportation

Interstate Highway	87
U.S. Highway	8
State Road	3
County/Forest Road	CR 1 — FR 1
Unpaved Road	=====
Railroad	+—+—+
Featured Trail	--------
Featured Trail on Road	═══════
Other Trail	- - - - - -

Hydrology

Lake/Large River	
River/Stream	
Marsh/Swamp	
Waterfall	

Land Use

National Park	

Symbols

Boat Ramp	
Bridge	
Campground	▲
City/Town	○
Gap/Pass	
Gate	•—•
Headquarters	
Lodging	
Mountain/Peak	▲
Parking	P
Picnic Area	
Point of Interest	■
Primitive Campsite	▲
Restroom/Latrine	
Scenic View	
Shelter	
Tower	
Trailhead (Start)	11

Northern Adirondacks

The northern section encompasses all of the Adirondack Park north and west of NY 3 to Coreys at the southern tip of Upper Saranac Lake. From Coreys, it continues south along the edge of the High Peaks Wilderness to Long Lake and then along NY 30 to Blue Mountain Lake. From there, the boundary cuts directly west to Stillwater Reservoir and the western edge of the Adirondack Park. The villages of Tupper Lake, Star Lake, and Cranberry Lake, and lakes of the same names, lie within the region. It also includes Paul Smiths and the popular Saint Regis Canoe Area.

The farther you go in the northern Adirondacks away from the center of the Adirondack Park, the flatter the land becomes. This region is better known for its extensive canoeing and fishing routes than its hiking trails. Many of the maintained trails are canoe carries or access trails to the myriad of area lakes, ponds, and rivers. While the region does not have the dramatic topography nor the multitude of bare summits found in other parts of the Adirondack Park, there are several interesting peaks to climb, including Lyon, Arab, Saint Regis, and Cat Mountains, which are described in this book. Lyon Mountain near Dannemora is the highest at 3,830 feet. The other mountains in the region are under 3,000 feet, though the views are still superb from atop a fire tower or a bald cliffy perch.

There are a few things to keep in mind when venturing into the northern Adirondacks. The region is remote and susceptible to some of the worst winter weather in the park. During the winter, the temperature can dip to minus 40 degrees Fahrenheit, and the snow can be exceptionally deep snow due to lake-effect storms off the Great Lakes. On the bright side, poison ivy and ticks carrying Lyme disease cannot survive here. You'll find few people on the trails yet many waterside destinations.

Be aware that this is a popular area for hunting bear and deer in the fall. Sport hunting is permitted on all public land within the Adirondack Park, so it's a good idea to wear brightly colored clothing if you are hiking here from mid-September through December 31.

The biggest hazard to hikers is death by mosquito. Not really, but the insect population thrives on the abundance of water in the region. Some people wear bug netting, but a ball cap and a coating of bug spray with 30 percent DEET is usually enough to deter the swarm and maintain mental sanity.

View of Chazy Lake from the fire tower atop Lyon Mountain (Hike 3)

1 Mount Arab

A short, kid-friendly hike to a restored fire tower, with lake views in every direction.

Nearest town: Mount Arab
Total distance: 2.0 miles, out and back
Highest point: 2,533 feet
Vertical gain: 760 feet

Approximate hiking time: 2.5 hours
Difficulty: Easy
Canine compatibility: Dog-friendly
Map: USGS Piercefield Quad

Finding the trailhead: In Tupper Lake, from the junction of NY 3 and NY 30, take NY 3 west for 6.9 miles to Piercefield. Bear left in Piercefield on St. Lawrence CR 62, following the sign to Mount Arab (the hamlet). Go 1.8 miles. Turn left on Mount Arab Road. Go 0.8 mile to the trailhead, on the left. Trailhead parking is on the right. Trailhead: N44 12.819' / W74 35.754'

The Hike

Mount Arab is a perfect hike for young children and other inexperienced hikers. There is a big reward—climbing the fire tower—for relatively little effort, as the rate of ascent ranges from hardly detectable to moderate. One eight-year-old rated the hike a 9 out of 10, deducting one point because he got a couple of bug bites and because there were a few slippery spots.

In the fire tower on Mount Arab

Swamp dewberry on Mount Arab

The trail begins on a state conservation easement called the Conifer Easement Lands. Following the red NYSDEC markers, the smooth path heads up a steady incline through a mixed hardwood forest. The undergrowth is lush, with grass, ferns, and various shrubs, including wild raspberries, under the airy canopy. At 0.3 mile the incline mellows as it crosses into the Adirondack Preserve. Don't be startled if you flush a couple of grouse walking through this classic upland habitat.

The route soon turns up again, though nothing extreme, as it crosses intermittent lengths of slab. In late spring trillium poke their tri-petalled flowers toward the sky along this section of trail. The path continues to climb, helped by a few rock steps. The trail is older and more worn in this area, but the footing is still good and soon becomes smooth again as you head up a steeper section of the slope.

At 0.5 mile the trail crosses a small shoulder of the mountain where grass grows along the side of the trail. The canopy, though not clear to the sky, is more open here, and there are berry bushes, so beware of prickers.

The trees soon thicken again, but not enough to block a glimpse of neighboring Wheeler, Buck, and Haystack Mountains to the left (southwest) just before you cross a wet area on short lengths of logs embedded in the trail.

At about 0.7 mile the trail climbs moderately, passing a rock outcropping, which forms a pretty, moss-covered wall on your left. Then the trail flattens as it goes around a large boulder. Views to the southeast open to the right through the scrubby maples and sumac.

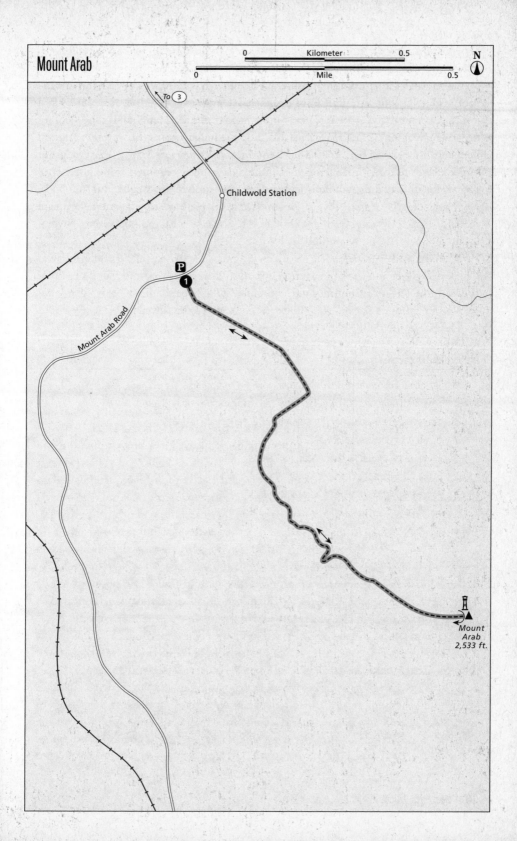

Mount Arab

To ③

Childwold Station

Mount Arab Road

Mount Arab 2,533 ft.

The trail makes a half-circle to the northeast before bending to the right, returning to its original southeasterly direction. At 0.9 mile the trail heads up a rise and comes to a short steep section of slab. You can either go up the slab or take the switchback around it. The summit is just beyond at 1.0 mile.

The former fire-watcher's cabin is at the edge of the summit clearing, the result of fires many years ago. The fire tower stands atop the high point of the rock slab. It stood in disrepair for a number of years until the Friends of Mount Arab, a local nonprofit organization, restored it. Though the summit clearing is hemmed in by red spruce and mountain ash, there is a 360-degree view from atop the tower. Mount Arab Lake and Eagle Crag Lake are below to the southwest. Tupper Lake and Raquette Pond are the large bodies of water dotted with islands to the east, with the High Peaks beyond in the distance. Mount Matumbla stands due north.

There is a lot of open rock for picnicking around the tower. A garden of wild blueberries, Queen Anne's lace, buttercup, and Indian paintbrush surround the cabin in late June. The true summit, with its telltale USGS benchmark—a circular brass disc—is on an open flat bit of bedrock to the north of the tower.

Return to the trailhead by the same route.

Miles and Directions

0.0 Trailhead. Follow the red NYSDEC markers up a smooth rise.

0.3 Enter into Adirondack Forest Preserve, traversing through upland forest.

0.5 Cross a small shoulder of the mountain. The canopy thins briefly.

0.7 Climb past a mossy rock wall.

0.9 Go up or go around a short steep rock slab.

1.0 SUMMIT! Climb the fire tower. Return by same route.

2.0 Arrive back at the trailhead and parking lot.

Adirondack Fire Towers

Many of the mountains in the Adirondacks still have fire towers on their summits or were the sites of former fire towers and now only their footings remain. Many of the surviving towers are open for hikers to climb, and the 360-degree views are truly incredible. Some towers that are still standing are closed. The lower steps have been removed because the towers are no longer safe to ascend.

Fire towers played an important role during the early and mid-twentieth century in the detection of forest fires. Lightning has ignited fires in the Adirondacks since the beginning of time. Then, as the railroads came through in the late 1800s, sparks from the locomotive engines increased the number of fires, especially when they passed through areas of heavy logging activity. At the same time, towns grew up and tourism increased, putting more people and property at risk. In 1903 and again in 1908, two exceptionally devastating forest fires burned through the Adirondack Park, pressuring the state to create a warning-and-containment system to keep future fires away from population centers.

At first, fire-watchers used crude log scaffolding with an open platform on top. By 1920 the state replaced most of these tenuous log structures with the steel scaffolding and metal cabins, some up to 70 feet high, that survive today. By the early 1970s light aircraft took over as the method of choice for monitoring forest fires. The fire towers became obsolete, at least for fire watching, but remain popular destinations for hikers.

Fire tower on Mount Arab

2 High Falls-Cat Mountain Loop

A pleasant three-day backpacking trip with two waterfront campsites, one by the legendary Oswegatchie River and the other by Cranberry Lake, plus an expansive view from atop Cat Mountain.

Nearest town: Wanakena
Total distance: 20.2 miles, loop with out and back up Cat Mountain
Highest point: 2,267 feet (summit of Cat Mountain)
Vertical gain: 640 feet

Approximate hiking time: 3 days/2 nights
Difficulty: Moderate
Canine compatibility: Dog-friendly
Maps: USGS Newton Falls Quad (trailhead, High Falls); USGS Wolf Mountain Quad (Cat Mountain)

Finding the trailhead: From the village of Cranberry Lake, travel west on NY 3 to the Wanakena turnoff. Turn left (south) on CR 61. Go 0.8 mile. Bear right at the fork and the sign reading WANAKENA, EST. 1902. Go 0.4 mile. Bear right again at the next fork, over a metal bridge, ignoring the dead end sign. Go 0.1 mile. A NYSDEC sign points the way to the trailhead up a driveway-like road on the right. Trailhead parking is just beyond the sign. There's also parking on the right past the Wanakena community tennis courts. Trailhead: N44 07.863' / W74 55.365'

The Hike

The High Falls Loop and the side trip to Cat Mountain lie in the heart of the Five Ponds Wilderness. Few trails penetrate this remote area, which is known for its frequently flooded beaver ponds; fishing on the Oswegatchie River; and High Falls, where the meandering Oswegatchie briefly becomes a torrent as it crashes down a broad rock ledge. You'll spend your last night by Cranberry Lake, the third-largest lake in the park (7,040 acres of water) and one of the least populated. By midsummer both the river and the lake warm into the 70s Fahrenheit, which makes for a refreshing swim at the end of a day on the trail. This is also one of the easiest backpacking trips in the Adirondacks because the route has little vertical gain. Even the climb up Cat Mountain on the last morning is modest, under 500 vertical feet, and you can do it without your pack.

Day One: Wanakena to High Rock

From the parking area, the route begins on a short paved road that ends at a stop sign by a metal gate. Walk around the gate, continuing down the grassy road along Skate Creek, following the red NYSDEC markers. The road was originally a railroad bed. Built in 1902, the Rich Lumber Company used the railroad for about ten years to transport timber out of the forest. A couple of curious antique logging apparatuses lie rusting farther down the trail as evidence of the abandoned lumber operation.

The state acquired the land in 1919 and then upgraded the railroad bed to a truck trail in the 1930s. Today it is known as the Wanakena Primitive Corridor and is limited to foot traffic. It's easy to imagine a railroad where you are walking. The grade is level through a corridor about as wide as a railroad bed. The trail passes between a number of berms that allow the route to cut through, rather than go over, some minor rises in the land, and it is unnaturally straight. Yet nature has encroached on the path in many ways. In midsummer the corridor is a wildflower garden, with yellow buttercups, orange jewelweed, white Queen Anne's lace, and blue chicory among the colorful display. There are also enough wild blueberries in the first mile to make ten pies.

At 3.7 miles you reach the spur to High Rock. Bear right and go the short 0.1 mile to an obvious

Pearly Everlasting, one of the many wildflowers along the Wanakena Primitive Corridor

clearing and fire ring. This is your first campsite, and it's a special one. High Rock is literally a gigantic boulder partially embedded in the earth. From it, you can see a long stretch of the Oswegatchie River to the north. The Onondaga Indians who once lived in this area named the Oswegatchie, which means "black river." The water is indeed very dark due to a high level of natural tannins, but it is considered one of the cleanest rivers in the state. The other accepted translation of the name is "going around the hill," which from this point is apparent, as the river bends gently around High Rock.

For a view to the south, you need to walk down the rock toward the water. The view is not mountainous, but it's beautiful just the same, mainly of the expansive wetlands and the river, which braids and winds across the open valley. The best access to the water for fishing and swimming is via a short path from the tent site.

Day Two: High Rock to Janack's Landing

On day two return to the High Falls Trail at 3.9 miles (from the trailhead). Turn right, heading southeast toward High Falls. At 4.2 miles the trail crosses an old stone railroad bridge with a pretty cascade flowing down the smooth broad rock on your left.

In general the path is hemmed in by ferns and tall grass as it cuts through the forest, though the trees soon open up as you pass by the first of four beaver ponds en route to High Falls.

Few people hike to High Rock and even fewer go beyond it on this loop. Scars to the forest in this area are mainly due to Mother Nature. Over the years there have been several violent wind storms. At 6.0 miles the trail passes evidence of the last major blowdown, which occurred in 1995 and required a mammoth effort to reopen the route you now trek.

Backpacker on flooded trail by a beaver pond

The trail continues to the southeast, passing a second beaver pond. At 6.8 miles it comes alongside the Oswegatchie River at a small grassy clearing. This is a nice place to camp if you desire more mileage your first day. The trail has been loosely following the river since mile 3.0 yesterday and will continue to do so to High Falls. At times you may hear canoeists on the water.

From here, the trail changes direction, bending to the northeast and passing a third beaver pond. The pond appears grassed in but is actually very boggy. At 7.4 miles the trail to Little Shallow Pond departs to the right. Continue straight (east) toward High Falls, soon cutting through the middle of another huge beaver pond. It's a wet stretch, but your feet will stay dry if you step carefully.

At 8.0 miles the trail reaches a narrow, dark stream. This is not the Oswegatchie River but Glasby Creek, just above its confluence with the larger Oswegatchie. A campsite hides in the trees to the left at the end of a faint spur trail. From here, the trail bends back to the southeast and crosses through more open grassy wetlands known as The Plains. Birders should bring binoculars to get a closer look at the wrens, chickadees, and catbirds. You can also glimpse hermit thrushes, various sparrows, warblers, and cedar waxwings.

The trail soon climbs a gentle rise to drier ground. Though a mere 25 feet of vertical gain, it is a welcome change in topography. From here, you pass through an impressive old-growth pine forest. One tree by the trail is over 4 feet in diameter! This is the edge of one of the largest virgin forests in the northeastern United States, which continues across the wilderness to the south of High Falls.

At 8.5 miles you reach the junction with the short spur to High Falls. To reach the falls, go straight (south). Red NYSDEC discs mark both the spur trail to the falls and the Dead Creek Flow Trail, which is the continuation of the main trail from here. The trail descends gently, passing a one-hundred-year-old skidder in the woods, quite a contraption with its exposed chains and gearing. You can hear the rushing water as you climb a short rise to a clearing and a campsite. Yellow canoe-carry markers point the way along the falls. There are several other tent sites scattered along the canoe carry, some illegal (too close to the river) and all enticing.

At 8.9 miles the trail comes to a perfect lunch spot at the falls. While High Falls is not very high (under 20 feet), it is broad, at about 50 feet across. The rushing water has worn the rock smooth as it flows between the towering pines that guard both sides of the powerful cascadelike wooden sentinels.

After enjoying the falls, retrace your steps back to the main trail at 9.3 miles, and then bear right (northeast) toward Dead Creek Flow. This portion of the loop feels more like a footpath than a railroad bed, but it was in fact another railroad bed turned truck trail. Built during the Great Depression by the Civilian Conservation Corps (CCC), the Dead Creek Flow Trail climbs gently over a small rise as it winds through dense forest and then gently descends the other side. It's a marshy 2.4 miles from High Falls to the junction with the trail to Cat Mountain. The trail heads generally to the northeast following Glasby Creek, which seems more a series of beaver ponds than a stream. In some places the crossings are makeshift on sturdy sticks and fallen logs. In other places low bog bridges help keep your feet dry. At one point the trail crosses the top of an old beaver dam. This large wetland habitat lies between two low peaks, Roundtop Mountain (elevation 2,119 feet) to the northwest and Threemile Mountain (elevation 2,093 feet), the long low ridge to the east.

At 11.5 miles the trail crosses a narrow creek on a constructed two-log bridge stabilized by heavy riprap on both banks. From here, it's a gentle climb to the junction with the Cat Mountain Trail at 11.7 miles. This junction is called Sand Hill, probably because the trail turns smooth and sandy as it climbs easily to a height of land. Go straight (north) at the junction toward Janack's Landing, continuing uphill on a shallow incline to the top of the hill and then descending the other side. It's a welcome though brief change of scenery through upland forest.

After Sand Hill the trail begins to feel like an endless slog through beaver ponds and bogs and over bog bridges, though it's less than a mile from Sand Hill to Janack's Landing. At 12.5 miles turn right at the junction onto the short trail to Janack's Landing (yellow NYSDEC markers). The path traverses a long bog bridge and then turns left off the bridge alongside a marsh. It reaches a finger of Cranberry Lake at the top of a small rise and soon afterward a fork in the trail. Go straight at the fork to reach the lean-to just ahead at 12.7 miles. The other side of the fork goes to the landing, a small sandy beach where canoe-campers and others approaching by small motorboat might compete for the lean-to, but there is plenty of space around the shelter for tents if it is full. The pleasant grassy clearing at the landing is an even nicer place to pitch a tent. It's called Janack's Landing after the Janack family that used to reside here and man the fire tower atop Cat Mountain.

Day Three: Janack's Landing to Cat Mountain to Wanakena

Start the day with the climb up Cat Mountain. It's a moderate 4.4 miles round-trip from the junction with the Dead Creek Flow Trail near Janack's Landing and well worth the trek for the expansive view from its ledgy summit.

From the lean-to at Janack's Landing, return to the Dead Creek Flow Trail at 12.9 miles, and stash your heavy pack in the woods. You'll need only some water, a snack, and a jacket for the ascent of Cat Mountain. Turn left (south), retracing the route to Sand Hill.

At 13.7 miles bear left (east) at the junction with the Cat Mountain Trail. The narrow footpath (yellow NYSDEC markers) climbs moderately at first. Soon the canopy breaks for a moment as you cross a bit of slab. Then the trail swings left, passing a pretty 4-foot waterfall between two boulders, and levels off.

Hiker on Cat Mountain summit

At 13.9 miles the trail comes to a campsite in a small clearing by Glasby Pond with a view of Cat Mountain and its rocky scar across the water. Though remote, Glasby Pond is a well-known trout pond among anglers in the Adirondacks. It is categorized as "special trout water," which means only artificial lures and flies are permitted and there's a daily catch limit. Continue east along the edge of the pond toward Cat Mountain.

At 14.3 miles you arrive at a fork. The path to the right goes to Cowhorn Junction. Bear left (northeast), continuing toward Cat Mountain (red NYSDEC markers). After the fork the trail swings back to the east and then climbs more steadily. It's washed out in places and crosses some lengths of slab, which can be slick if wet. The trail ascends in waves, eventually traversing under a large boulder and then by two fern "lawns." After passing the rock scar visible from the pond, the dirt path climbs steeply up the right side of a cliff and then turns 90 degrees left across the top of the cliff. There is an unofficial spur trail on your left that traverses the 20 yards to the edge of this rocky perch and nice view to the west of Glasby Pond and Dead Creek Flow. Threemile Mountain is the long ridge to the left.

From here, the trail bends to the right away from the cliff, into the woods, and flattens out. At 15.0 miles it breaks open onto the summit of Cat Mountain, a long open ledge with an endless view to the south. The fire tower has been removed, but its concrete footings remain. You can understand how remote the Five Ponds Wilderness is from this vantage point. Acre upon acre of untouched green forest lies before you. There is a campsite tucked into the trees farther along the cliff. No water, but an awesome spot to spend the night!

From the summit of Cat Mountain, retrace your steps back to the Dead Creek Flow Trail and the junction with the trail to Janack's Landing. Grab your pack and head west on the Dead Creek Flow Trail following the shoreline of Cranberry Lake. At 17.6 miles the trail rounds the tip of the long inlet, crossing the spot where Dead Creek Flow enters the lake. The trail bends north continuing along the lake. Cranberry Lake has 55 miles of shoreline of which 40 miles are state-owned. There are over forty public campsites on the lake. You pass a number of them along this stretch of trail.

At 18.3 miles the trail leaves the lake heading northwest. It traverses another long 1.5 miles of marshy, flooded land. Even if you don't normally hike with trekking poles, it's a good idea to bring them on this trip for balance on the many slippery logs and makeshift bog crossings.

At 19.8 miles you reach the trailhead for the Dead Creek Flow Trail in Wanakena. Turn left (west) on the paved road. Close the loop at 20.2 miles, back at your car at the trailhead parking lot for the Wanakena Primitive Corridor.

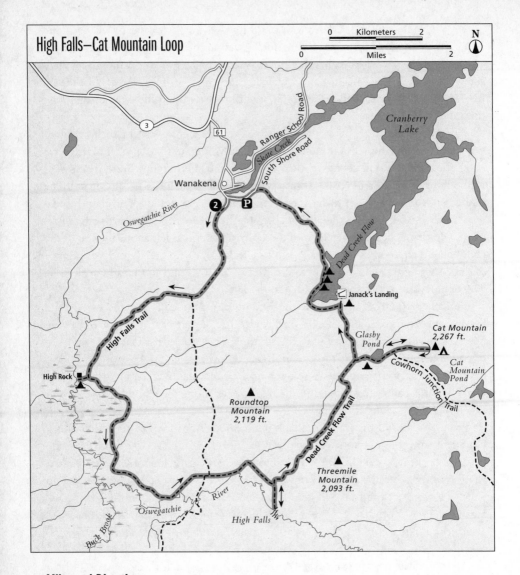

High Falls–Cat Mountain Loop

Miles and Directions

Day One

0.0 Trailhead. Walk around the gate, heading down the Wanakena Primitive Corridor on the High Falls Trail.

3.7 Bear right at the spur to High Rock.

3.8 HIGH ROCK! Camp here the first night.

Day Two

3.9 Return to the junction with the High Falls Trail. Turn right (southeast).

4.2 Cross over an old stone railroad bridge.

6.0 Pass by evidence of an old blowdown.

6.8 Pass through a small clearing beside the Oswegatchie River.

7.4 Continue straight (east) at the junction with the trail to Little Shallow Pond.

8.0 Come alongside Glasby Creek.

8.5 At the junction with the trail to High Falls, go straight (south) toward High Falls.

8.9 High Falls! Enjoy the falls and a picnic. Return to the junction with the main trail.

9.3 Arrive at the junction with the main trail, which is called the Dead Creek Flow Trail beyond this point. Bear right (northeast) on the Dead Creek Flow Trail.

11.5 Cross a constructed bridge over Glasby Creek.

11.7 Arrive at the junction with the Cat Mountain Trail at Sand Hill. Continue straight (north) toward Janack's Landing.

12.5 Turn right at the junction, heading toward Janack's Landing on the shore of Cranberry Lake.

12.7 JANACK'S LANDING! Camp here the second night.

Day Three

12.9 Return to the junction with the Dead Creek Flow Trail. Hide your packs near the junction. Turn left (south), retracing your steps to Sand Hill.

13.7 At the junction with the Cat Mountain Trail at Sand Hill, bear left (east) toward Cat Mountain.

13.9 Pass through a campsite beside Glasby Pond.

14.3 At the fork with the trail to Cowhorn Junction, bear left (northeast) toward Cat Mountain and begin climbing.

15.0 SUMMIT of Cat Mountain! On the Dead Creek Flow Trail, retrace back to the junction with the trail to Janack's Landing.

17.1 Arrive at the junction with the trail to Janack's Landing. Retrieve your pack. Turn left (west), following the shoreline of Cranberry Lake.

17.6 Cross the outlet of Dead Creek Flow. Continue north along the lake.

18.3 Leave the lakeshore, heading northwest through more flooded beaver ponds.

19.8 Arrive at the trailhead for Dead Creek Flow Trail in Wanakena. Turn left (west) on the road.

20.2 Close the loop at your car at the trailhead parking area for the Wanakena Primitive Corridor.

3 Lyon Mountain

A steep hike to a fire tower and an open rocky summit with views into Canada, Vermont, and the High Peaks region of the Adirondacks.

Nearest town: Chazy Lake
Total distance: 6.4 miles, out and back
Highest point: 3,829 feet
Vertical gain: 1,904 feet

Approximate hiking time: 4 hours
Difficulty: Strenuous
Canine compatibility: Dog-friendly
Map: USGS Lyon Mountain Quad

Finding the trailhead: From the junction of NY 374 and Standish Road in the hamlet of Lyon Mountain, take NY 374 east for 3.6 miles. Turn right (south) on Chazy Lake Road. Go 1.7 miles. Turn right on a seasonal dirt road (no sign, but formerly called Lowenburg Road). Go 0.9 mile to the end of the road. The trailhead is on the left, a continuation of the dirt road. Parking is on the right. Trailhead: N44 43.424' / W73 50.519'

The Hike

Lyon Mountain is only 171 feet short of making the 4,000-footer list. It is a monadnock—a peak that stands alone—about 30 miles west of Plattsburgh, crowning the southwestern shore of Chazy Lake. From 1870 to 1967, iron ore was mined from the mountain. Considered some of the finest iron ore in the world, it was used in structures such as the Golden Gate Bridge in San Francisco. Nine years after the

Remains of fire-watcher's cabin on Lyon Mountain

mine opened, Verplanck Colvin located the headquarters for his Adirondack survey at Lyon Mountain. In 2005 the state of New York purchased 20,000 acres of land in the northern Adirondacks, including Lyon Mountain, from the Nature Conservancy for $9.8 million, which was about the time that restoration work on the fire tower began.

The original trail up Lyon Mountain was relatively short and steep, just under 2 miles but averaging 1,000 vertical feet per mile. A new trail was opened in 2009, which is more than a mile longer but much easier, with modern-day switchbacks and a moderate incline until it meets the old trail just below the summit. Your heart will pound as you scramble up the upper slopes. But it's a worthwhile effort. The panorama from atop Lyon Mountain is the king of views in the northern Adirondacks if you like to look at mountains. You can see the highest peaks in both New York and Vermont from atop its fire tower as well as Montreal, Quebec, on a clear day.

From the parking lot, continue up the dirt road on foot. It immediately turns to large uneven cobblestones, climbing gently. The route (red NYSDEC markers) is a wide, unmaintained jeep road that rises through a hardwood forest with both paper and yellow birch and many striped maple in the mix. At 0.3 mile the trail splits briefly around a stand of paper birches, then comes to a pile of sticks and logs blocking the trail. Turn left at the sign onto the new route, crossing a stream on a footbridge.

The trail is soft and muddy but easygoing. It continues to climb moderately, around a long switchback. As you ascend along an angled traverse to the southwest, it's striking how different this trail is from other older trails in the Adirondacks, which were built on a direct line up a mountain.

The trail bends left as it rounds another switchback and levels off on a lazy arc to the right. But it soon resumes S-ing through the ferns and forest, heading to the southwest.

After a slight downhill, it skirts a hillside, passing by mature hemlocks. After one particularly muddy section, stepping stones aid the climb. At 0.7 mile the trail dips again, crossing a stream on a second footbridge. It then begins climbing again, though moderately and at the same angle to the southwest.

At 1.0 mile you cross the first lengths of slab where a couple of fir trees have toppled over, exposing the bedrock below. The trail bends right, still climbing moderately, then traverses more rock-strewn mud. After another long switchback, the trail zigzags around trees. The canopy opens briefly as you wind through a small clearing of ferns. Then it heads downhill past a large glacial erratic on the right side of the trail. This huge boulder has a cleft in its side, creating a shallow overhang.

The downhill is thankfully short, then the trail levels off, passing over a small freshet. After a couple of switchbacks, it ascends more persistently, heading to the southwest. It bends to the north, passing through a grove of birch and ferns, and soon enters the lower boreal. Hemlocks and paper birch take over the forest mix.

As you pass through a few more switchbacks, your elevation gain becomes more evident as you begin to see sky through the trees on your left, rather than just above

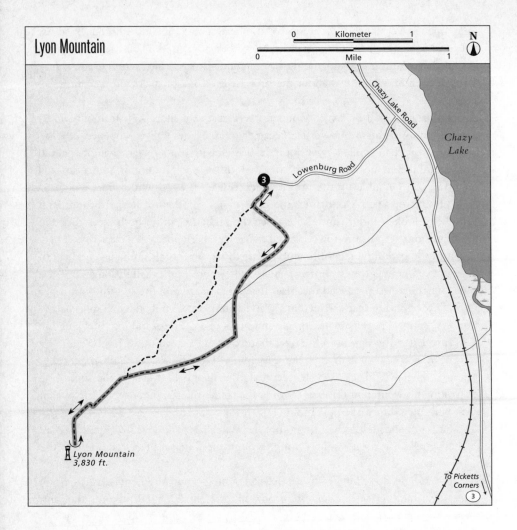

Kilometer

Mile

N

Chazy Lake Road

Lowenburg Road

3

Chazy Lake

Lyon Mountain
3,830 ft.

To Picketts Corners

3

the treetops. The trail passes a moss-topped boulder, which forms a short wall next to the trail on a longish traverse, coming to a junction with the old route at 2.5 miles. Turn left, heading up the broad, washed-out trail.

The trail is steep and heads directly up the side of the mountain. It's eroded and uneven, with exposed roots winding across the path among the rocks. Indian pipe, asters, and clintonia peak up from among the rocks and roots. At 2.7 miles the trail passes the remains of the small fire-watcher's cabin, of which only two front steps, two footings, and the foundation wall on the uphill side remain. Beyond the cabin site the eroded, braided trail continues its persistent ascent up the steepest section yet. It's also the wettest and muddiest section after a rainstorm, but the view of Chazy Lake, which starts to appear behind you to the northeast, helps keep enthusiasm high for reaching the summit.

At 2.8 miles the steep pitch begins to mellow. There are more sections of slab underfoot.

As the trail levels off, the trees become noticeably slimmer. The fire tower looms over the treetops at 3.2 miles. The 35-foot tower sits on an open rock on the broad summit. It was built in 1917 and served until 1988. There is a 360-degree view, but the eastern panorama, which includes Lake Champlain, plus Mount Mansfield and Camel's Hump across the water in Vermont, draws your eye the most. The High Peaks crown the horizon to the south. Chazy Lake is the large, close body of water to the northeast. The white windmills that dot the countryside to the north produce electricity for the surrounding communities. After looking around, descend the tower and head toward the lake view, where there are open ledges and several perfect picnic spots. The view is much better here than on the west side of the summit, which is covered with thin, scrubby trees.

Return to the trailhead by the same route.

Miles and Directions

0.0   Trailhead. Continue on the dirt road, now an unmaintained jeep road.

0.3   Turn left onto the new route, crossing a stream on a footbridge.

0.7   Dip down to a second footbridge over another stream.

1.0   Pass over slab where fallen trees have peeled the soil away.

2.5   Turn left at the junction with the old route, climbing the wide, washed-out trail.

2.7   Pass the remains of the fire-watcher's cabin.

2.8   The pitch mellows.

3.2   FIRE TOWER! Return by the same route.

6.4   Arrive back at the trailhead.

4 Saint Regis Mountain

A relatively easy hike, considering the mileage, to an abandoned fire tower and the best view of the Saint Regis Canoe Area.

Nearest town: Paul Smiths
Total distance: 6.0 miles, out and back
Highest point: 2,858 feet
Vertical gain: 1,381 feet

Approximate hiking time: 5.5 hours
Difficulty: Moderate
Canine compatibility: Dog-friendly
Maps: USGS Saint Regis Mountain Quad

Finding the trailhead: At the junction of NY 86 and NY 30 in Paul Smiths, turn right (north) on NY 30. Go 100 yards. Turn left (west) on Keese Mills Road. *Note:* The road sign may be missing, but there is a large brown sign that says "St. Regis Presbyterian Church" at the turn. Go 2.7 miles. The trailhead parking lot is on the left side of the road just beyond the turn for Topridge Road. Walk 0.1 mile down Topridge Road to the trailhead. Trailhead parking: N44 25.923' / W74 18.011'

The Hike

Saint Regis Mountain is a short hike if you take a boat across Upper Saint Regis Lake, but if you must go by car, you'll need to follow the full route, which is described here. It's a 6-miler, but it's easy terrain-wise, as most of the route is the approach to the mountain, not the ascent. And it's very pretty, especially when the leaves reach their peak color in the fall (late September here) due to the many maples in the forest mix. The path is serene, and there's a fantastic view from the open rock summit even though the fire tower is closed. Although on the long side for young children, this is a great one for older kids and dogs. It's also a perfect prelude to more ambitious outings.

From the parking lot on Keese Mills Road, cross over the metal bridge on foot and walk the short 0.1 mile down the dirt road to the trailhead, which is on the right. From the sign-in box, cross a streamlet on a long constructed bridge and climb a few stone steps following the red NYSDEC markers. The trail bends left (south) and continues to climb moderately up the small hillside. It quickly flattens out and then dips past a small grassy wetland on your left. The footing is smooth as you wind through the classic mixed northern forest.

At 0.2 mile (from the trailhead), the trail swings right (northwest) on another easy, short climb and then levels off on a woods road. A moment later watch for a short detour over a large low boulder. The woods road goes straight, but it's blocked by sticks. The trail merges with the road again on the other side of the elongated boulder and then narrows to a footpath over a length of slab as it continues deeper into the forest, climbing moderately.

At 0.7 mile the path passes through a grove of mature hemlocks where the ground is clear of flora and debris except for a soft carpet of needles—a sharp contrast to the earlier portion of the trail, which was hemmed in by ferns and hobblebushes. Then the trail begins a long, gradual downhill and hardwoods return to the mix. Eventually the path bends to the south on a sustained undulating traverse.

At 1.9 miles the trail crosses a footbridge over a pretty streamlet and bends to the southwest. Soon afterward it finally begins to climb the mountain. Though a steady pitch, the footing is smooth and not overly strenuous. After a dip the climb resumes, now with roots and stones strewn along the path.

At 2.2 miles the trail climbs more persistently up through a young forest onto the shoulder of the mountain. A few stone steps aid the ascent. At 2.6 miles the trail bends northwest up a much longer stone staircase and then more stone steps just beyond a low mossy rock outcropping. Look back to glimpse Spitfire Lake through the trees. You'll begin to notice the elevation gain as the forest brightens and the canopy thins.

The ascent is direct, passing under another low rock wall and then heading up through a well-traveled, eroded section. A few minutes later the trail passes

Hiker crosses a footbridge en route to the top of Saint Regis Mountain

through a boulder pile on its path toward the sky. After scrambling over a rock jumble, the ascent eases on a small high shelf. There are many bent and broken paper and white birches, evidence of a past ice storm.

The trail winds around the north side of the mountain. At 2.8 miles there is an unmarked but obvious spur trail on the right, which leads to a view to the west and north. The fire tower is just above you at 3.0 miles.

The lower steps have been removed from the fire tower to prevent hikers from ascending, but don't feel deprived. From the broad open summit, there is an unobstructed view of the 19,000-acre Saint Regis Canoe Area, the largest wilderness canoe area in the northeastern United States and the only one in New York. It is closed to motor vehicles, motorboats, and floatplanes. The fire tower was erected in 1918, then closed in 1990, one of the last manned towers in the Adirondacks. Its fate is undecided. It is considered a nonconforming structure under Adirondack Park guidelines, which prohibit man-made structures in designated wilderness areas of the park. However, it is listed on the registry for National Historic Places. A nonprofit

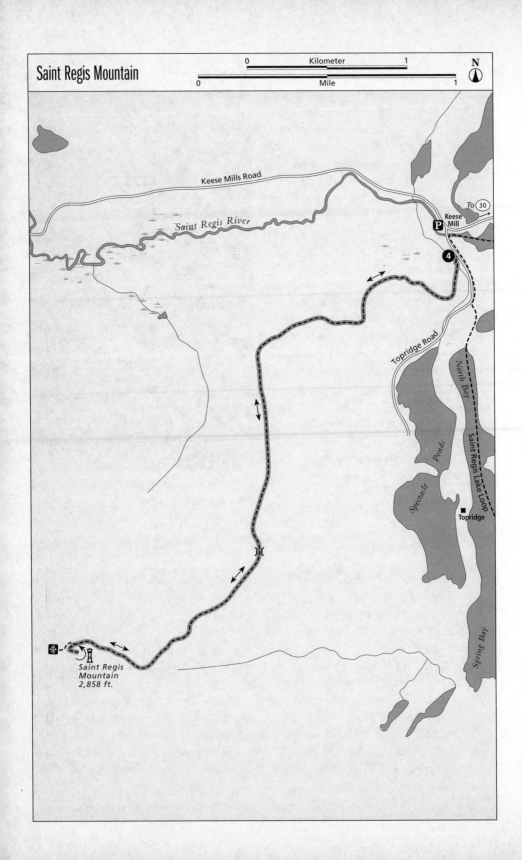

group called Friends of Saint Regis Mountain Fire Tower has collected over 2,500 signatures petitioning the state to allow the tower to remain and be restored for the enjoyment of hikers.

Return to the trailhead by the same route.

Miles and Directions

0.0 Trailhead. Enter the woods on a long footbridge.

0.2 Swing right and climb a short way to a woods road.

0.7 Pass through a grove of tall hemlocks.

1.9 Cross a footbridge and begin climbing.

2.2 Reach a shoulder of the mountain.

2.6 Continue the steep ascent aided by stone steps.

2.8 Turn right onto a short spur to a rock outcropping just below the summit for a view to the north and west.

3.0 SUMMIT! Enjoy the view. Return by the same route.

6.0 Arrive back at the trailhead. Walk the short way down Topridge Road back to your car.

High Peaks Region

A Sampling of 4,000-Footers

The High Peaks region of the Adirondacks is accurately named. All of the mountains in the Adirondack Park that are over 4,000 feet are located in this area, which is defined by NY 3 to the northwest, which passes through Saranac Lake; NY 28N and NY 28 to the south, which passes through Newcomb; and US 9 to the east. The villages of Lake Placid, Elizabethtown, and Keene Valley lie in the middle of the region.

When the Adirondacks were first surveyed, forty-six peaks were deemed 4,000 feet or higher. Modern measuring techniques have since determined that four of those original forty-six—Blake Peak, Cliff Mountain, Nye Mountain, and Couchsachraga Peak—are actually lower than 4,000 feet, and that MacNaughton Mountain makes the cut. However, becoming an Adirondack forty-sixer requires bagging the summits on the historical list. It is a challenging quest, as twenty of the peaks are extremely remote, even by Adirondack standards, and trail-less, though unofficial "herd paths" now lead to all of the trail-less summits.

Most of the High Peaks are grouped into various ranges, such as the Santanoni Range, the MacIntyre Range, and the Sentinel Range. There are also wilderness areas such as the Giant Mountain Wilderness and the Dix Mountain Wilderness, and primitive areas such as the Hurricane Mountain Primitive Area and the Johns Brook Primitive Corridor. These ranges, wilderness areas, and primitive areas are simply a means of identifying tracts of land, mostly state-owned, within the High Peaks region. Regardless of their designation, these mountains offer some of the most spectacular and challenging hiking in the northeastern United States. Mount Marcy, the highest peak in New York State, is the most famous, but there are many other exceptional

◀ *Avalanche Lake (Hike 6)*

summits. This entire guidebook could have covered only the 4,000-footers in the High Peaks region. Instead, it cherry-picks the "must do" peaks, the iconic destinations that all hikers who spend time in the Adirondacks ascend.

From the top of each mountain, you will find an open rocky summit and a view of a lifetime, but you'll have to work for it. With the exception of Cascade Mountain, these are long hikes over challenging terrain with vertical gains over 2,000 feet. Only fit, experienced hikers should attempt to climb a 4,000-footer.

You'll walk in true alpine zones above tree line, but you could also be exposed to wild wind and weather, even in midsummer. Many days the sun shines in town while clouds hang over the High Peaks. Save a trek up a 4,000-footer for a clear day.

Also be aware that many of the 4,000-footers are not dog-friendly. The smooth rock chimneys, ladders, and rough, bouldery trails common to this region are tough on canines. That said, hiking to the top of any of these mountains is a challenge worth taking.

5 Algonquin Peak

A popular though challenging climb to a broad rock summit, with excellent views of Mount Marcy, the Great Range, the slides on Mount Colden, Avalanche Lake, and Lake Colden.

Nearest town: Lake Placid
Total distance: 7.2 miles, out and back
Highest point: 5,114 feet
Vertical gain: 2,969 feet
Approximate hiking time: 7.5 hours
Difficulty: Strenuous

Canine compatibility: Experienced, fit hiker-dogs only, due to rocky scrambles on the upper mountain. Dogs must be leashed in the alpine zone.
Map: USGS Keene Valley Quad

Finding the trailhead: From Lake Placid, take NY 73 east toward Keene. About 1.2 miles past the Olympic ski jump complex, turn right (south) on Adirondack Loj Road. Go 4.7 miles to the end of the road and the sizable parking lot at Adirondak Loj. The trailhead is at the opposite side of the parking lot farthest to the right, directly in front of the information building. *Note:* There is a fee for parking here, which is discounted for members of the Adirondack Mountain Club. Trailhead: N44 11.094' / W73 57.810'

The Hike

Algonquin Peak is the second-highest mountain in New York State after Mount Marcy, and the only other 5,000-footer. It dominates the MacIntyre Range, which also includes Boundary Peak, Iroquois Peak, Wright Peak, and Mount Marshall. The long-standing reason for the name, Algonquin Peak, was the belief that it was the southern boundary of the Algonquin nation. In fact, the Algonquins lived much farther north, but the name stuck.

From the trailhead, follow the blue NYSDEC markers into the woods on the smooth, wide dirt path called the Van Hoevenberg Trail. This is the same trailhead for the hikes up Wright Peak and the Avalanche Lake–Mount Marcy Loop. The trail heads slightly downhill at first, crossing the Mr. Van Ski Trail at less than 0.1 mile. From there, the trail narrows briefly through a stand of young hemlocks, continuing in its gentle descent.

At 0.4 mile the trail levels off and crosses over a small footbridge. It climbs three elongated steps and then crosses a long, highly constructed footbridge through a wet area. The trail turns gently upward off the bridge over several log water bars, heading generally to the south. After passing a couple more ski trails, it reaches the boundary of the High Peaks Wilderness.

At 0.9 mile the trail comes to a fork. The left path goes to Marcy Dam. Take the right (southwest) path toward Algonquin and Wright Peaks. The trail soon becomes rockier and the ascent more noticeable.

Trail from the summit of Algonquin Peak toward Mount Iroquois

At 1.3 miles the Whales Tail Ski Trail departs to the left. Continue straight on the Van Hoevenberg Trail. The climb is steady now, coming alongside a seasonal stream. At 1.8 miles the trail turns 90 degrees right, crossing the stream at a yellow arrow, then curls back to the southwest. The trail is old, worn, and eroded now. A few well-placed stonelike steps aid the climb, which passes out of the mixed northern forest and into the lower boreal zone, mainly softwoods and paper birch.

After crossing a section of steep rock slab, you pass a spur trail to a primitive campsite on the left. The trail dips back to the stream and crosses under a 50-foot cascade at 2.3 miles. There is a nice pool at its base when the waterfall is running, though it might be just a small trickle down the rock face during a dry spell.

Shortly after the waterfall the trail levels off through a muddy area. At 2.8 miles it bends sharp left up a short rock chimney and then crosses lengths of slab toward the summit hump of Algonquin, still almost a mile away.

The trees become shorter, though you are not above tree line yet. You can glimpse neighboring peaks through the branches, but you'll want to pay attention to the route, which requires some low-angle friction climbing.

At 2.9 miles the Wright Peak trail departs to the left. Continue straight following the yellow NYSDEC markers up more rock slab. Clamber up and over several large boulders, and then cross some logs laid over a mud hole. Side-hill slab greets you on the other side as you ascend through a corridor of conifers. After a brief flat reprieve, you will climb another long stretch of slab into a patch of krummholz, the gnarled dwarf trees typically found just at tree line. Look back to see Lake Placid, the Olympic ski jump complex, and Whiteface Mountain to the northeast.

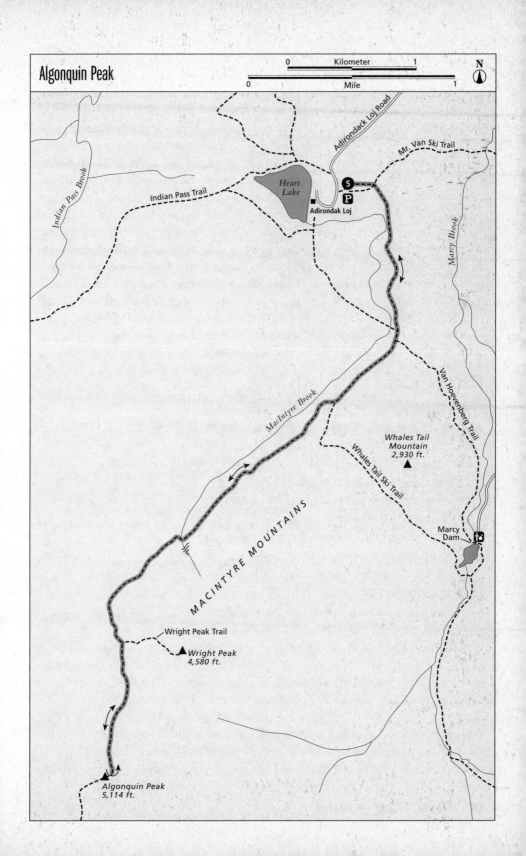

Soon the broad, bald summit of Wright Peak appears behind you to the right (east). The climb mellows as it continues through the shrinking spruce trees. After crossing a muddy area, you'll pass a sign that says "Entering an arctic plant zone." After more rocky scrambling, you clear the trees for good. Watch for yellow painted blazes on the bedrock and rock cairns (manmade piles of rock) to stay on the route.

The view gets grander and grander. By 3.5 miles you can see the cliffs above Indian Pass to the west and many of the High Peaks to the east. A rock depository for the "leave-your-rock-here" program lies just below the summit. Trail maintenance crews use these rocks to outline the trail and to build cairns in the alpine zone to prevent people from walking on the fragile revegetation areas.

At 3.6 miles the trail crests the summit. It's a broad expanse of rock, which requires you to walk to different vantage points to take in the entire 360-degree view. Avalanche Lake, Lake Colden, and Flowed Lake lie below to the southeast wedged between Algonquin and Mount Colden, with Mount Marcy's bald pate rising behind Colden. The slides of the Great Range stand out to the east, with the distinct cirque of Giant Mountain farther to the east. The trail continues southwest off Algonquin to Iroquois Peak. The Santanoni Range lies in the distance beyond Iroquois. It is arguably one of the best views from the heart of the High Peaks.

Miles and Directions

0.0 Start at the trailhead. Follow the trail toward Marcy Dam.

0.1 Continue straight at the junction with the Mr. Van Ski Trail.

0.4 Cross a long, well-constructed footbridge over a wet area.

0.9 At the junction with the trail to Marcy Dam, bear right toward Algonquin and Wright Peaks.

1.3 The Whales Tail Ski Trail departs to the left.

1.8 Cross a stream and then curl back to the southwest.

2.3 Pass by a 50-foot waterfall.

2.9 At the junction with Wright Peak Trail, continue straight toward Algonquin Peak.

3.5 Leave a rock in the leave-a-rock-here depository.

3.6 SUMMIT! Return by the same route.

7.2 Arrive back at the trailhead.

THE ALPINE ZONE

There are four climate zones in the High Peaks Wilderness: northern hardwood, boreal, krummholz, and alpine. The zone is determined primarily by elevation, but it is also influenced by exposure to the elements and soil quality.

The northern hardwood forests, predominantly sugar maple, American beech, and yellow birch, lie at the lowest elevations, below 2,500 feet. Here the soil is the most fertile and well drained, and the slopes are not too steep. Hobblebush is among the more common shrubs beside hiking trails in this zone.

The boreal forest lies between 2,500 and 4,000 feet. Red spruce and balsam fir are the most common conifers. Paper birch (white birch) also grow abundantly, especially in the low to mid-elevations in this zone. Bunchberry and goldenthread are among the wildflowers that carpet the forest floor.

Above 4,000 feet the soil thins dramatically and the exposure to strong wind and harsh weather is unavoidable. Balsam fir and black spruce are the main species of trees here, though as you near tree line, they are really just misshapen bushes, known as krummholz or "twisted trees." It's easy to determine the prevailing wind as their gnarled branches grow off one side of the trees, away from the wind.

Sedges in the alpine zone in autumn

Krummholz

Tree line in the Adirondacks is about 4,500 feet. Bare summits below this elevation, which may be home to alpine and subalpine plants, probably lost their forestation due to forest fire and then lost their soil due to erosion. The flora in the alpine zone is true alpine tundra similar to the tundra found near the Arctic Circle. The alpine flora in the Adirondacks became isolated when the last ice age began to recede 12,000 years ago. Today these precious plants that remain are important both for their ecological history and for the biodiversity of the region.

About eighty-five acres of alpine tundra exist in the High Peaks region among twenty mountaintops, but that figure includes the bare rock, too. The actual acreage of alpine plant life is half that. It is the southernmost area of alpine flora in the eastern United States. Though these plants survive under extreme conditions, they are fragile. Many are rare or endangered, such as diapensia, three-footed cinquefoil, and mountain sandwort. Some species, like deer's hair sedge and Bigelow's sedge, look like simple grasses, but one root-damaging footstep can kill them.

In order to preserve this sensitive ecosystem, always remain on the trail in the alpine zone, sticking to durable surfaces (rock). This is one of the reasons why it is illegal to camp above 4,000 feet in the High Peaks Wilderness and only at designated campsites above 3,500 feet.

The Adirondack Mountain Club, the Nature Conservancy, and the NYSDEC have instituted the Summit Steward Program to help preserve the alpine mountaintops. Uniformed representatives of these organizations visit the top of Algonquin Peak and Mount Marcy every day during the summer hiking season and periodically visit other summits as well. Their purpose is to educate hikers and to do trail maintenance work to aid the existing plants and facilitate revegetation of damaged areas.

Some of the other alpine species found above tree line in the Adirondacks include dwarf willow, dwarf tundra birch, small birch, Lapland rosebay, alpine azalea, and alpine blueberry.

In addition, some subalpine plants and lowland bog species can appear in the alpine zone in sheltered areas where the soil is mossy and acidic, including false hellebore, golden-thread, bunchberry, starflower, closed gentians, Labrador tea, bog laurel, leatherleaf, small cranberry, and cotton sedge.

Staying on the trail and protecting the alpine zone is becoming more and more critical. A study conducted over the twenty-three-year period from 1984 to 2007 by the State University of New York at Albany revealed that subalpine species are becoming increasingly prevalent in the alpine zone, which seems to be shrinking not only due to hiker impact but also atmospheric pollution and global warming.

Boreal forest

6 Avalanche Lake–Mount Marcy Loop

A challenging three-day loop past Avalanche Lake, Lake Colden, and Lake Tear in the Clouds, plus a climb over Mount Marcy, the tallest peak in New York State.

Nearest town: Lake Placid
Total distance: 15.6 miles, lollipop
Highest point: 5,344 feet
Vertical gain: 4,200 feet
Approximate hiking time: 3 days/2 nights

Difficulty: Experts only
Canine compatibility: Not dog-friendly due to bouldery shorelines and several tall ladders
Map: *USGS Heart Lake Quad* (trailhead); *USGS Mount Marcy Quad*

Finding the trailhead: From Lake Placid, take NY 73 east toward Keene. Go 1.2 miles past the Olympic ski jump complex. Turn right (south) on Adirondack Loj Road. Go 4.7 miles to the end of the road and the sizable parking lot at Adirondak Loj. The trailhead is at the opposite side of the parking lot farthest to the right, directly in front of the information building. Trailhead: N44 11.094' / W73 57.810'

The Hike

Mount Marcy is a mecca for hikers in the Adirondacks because it is the tallest mountain in the state and because it has a grand open summit with views over 50 miles in every direction on a clear day. Though many people hike up Mount Marcy as a day trip, it is a *long* 14-mile day up the most popular route, the Van Hoevenberg

Kids on "Hitch Up Matilda" along the shore of Avalanche Lake

Trail, from Adirondak Loj. The region around Mount Marcy is a web of trails that lead to six other prominent peaks—Algonquin, Wright, Iroquois, Colden, Phelps, and Skylight—as well as four trail-less 4,000-footers, Gray, Redfield, Marshall, and Table Top. It is also the primary access point to Avalanche Pass, Avalanche Lake, and Lake Colden, one of the most dramatic and beautiful passages in the High Peaks and another "must do" hike. There are an infinite number of routes that you can piece together depending on what backcountry destinations you want to see on a particular trip. The route described here takes you through Avalanche Pass to Avalanche Lake and Lake Colden, over the summit of Mount Marcy, and then back to Adirondak Loj via the Van Hoevenberg Trail.

A super-fit experienced backpacker with a relatively light pack could do this trip in two days. A few bionic hikers have done it in one. But mere mortals with a few extra creature comforts stashed in their loads will appreciate the extra night out. The mileage is not long, but the route is arduous, particularly the stretch along Avalanche Lake and Lake Colden. The terrain by lakes is fun and interesting with little vertical gain, but there are many large rocks and small boulders to scramble over and around, which greatly slows the pace. The climb over Marcy is steep, plus there are many, many places along this route that beg for a break to enjoy the spectacular views.

Day One

From the trailhead, follow the blue NYSDEC markers into the woods on the smooth wide dirt path called the Van Hoevenberg Trail. It heads slightly downhill at first, crossing the Mr. Van Ski Trail at less than 0.1 mile. From there, the trail narrows briefly through a stand of young hemlocks, continuing on its gentle descent.

At 0.4 mile the trail levels off and crosses over a small footbridge. It climbs three elongated log steps and then crosses a long boardwalk over a stream and a marshy area. The trail turns gently upward off the bridge over several log water bars, heading generally to the south. After passing a couple more ski trails, it crosses the boundary into the High Peaks Wilderness.

At 0.9 mile the trail comes to a fork. The right path goes to Algonquin and Wright Peaks. Take the left path toward Marcy Dam. The trail rolls along through dappled sunlight. Don't be surprised if a whitetail deer peers at you through the undergrowth.

The trail dips across a footbridge over a streamlet, a prelude to many more bog bridges and other substantial trail work on this high-traffic route. It's easy going here, flat and smooth. At 1.8 miles a short spur on the left leads to the side of Marcy Brook. It's a pretty spot for a break, where water rushes around the many rocks and boulders. From here, the trail climbs a couple of rises paralleling the brook, then descends a set of stairs and immediately climbs out of the depression on another set of stairs. Marcy Dam is just ahead at 2.1 miles.

From Marcy Dam, you can see Avalanche Mountain, Algonquin Peak, Wright Peak, and Whales Tail Mountain across the pond on the right. Loggers first began building removable dams on this site in the late 1800s. When water was needed to move timber down lower Marcy Brook, they broke the dam apart. Although logging here ended in the early 1900s, the state continued to keep the dam, building the permanent structure that stands today in the 1960s.

Bear right off the bridge, following the yellow NYSDEC markers toward Avalanche Lake. You will pass several tent sites on your left, which might be nice options tomorrow night. Immediately after the tent sites, the Phelps Trail departs to the left at 2.2 miles. Bear right, passing a lean-to on your right. The trail comes alongside Marcy Brook and soon becomes more worn and rocky like a streambed itself. Though rougher, the terrain is still relatively flat.

Eventually the trail distances itself from the brook. At 3.0 miles you pass the Avalanche Camp lean-to on your right and a tent site on your left. Paper birch and evergreens take over as the dominant trees, signaling your entry into the boreal zone. After crossing the brook on a well-constructed bridge, you come to the junction with the north trail to Mount Colden. Bear right on the Avalanche Lake Trail. The path crosses over puncheon and then ascends some log work and a short beefy ladder, in place more to protect the soil than to scale rock. From here the trail becomes rougher and rockier and finally feels like an earnest ascent.

At 3.8 miles the trail flattens over lengths of puncheon, zigzagging into to the mouth of Avalanche Pass. A massive bare slope towers above you on the left, rising from a giant blowdown that slid down the steep mountainside and now forms a 12-foot wall of sawed-off logs. From here the path squeezes through an unforgettable ravine. Pick your way across the bog bridges following the stream that cuts through the bottom of the pass. The atmosphere is thick with humidity trapped by the rock walls. Water drips down the tall cliffs, which are lush with moss. Avalanche Pass feels like a secret rain forest hidden between two tall peaks.

As the ravine opens towards the lake, the trail descends gradually through an even wetter area, becoming streamlike in places, with large rocks to negotiate in one section. At 4.2 miles the trail passes a large glacial erratic (boulder) balancing on your left and then arrives at Avalanche Lake. The narrow lake is hemmed in on both sides by 500-foot cliffs. Green shrubs cling impossibly from the sheer gray walls. The trail heads down the right side of the lake, beginning with a ladder. This is a challenging section, with several more ladders, lots of scrambling over boulders, and a series of footbridges known as the "Hitch Up Matildas." Local lore claims that a guide led two sisters along this route in the late 1800s. As the water level of the lake began to rise, their skirts started to get wet, prompting one sister to say to the other, "Hitch up, Matilda!" Don't expect to break any speed records along this section of the trail, especially with a large pack. Take your time and be sure of your footing.

At 4.6 miles the trail comes to the south end of Avalanche Lake. It parallels a stream, descending gradually through wetlands en route to Lake Colden. At 4.9 miles the south trail to Mount Colden departs to the left. Then at 5.2 miles, as the trail starts down the west shore of Lake Colden, the Algonquin Peak Trail departs to your right. The trail markers become blue again as you follow the shoreline of Lake Colden.

At 5.3 miles the trail passes a NYSDEC Interior Outpost that's manned by a ranger, just before the junction with the Cold Brook Pass Trail and the bridge over Cold Brook. Bear left, continuing south along the shore of Lake Colden. There are several lean-tos and primitive campsites in this area and farther along the shore of the lake. The Beaver Point lean-tos, at 5.6 miles, and then the Cedar Point lean-tos a little farther along path, are both particularly nice spots with views across the water of Mount Colden. There are also several primitive campsites tucked into the woods near the lean-tos. Spend your first night here.

Day Two

The trail along the shore of Lake Colden is a mixture of puncheon and a rock obstacle course. At 5.7 miles (from the trailhead), the trail splits at Lake Colden Dam. Turn left (east), then descend the ladder and across the dam, following the yellow markers. The trails forks at the opposite end of the dam. Bear left toward the bridge as noted on the sign. There are additional campsites here if the ones near Beaver Point are taken.

A short time later, at 5.8 miles, a trail back to Avalanche Lake and to Mount Colden departs to the left. Stay right (southeast) toward Mount Marcy, now following red markers. After the rough terrain along Avalanche Lake and Lake Colden, the trail here is thankfully smooth and dry and soon comes alongside the Opalescent River.

At 5.9 miles cross the river on a suspension bridge and then arrive at a beautiful waterfall. It's a wide cascade with many rock perches from which to enjoy it, but linger only briefly as you have a big climb ahead.

The trail turns rough again as it veers along a tributary streamlet. After crossing the streamlet it passes another cascade by a dripping rock wall and returns to the main river, which funnels through a gorge below you. After a muddy stretch and a few log steps, the path climbs steadily, still following the river. A few minutes later it flattens on a landing where the water dives into a rock chasm. The roar of the ravine provides enough distraction that you'll hardly notice the muddy path.

The trail mellows as the ravine mellows, climbing moderately. Hiking poles and Gore-Tex boots are helpful through this wet uneven section. At 7.2 miles the trail passes through a campsite near the confluence of Uphill Brook and the Opalescent River. It bends northeast, and the markers become yellow again. Cross over the brook, a wet crossing if the water is high, and then traverse long lengths of bog bridges, continuing to follow the river.

At 7.5 miles the trail comes to the junction with the southern trail to Lake Arnold. Bear right (east), continuing to follow the yellow markers toward Lake Tear in the Clouds and Mount Marcy. After another stream crossing the trail climbs moderately again through a thick hedge of hemlocks and spruce, which seem to close in on the trail. A few minutes later a sign notes the elevation at 3,500 feet.

As the ascent gets more persistent, Gray Peak becomes visible through the trees to the north, across from you rather than above you. The trail becomes smoother as the trees shrink. At 8.1 miles another sign marks the 4,000-foot level and warns that camping is not allowed above this point.

A few minutes later the trail levels off and bunchberries bloom by your feet. You pass an open marshy area on your left, signaling your approach to Lake Tear in the Clouds. At 8.9 miles you can see the bald cone of Mount Marcy on your left. Despite its fame as the source of the mighty Hudson River, Lake Tear in the Clouds is only a small tarn with an unwelcoming shoreline and a vibrant mosquito population.

Just past Lake Tear in the Clouds, at 9.1 miles, the trail comes to a four-way junction with the trails to Mount Skylight and Panther Gorge. Turn left (north). From this junction, it's a direct, steady climb to the summit of Mount Marcy. The trees quickly shrink to head height, and the footing turns to slab. Just after the sign for the alpine zone, the trees shrink even further to krummholz, and the views begin to grow. The Great Range is to the east past Mount Haystack, and the hump of Skylight appears behind you to the south. There is a special perch just above tree line called Schofield Cobble with a breathtaking view to the east. It's a quiet place to rest during the climb to the summit, which will undoubtedly have other hikers on it.

Ladders aid passage through boulder-laden woods.

The climb from here, though fairly steep, is a rare treat—0.7 mile of open rock. At 9.8 miles the bedrock levels off at the top of New York State. Mount Marcy is named for William L. Marcy, a former governor of New York who authorized the original survey of the area. The mountain is sometimes called "Tahawus," an Indian word for "cloud splitter" that was probably given to the mountain by early Europeans, not Indians, as they rarely came into this area. Ebenezer Emmons is credited with the first recorded ascent of the mountain, in 1837.

Continue northeast across the broad summit and then descend following the cairns back to tree line on the opposite side of the mountain. As the trees become head high, the trail crosses a wet, grassy area on boards. Soon spruce trees close in on both sides. At 10.3 miles the trail forks. The right path heads to Slant Rock. Bear left (north) toward Indian Falls and Marcy Dam.

As the trees get taller, you'll find more long lengths of slab underfoot as well as some muddy areas where logs have been set width-wise across the trail like railroad ties to help stabilize your footing. At 10.9 miles the trail forks again at a muddy junction with the Bushnell Falls Trail. Bear left (northwest), continuing toward Indian Falls.

At 12.4 miles the northern trail to Lake Arnold splits off to the left. Continue straight (north). A few moments later, at 12.5 miles, the short spur to Indian Falls departs to the left. Indian Falls is a beautiful spot in the afternoon. You are actually at the top of the falls, with Iroquois, Algonquin, and Wright Peaks bathed in golden light across the valley. It's just under 2 miles from here to Marcy Dam. Depending on your energy level, plan to find a place to camp between here and Marcy Dam that is at least 150 feet from the trail or from water sources or go all the way to the campsite and lean-tos by the dam. The trail on this side of Marcy is not as bouldery as the other side of the mountain, and the slope is relatively moderate for down-hiking. It can be slippery in places if wet, but on the whole you can make better time.

Day Three

As you continue toward Marcy Dam, you cross a bridge over Phelps Brook at 13.2 miles. At 13.4 miles the Phelps Mountain Trail departs to the right. Continue straight toward Marcy Dam. At 14.1 miles you come to the junction with the High Water Trail. If the water is high, take the High Water Trail. Otherwise cross the bridge over the stream and continue down the other side.

After passing the second high-water bridge, the trail widens and drifts away from the stream. Then it smoothes out and flattens, passing several primitive campsites. At 14.3 miles the loop closes at the trail to Avalanche Lake. Turn right and retrace your steps from here over Marcy Dam, arriving back at the trailhead by Adirondak Loj at 15.6 miles.

Miles and Directions

Day One

0.0 Start at the trailhead. Follow the trail toward Marcy Dam on the Van Hoevenberg Trail.

0.1 Continue straight at the junction with the Mr. Van Ski Trail.

0.4 Cross a long, well-constructed footbridge over a wet area.

0.9 At the junction with the trail to Algonquin and Wright Peaks, bear left toward Marcy Dam.

1.8 Arrive at a short spur trail to the edge of Marcy Brook.

2.1 MARCY DAM! Walk across the dam and continue on the Van Hoevenberg Trail toward Mount Marcy.

2.2 Ignore the junction with Phelps Trail, then bear right 200 feet later on the Avalanche Pass Trail.

3.0 Pass the Avalanche Camp lean-to.

3.3 At the junction with the north trail to Mount Colden, bear right toward Avalanche Lake.

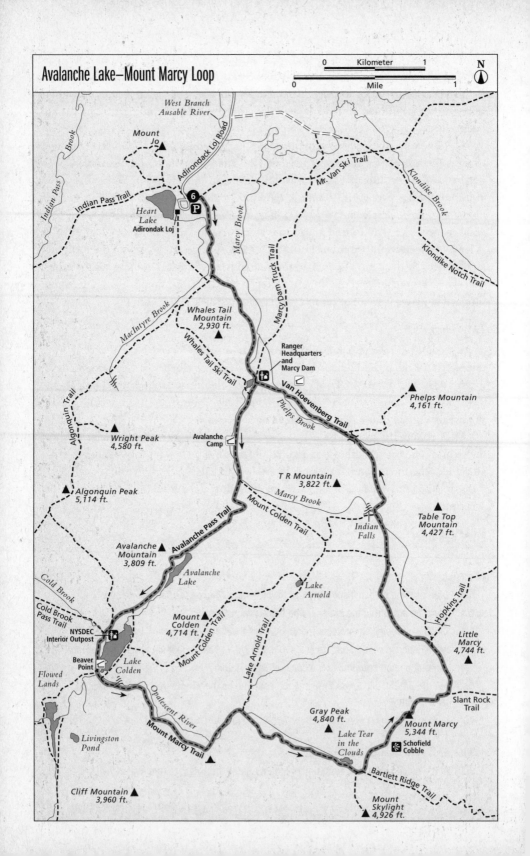

Avalanche Lake–Mount Marcy Loop

Kilometer

0   1

Mile

0   1

N

West Branch Ausable River

Mount Jo

Indian Pass

Brook

Adirondack Loj Road

Indian Pass Trail

Mr. Van Ski Trail

Klondike Brook

6 P

Heart Lake

Adirondak Loj

Marcy Brook

Klondike Notch Trail

MacIntyre Brook

Marcy Dam Truck Trail

Whales Tail Mountain 2,930 ft.

Whales Tail Ski Trail

Ranger Headquarters and Marcy Dam

Van Hoevenberg Trail

Phelps Mountain 4,161 ft.

Algonquin Trail

Wright Peak 4,580 ft.

Avalanche Camp

Phelps Brook

Algonquin Peak 5,114 ft.

T R Mountain 3,822 ft.

Marcy Brook

Table Top Mountain 4,427 ft.

Mount Colden Trail

Avalanche Pass Trail

Indian Falls

Avalanche Mountain 3,809 ft.

Avalanche Lake

Lake Arnold

Cold Brook

Cold Brook Pass Trail

Mount Colden 4,714 ft.

Hopkins Trail

Little Marcy 4,744 ft.

NYSDEC Interior Outpost

Mount Colden Trail

Lake Arnold Trail

Beaver Point

Lake Colden

Flowed Lands

Opalescent River

Gray Peak 4,840 ft.

Lake Tear in the Clouds

Mount Marcy 5,344 ft.

Schofield Cobble

Slant Rock Trail

Livingston Pond

Mount Marcy Trail

Bartlett Ridge Trail

Cliff Mountain 3,960 ft.

Mount Skylight 4,926 ft.

3.8 AVALANCHE PASS! Continue through the pass to Avalanche Lake.

4.2 AVALANCHE LAKE! Bear right, following the trail along the west shore of Avalanche Lake.

4.6 Reach the south end of Avalanche Lake. Continue southwest toward Lake Colden.

4.9 Pass a junction with the south trail to Mount Colden on the left.

5.2 Pass the junction with Algonquin Peak Trail on the right. Continue on the "Hitch Up Matildas" along the west shore of Lake Colden.

5.3 Arrive at the NYSDEC Interior Outpost and junction with the Cold Brook Pass Trail. Cross the bridge and turn left, continuing along the shore of Lake Colden.

5.6 Come to the Beaver Point lean-tos. Camp here.

Day Two

5.7 Cross Lake Colden Dam.

5.8 At the junction with Avalanche Lake/Mount Colden Trail, continue straight (southeast).

5.9 Cross the suspension bridge over Opalescent River.

6.0 WATERFALL! Continue toward NYSDEC Interior Outpost.

6.3 Ascend log steps.

7.5 Junction with southern trail to Lake Arnold. Bear right (east) toward Mount Marcy.

8.9 LAKE TEAR IN THE CLOUDS! Continue straight.

9.1 At the "Four Corners" junction with trails to Mount Skylight and Panther Gorge, turn left toward the summit of Mount Marcy.

9.8 SUMMIT! Welcome to the top of New York State. Continue straight over the top of the mountain, heading northwest.

10.3 At the junction with Slant Rock Trail, bear left toward Indian Falls and Marcy Dam.

10.9 At the junction with Bushnell Falls Trail, bear left toward Indian Falls and Marcy Dam.

12.4 At the junction with the northern trail to Lake Arnold, continue straight (north) toward Indian Falls and Marcy Dam.

12.5 INDIAN FALLS! Camp near here or continue north to lean-tos and campsites near Marcy Dam.

Day Three

13.2 Cross the bridge over Phelps Brook.

13.4 At the junction with Phelps Mountain Trail, continue straight (left).

14.1 Cross the stream at the junction with High Water Trail.

14.3 Close the loop at the trail to Avalanche Lake. Turn right toward Marcy Dam. This is your last chance to camp (in a lean-to near Marcy Dam).

15.6 Arrive back at the trailhead at Adirondak Loj.

7 Big Slide-Yard Mountain Loop

An Adirondack classic that rewards with multiple views from a series of rock ledges and from a landmark peak and then ends with a chance to see Johns Brook Lodge.

Nearest town: Keene Valley
Total distance: 10.2 miles, loop
Highest point: 4,199 feet
Vertical gain: 2,830 feet
Approximate hiking time: 8 hours

Difficulty: Experts only
Canine compatibility: Not dog-friendly due to ladders and a couple of rock chimneys
Map: *USGS Keene Valley Quad*

Finding the trailhead: From NY 73 in Keene Valley, turn right (west) on Adirondack Street. Go 1.6 miles. The road narrows and turns to dirt, becoming Johns Brook Lane, which ends at the trailhead called the Garden. If the parking lot is full, there is an overflow lot at Marcy airfield, north of Keene Valley on NY 73, with a hiker shuttle to the Garden. Trailhead: N44 11.224' / W73 48.875'

The Hike

In 1830 a large landslide cleared the steep southeast face of Big Slide Mountain down to bedrock. That permanent scar is the simple reason for this mountain's name. It's one of the more popular hikes in the High Peaks region, and with good reason. The approach via The Brothers, a series of ledges laden with blueberries and offering

Lean-to

increasingly impressive views, makes the ascent as pleasurable as 2,800 vertical feet can be. One could argue that including the traverse to Yard Mountain doesn't add much, but because you are so close, you might as well see it, and it gives you a chance to see Johns Brook Lodge (JBL), the Adirondack Mountain Club's longtime backcountry base camp. Yard Mountain (elevation 3,990 feet) is not considered a separate peak because it is too close to Big Slide.

From the trailhead, take the right trail (blue NYSDEC markers) toward The Brothers. It's a steady climb from the start. The footing is good at first, with only some roots crisscrossing the trail through a forest dominated by maple and paper birch.

At 0.3 mile the trail to Porter Mountain departs to the right. Continue straight toward the first of the three Brothers. The trail ascends moderately to a height of land, then dips down over a streamlet, which might be dry. From here, the climb continues, soon becoming more persistent and rocky.

At 0.6 mile the trail opens on a rock shoulder of The Brothers where there is a view to the southwest to neighboring Rooster Comb across a narrow valley. From here, the trail hangs on the side of the mountain for a short way and then bends back into the woods around a rock outcropping.

The trail continues to climb over the first Brother. The view is eye-popping and just gets better as you go higher. Wild blueberries are everywhere in early August. It's tempting to pick a ledge, eat blueberries, and forget about the rest of the loop. At 1.0 mile the trail bends back into the woods briefly and then returns to the edge of the cliff, ascending a short rock chimney. By the second Brother the view is almost 360 degrees. You can see the hump of Big Slide ahead to the west. *Note:* Although the painted blazes on the rocks are yellow, the NYSDEC markers remain blue.

The trail continues through a small depression and then heads over the third Brother. From there, it traverses into the woods and then climbs through paper birch and softwoods. At 2.7 miles the trail descends into a shallow col where you can glimpse the impressive scar on Big Slide before heading into thicker trees. After a fairly long traverse, which includes crossing a mossy streamlet and then a muddy area, the trail climbs again, though gently at first. It's rougher and more eroded than the lower portion of the route.

At 3.4 miles the trail comes to a junction with the first of two paths to Johns Brook Lodge off the summit of Big Slide. This one is more direct and saves 2.0 miles if you decide to skip Yard Mountain. Bear right at the junction (northwest), heading uphill toward the summit of Big Slide, still following the blue markers.

The last 0.2 mile to the summit is steep and rocky. A series of weathered log ladders aides your climb up a long stretch of steep slab. Watch the trail carefully above the ladders. The trail cuts through scrubby trees rather than heading out on a ledge, just before reaching some side-hill slab. After a spur to a cliff top, where you'll find a fine view to the south, climb one more rock wall to reach the summit at 3.6 miles.

The summit has a 180-degree view from the main open rock, but you can walk around a small pinnacle to get the rest of it. The Great Range is directly to the south-

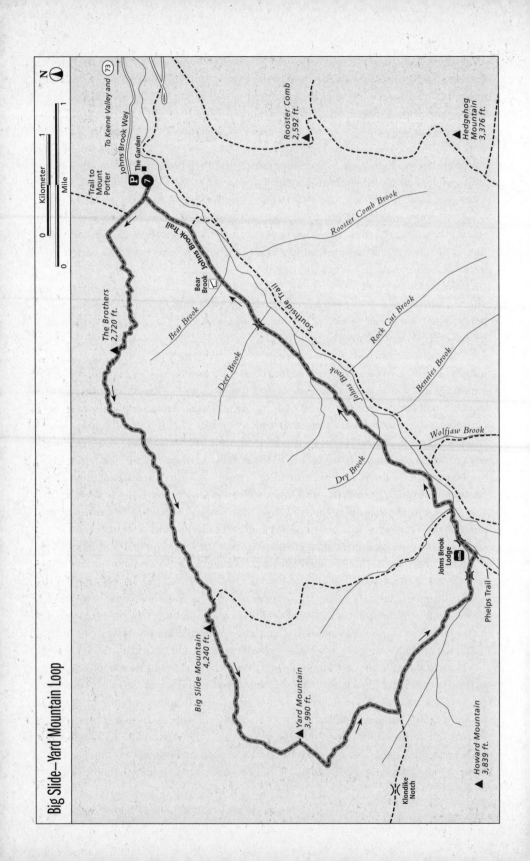

Big Slide–Yard Mountain Loop

N

0 1 Kilometer
0 1 Mile

To Keene Valley and 73

Johns Brook Way

The Garden

Trail to Mount Porter

P 7

Rooster Comb 2,592 ft.

Hedgehog Mountain 3,376 ft.

Rooster Comb Brook

Johns Brook Trail

Bear Brook

Bear Brook

Southside Trail

Deer Brook

Rock Cut Brook

Bennies Brook

Johns Brook

Wolfjaw Brook

Dry Brook

The Brothers 2,720 ft.

Big Slide Mountain 4,240 ft.

Yard Mountain 3,990 ft.

Johns Brook Lodge

Phelps Trail

Howard Mountain 3,839 ft.

Klondike Notch

east across the Johns Brook drainage. Mount Marcy is to the far right (south) of the panorama. You can see a number of other 4,000-footers, including Giant to the east and Algonquin to the west.

From the summit of Big Slide, continue south off the summit knob toward Yard Mountain. Softwoods and ferns surround you as you cross a high ridge. The trail descends a little, traverses, and then descends a little again. The footing is nice, probably because it doesn't see much traffic compared to The Brothers trail. Eventually the path turns upward, though moderately, reaching the short spur to the summit of Yard Mountain at 4.7 miles. The limited view is anticlimactic after Big Slide, but you can glimpse the prominent rock slides on Gothics through the scrubby trees from a slightly different perspective.

From the summit of Yard, the trail drops down below a rocky precipice, passing through a washed-out area, and then coming to a blowdown. Watch carefully for the blue NYSDEC discs. At 5.7 miles Yard Mountain Trail ends at a T with the Klondike Trail. Turn left (southeast), now following red markers toward Johns Brook Lodge on a long, easy downhill traverse.

At 6.6 miles a tributary stream of Johns Brook flows below you on your right. The grass-lined trail runs parallel to the stream, crossing puncheon and stepping stones in wetter areas. At 6.8 miles it crosses the stream on a double log bridge and continues the gentle descent on the opposite side of the stream. JBL is just ahead at 6.9 miles.

JBL is a rustic backcountry lodge owned by the Adirondack Mountain Club. It is a well-known retreat for hikers in the heart of the High Peaks and accessible only on foot. It has two bunkrooms and serves three meals per day to people staying there during the summer. A caretaker remains during the spring and fall. There is an outdoor faucet at JBL where you can refill your water bottle.

Many trails fan out from JBL. Head along the front of the building to the northeast, past an information board and the crew's cabin, following the yellow discs. Johns Brook should be on your right. The trail is wide and obvious, with good footing. There are many places to soak your feet in the 40-degree brook as you gradually descend back to the Garden. At 7.3 miles the trail passes a substantial footbridge to Camp Grace and Camp Peggy O'Brien, two cabins that can also be reserved through the Adirondack Mountain Club. A hundred yards later you come to the junction with the alternate trail from Big Slide that omits Yard.

After crossing a large tributary stream, you pass a spur on your right to the William G. Howard lean-tos, which were named for the former New York State assistant superintendent of forests, who was involved with the founding of the Adirondack Mountain Club in 1922. Continue on the main trail, crossing puncheon and then passing by a tent site next to the brook. A NYSDEC Interior Outpost is just ahead. Turn left at the outpost heading toward the Garden. The trail follows the brook all the way to the trailhead, though it climbs away from it here. At a height of land, the trail passes through another tent site and then bends right (east), heading downhill again.

At 9.1 miles the trail passes over a double footbridge across two channels of Deer Brook and then rises to the Deer Brook lean-to before descending again. At 9.5 miles it passes the Bear Brook lean-to, and at 9.8 miles it comes to the junction with the South Side Trail. The South Side Trail also heads to the Garden, but on the opposite side of Johns Brook. Stay left, closing the loop at 10.0 miles at the junction with the trail to Porter Mountain. Turn right, arriving at the trailhead at 10.2 miles.

Miles and Directions

0.0 Start at the Garden. Take the trail toward Porter Mountain and The Brothers.

0.3 At the junction with the trail to Porter Mountain, continue straight toward The Brothers.

1.0 Pass over The Brothers ledges.

2.7 Descend into a col and then traverse toward Big Slide.

3.4 Bear right at the junction with the trail to Johns Brook Lodge (JBL), heading uphill.

3.6 SUMMIT of Big Slide! Continue south off the summit.

4.7 SUMMIT of Yard Mountain! Take the short spur trail to the top of Yard Mountain, then descend below a rocky precipice.

5.7 Turn left (southeast) toward JBL.

6.6 Follow the tributary of Johns Brook on a gentle downhill traverse.

6.8 Cross a stream on a double log bridge.

6.9 Pass in front of JBL, following Johns Brook toward the Garden.

7.3 Pass the bridge to Camp Grace and Camp Peggy O'Brien and then the junction with the alternate trail from Big Slide.

9.1 Cross the bridge over Deer Brook.

9.5 Pass the Bear Brook lean-to.

9.8 Bear left at the junction with the South Side Trail, remaining on the north side of Johns Brook.

10.0 Close the loop at the trail to Porter Mountain and The Brothers. Turn right toward the Garden.

10.2 Arrive back at the Garden trailhead.

8 Cascade Mountain

The easiest of the 4,000-footers and a great "starter" hike, with a view of ~~~~ ~~~~
Adirondack peaks, plus Lake Champlain and the Green Mountains of Vermont.

Nearest town: Lake Placid
Total distance: 4.2 miles, out and back
Highest point: 4,098 feet
Vertical gain: 1,899 feet
Approximate hiking time: 4 hours

Difficulty: Moderate
Canine compatibility: Dog-friendly. Dogs must be on leash.
Map: USGS Keene Valley Quad

Finding the trailhead: From the junction of NY 73 and Old Military Road (by the fairgrounds in Lake Placid), follow NY 73 east past the Olympic ski jumps. Go 5.7 miles. The trailhead is on the right (south) side of the road at the second of three small parking areas, just before Upper Cascade Lake. Trailhead: N44 13.136' / W73 53.254'

The Hike

Cascade Mountain is a popular hike, so it's best to get an early start if you want a parking spot in one of the three turnouts by the trailhead. This is good one for older kids and for less-experienced hikers looking for a big reward without serious mileage. It's also the perfect hike for the road-weary looking for some exercise after a long drive into the Adirondack Park but without a big time commitment—plus you get credit for bagging a 4,000-footer.

Note: Though Cascade Mountain is considered entry-level by seasoned hikers, it is still a 4,000-footer, with an exposed summit. Expect wind, and be prepared for cold temperatures and sudden weather changes even on a fair summer day. In addition, there is a lot of open rock, which can be slick when wet. Save this one for a nice day.

From the trailhead, descend a log-framed staircase and then cross four short footbridges to reach the sign-in box. This obvious, well-used trail follows red NYSDEC markers, ascending

Rock cairns show the way to the summit of Cascade Mountain.

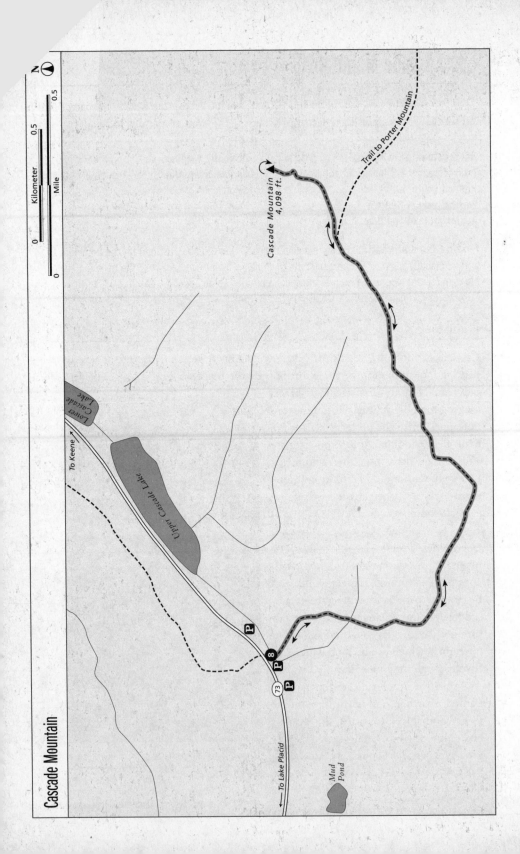

Cascade Mountain

Cascade Mountain
4,098 ft.

Trail to Porter Mountain

Lower Cascade Lake

Upper Cascade Lake

To Keene

To Lake Placid

73

Mud Pond

N

Kilometer
0   0.5

Mile
0   0.5

View of Great Range across Cascade Mountain's summit ridge

immediately from the box. There are lots of rocks and roots on the eroded trail, but they seem more like steps than inconvenient obstacles. Numerous water bars and well-placed stones help keep this popular trail in shape.

The trail climbs at a comfortable rate, heading south through a mixed northern forest of birch, striped maple, and beech. There are breaks in the ascent, first to cross a stream that flows down a pretty, mossy cascade just above the trail, and second to pass through a mud hole on large stepping stones. From the mud hole, the path heads deeper into the forest to the southeast. Soon it begins to climb steadily again and become rockier.

At 0.7 mile the pitch gets steeper, although two dozen stone steps aid the climb. It levels off as you pass a pointed-top boulder next to the trail, and then turns upward once again, becoming rocky and eroded again. As you near the boreal zone, birch "pillars" beckon you upward, with firs and other evergreens filling in the gaps, and the climb becomes more sustained.

At 0.9 mile the trail swings northeast and some slab appears underfoot. You can see more sky through the thinning canopy. The pitch moderates a little and then levels off briefly as you cross a wide mud pit, then it resumes its aggressive ascent.

At 1.2 miles, after one particularly washed-out slabby area, the trail bends to the east, passing a flat-top rock. There's no view, but it's a perfect place to take a break. Above the rock the trail eases as it winds through forest. You begin to sense the higher elevation, with some sky to either side of you. You are on a high buttress of the mountain. A cool breeze blows through the firs and the sporadic weather-beaten birches.

The eroded trail climbs steadily, eventually heading up a length of steep slab and then breaking out onto an open rock at 1.7 miles. Marcy looms large to the west, and there is a great view of the ski jumps and Lake Placid to the north.

The trail reenters the spindly trees, continuing to the northeast over more slab and mud. At 1.8 miles the trail forks at a broad, flat rock. The right fork goes to Porter Mountain. Bear left, following the red markers and the arrow toward Cascade Mountain.

The trail becomes fairly level, soon passing through a small grassy clearing. The trees end just ahead. Follow the yellow printed blazes and rock cairns up the expansive bald rock toward the summit. It's steep, requiring some scrambling and some easy friction climbing in places.

The trail ends at the summit at 2.1 miles, a broad, long ridge with many places to enjoy the view and have a picnic even if there are lots of people there. You can see the fire tower on Hurricane Mountain to the east, Memorial Highway snaking up Whiteface to the north, Lake Placid village and lake to the northwest, and a mesmerizing number of 4,000-footers to the south including the famous Great Range (Gothics, Armstrong, Upper Wolfjaw, and Lower Wolfjaw).

Return to the trailhead by the same route.

Miles and Directions

0.0 Start at the trailhead. Descend the log-framed stairs into the woods and cross four short lengths of puncheon.

0.7 Climb two dozen stone steps and then pass a pointed boulder.

0.9 Swing northeast as slab appears underfoot.

1.2 Pass a flat-top rock.

1.7 Reach the first view on the hike, from a patch of open rock.

1.8 Bear left toward the summit at the junction with the trail to Porter Mountain.

2.1 SUMMIT! Return by the same route.

4.2 Arrive back at the trailhead.

9 Giant Mountain via the Ridge Trail

A steep climb that passes a scenic mountain tarn then rewards with views of the Champlain Valley, the Great Range, and many landmark peaks.

Nearest town: Saint Huberts
Total distance: 5.2 miles, out and back
Highest point: 4,627 feet
Vertical gain: 3,000 feet
Approximate hiking time: 6.5 hours

Difficulty: Strenuous
Canine compatibility: Not recommended due to rock chimney just at tree line
Map: USGS Keene Valley Quad

Finding the trailhead: From the junction of NY 73 and Ausable Road (the road to the Ausable Club) in Saint Huberts, head south on NY 73 for 2.0 miles, past the second entrance to Ausable Road and the parking area for the Roaring Brook Trail. The trailhead for the Ridge Trail is just past Chapel Pond on the left (north) side of the road. There is parking on both sides of the road.

If approaching from I-87, take exit 30, then take NY 73 and US 9 north for 2.1 miles. Where NY 73 and US 9 split, continue on NY 73 for another 3.0 miles. Trailhead: N44 08.318' / W73 44.597'

The Hike

There is nothing little about Giant Mountain, the tallest peak in the Giant Mountain Wilderness. It's a cardio workout from the start, but with lots to see along the way, including wonderful open stretches of rock slab, a serene mountain tarn known as Giant Washbowl, the largest body of water in the Giant Mountain Wilderness, and for the grand finale, views from atop a dramatic cliff into the heart of the High Peaks. The Ridge Trail described here is the shortest route to the summit and one of two approaches from the west. The other, called the Roaring Brook Trail, is 1.2 miles longer round-trip and misses the Washbowl. Another favored approach is from the east over Rocky Peak Ridge, also a 4,000-footer, but that route is a much longer hike—15.8 miles round-trip.

Charles Broadhead is credited with the first ascent of Giant Mountain, in 1797, while running a survey line along the southern boundary of the Old Military Tract, a 665,000-acre parcel of land that was set aside by the State of New York in 1781 to give to soldiers who helped protect the northern part of the state from Indian attacks.

View of Great Range near tree line

View of the Great Range

This was the first recorded ascent of any major peak in the Adirondacks. The Ridge Trail was cut seventy-six years later in 1873.

From the trailhead, the path follows blue NYSDEC markers east into the woods over a couple of small footbridges to the sign-in box. From there, the trail climbs moderately through a hardwood forest typical of the Adirondacks at lower elevations. In early July wild raspberries bloom profusely along the trail.

The path bends left over an unreliable streamlet and then angles to the northeast following the streambed. Though the trail is strewn with rocks and roots, the footing is generally good as you climb. Patches of wood sorrel blossoms brighten the ground here and there. Soon the trail gets rockier and steeper. It crosses the streamlet again, angling up the slope. Everything around you appears green and lush.

After several switchbacks and some stone steps up a particularly steep pitch, the trail comes alongside the streamlet again and then crosses it. The slope eases a bit, crossing some sections of slab, heading north across a height of land. This is the top of the rock wall on the left side of the ravine above the trailhead. Once atop this plateau, the road noise seems far below and quickly fades away.

At 0.5 mile there is a nice rock perch with a view of Chapel Pond below and the Great Range (Gothics, Armstrong, Upper Wolfjaw, and Lower Wolfjaw Mountains) to the west. From here, the trail dips as it continues north back into the woods, away from Chapel Pond. Almost immediately, at 0.6 mile, it comes to Giant Washbowl and the junction with the lower traverse to the Roaring Brook Trail.

Nestled below a cliff, the Washbowl is a 4.2-acre pond that the state stocks with brook trout. Hidden frogs chirp among the water lilies that speckle the pond. It's a pleasant place to take a break if the rock perch you just passed is populated. There is a primitive campsite just beyond the pond on the right.

From Giant Washbowl, the trail continues to climb but more moderately. More hemlocks find their way into the forest mix as you wind back into the wilderness. The footing is good thanks to a lot of recent trail work here. At 0.9 mile the second connector to the Roaring Brook Trail, over an open rock hump known as Giant's Nubble, departs to the left (northwest). The 0.4 mile to Giant's Nubble is a worthwhile side trip for the view of Dial and Nippletop Mountains and a look at the Great Range from another angle. Wild blueberries grow among the rocks and Chapel Pond seems far below.

From the junction with the trail to Giant's Nubble, continue straight (left if coming from the Nubble), climbing up a steep eroded pitch. This older section of trail is soon aided by well-placed steps and switchbacks. This is the meat of the climb. Though some sections are newer and smoother and zigzag upward, it is still a heart-pounder.

Wild raspberry flowers beside the trail

At 1.2 miles the trail opens onto a section of bedrock. Follow the low rock cairns and painted arrows to stay on the route. The Great Range lies to the right of Round Mountain across the narrow valley.

The trail bends left (northeast) into the trees, though there is still rock slab underfoot. The canopy disappears almost immediately again as you scramble up a ledgy area. When a rock face appears ahead, the trail bends north. Watch for yellow blazes on the slab when you're not looking at the Great Range again.

There are more fun, ledgy scrambles as the trail goes in and out of the trees. Soon the views to the east and west open up, including a bird's-eye view of the historic Ausable Club's clubhouse, the large white building surrounded by grass. At 1.5 miles the trail splits. The trail to the right is called "Over the Bump," and the trail to the left is "Around the Bump." Bear left, going around the bump. "It's not worth going over the bump," stated one veteran Adirondack hiker. "The view is no better than the one you just had."

You are now in boreal forest. Bunchberries bloom by your feet along the path. The trail dips through a muddy spot and then climbs to another rocky area with views to the south and east. After traversing over bedrock the trail passes through a small glen of sumac, evergreens, and ferns in a low spot and then heads up through

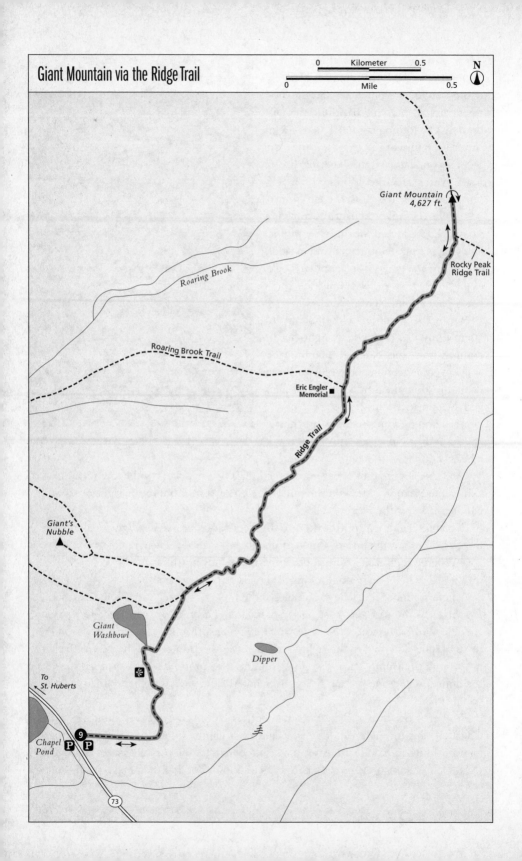

Giant Mountain via the Ridge Trail

0   Kilometer   0.5
0   Mile   0.5

N

Giant Mountain
4,627 ft.

Rocky Peak
Ridge Trail

Roaring Brook

Roaring Brook Trail

Eric Engler
Memorial

Ridge Trail

Giant's
Nubble

Giant
Washbowl

Dipper

To
St. Huberts

Chapel
Pond

9
P P

73

another washed-out section. As you climb you sense the ridge on either side of you although you are in the trees.

At 1.9 miles the trail passes a cross placed in memory of a Boy Scout named Eric Engler, who died here. Some believe Engler died of heatstroke, though his autopsy revealed that he died of heart failure. The cross was put on the mountain by the boy's grandparents, who were from Switzerland, where there is a tradition of placing crosses on mountains where people have died. However, they originally put it in the wrong spot. Several years later one of Engler's friends returned to the mountain and moved the cross to its current, accurate location. The NYSDEC does not permit memorials on state land in the Adirondack Park but has yet to remove the cross as of this book's publication. The Roaring Brook Trail merges with the Ridge Trail just after the cross.

After passing a large boulder on your left, the climb continues persistently up the slabby trail. It dips and bends left (north), providing a view of the summit hump. Clintonia sprouts among the bunchberries on this short reprieve across a high, narrow shoulder of the mountain.

The final grunt up the summit knob is a combination of rock, rubble, and slab, which can be slick when wet. A fun rock chimney lifts you into the krummholz. At 2.5 miles a sign denotes the beginning of the alpine zone at the junction with the Rocky Peak Ridge Trail. The route clears the tree line at 2.6 miles on the elongated open summit ledge, which is laced with mountain sandwort.

Giant Mountain is ranked twelfth among the Adirondack 4,000-footers. The breathtaking view of the Great Range with Mount Marcy poking up behind that iconic ridge is the highlight of Giant's summit panorama. The Ausable Club lies below, across the mountain's great cirque. Lake Champlain lies to the left (east). The ski trails on Whiteface Mountain are visible to the far right (west).

Return to the trailhead by the same route.

Miles and Directions

0.0 Start at the trailhead for the Ridge Trail. Head east into the woods over a couple of footbridges.

0.5 FIRST VIEW! Continue north into the woods.

0.6 GIANT WASHBOWL! At the junction with the lower traverse to the Roaring Brook Trail, continue straight (north).

0.9 Pass the trail to Giant's Nubble, continue straight (north), climbing a steep eroded pitch.

1.2 Follow the yellow arrows and low rock cairns across the open rock.

1.5 Bear left, "around the bump."

1.9 Pass a cross placed in memory of Boy Scout Eric Engler just before the Roaring Brook Trail merges with the Ridge Trail.

2.5 Enter the alpine zone as the Rocky Peak Ridge Trail departs to the right.

2.6 SUMMIT! Return by the same route.

5.2 Arrive back at the trailhead.

10 Great Range Loop

An epic hike along a river, past waterfalls, and across the most famous alpine ridge in the Adirondacks over four 4,000-footers—Gothics, Armstrong, Upper Wolfjaw, and Lower Wolfjaw Mountains.

Nearest town: Saint Huberts
Total distance: 11.5 miles, lollipop
Highest point: 4,331 feet (4,675 feet with option to summit of Gothics)
Vertical gain: 3,303 feet

Approximate hiking time: 10 hours
Difficulty: Experts only
Canine compatibility: Not dog-friendly due to ladders and rock chimneys
Map: USGS Keene Valley Quad

Finding the trailhead: From the bridge over Johns Brook in Keene Valley, travel 3.3 miles east on NY 73 to Saint Huberts. At the second junction with Ausable Road, turn right. Go about 100 yards. The trailhead parking lot is on the left. This is the same parking lot for the hike to Noonmark and Round Mountains. Parking is not permitted along Ausable Road. Walk up the dirt road to the trailhead. Trailhead parking: N44 08.982' / W73 46.078'

The Hike

This route is the longest day hike in this book, and that's excluding the options to the summits of Gothics and Lower Wolfjaw Mountains. Only experienced, physically fit hikers should attempt this loop. The hike, while very challenging, is also spectacular and includes a lot of everything Adirondack. You'll walk along the legendary East Branch Ausable River, rest by scenic waterfalls, and climb over at least two 4,000-footers— Armstrong Mountain and Upper Wolfjaw Mountain—along the landmark ridge that hikers on every other mountain at the High Peaks gaze at. And if you're really ambitious, you can add two more summits, Gothics and Lower Wolfjaw Mountains.

Given the mileage and the vertical climb, plan an early start and watch the clock and the weather, especially after Labor Day as the days get shorter. By early October expect ice on the northern side of each peak, which can make rocky areas extremely slick and challenging. For time benchmarks, plan to be at Gothics col by noon, the summit of Armstrong Mountain by 1:00 p.m., and on Upper Wolfjaw Mountain by 2:00 p.m. If you are ahead of this schedule and you have the endurance, you could bag Gothics and Lower Wolfjaw as well.

Save this hike for a clear day, and even then, be prepared for an unexpected change in the weather. You'll spend much of the time on one of the highest ridges in the Adirondacks, potentially exposed to strong winds, rain, and even ice and snow, though the valley might be calm and dry. This route tests your ability as a hiker, but it's worth the effort. You will return to your car after an extraordinary day.

From the trailhead parking lot, head up the dirt road into the Adirondack Mountain Reserve (AMR), aka Ausable Club. The AMR was founded in 1887 by William

East Branch Ausable River at its lowest flow, during the fall

G. Neilson at the height of the logging boom in the Adirondacks. Neilson, a prominent mining engineer from Philadelphia, and several friends purchased 25,000 acres, which included Upper and Lower Ausable Lake and the surrounding mountains, to keep them pristine. The AMR grew to 40,000 acres by 1910 but then sold two large tracts to New York State. Today the AMR encompasses 7,000 acres. The State of New York retains permission (an easement) from the AMR for the public to use its trails that connect with state land, a right that has existed since the AMR began. However, the AMR prohibits hunting, fishing, camping, boating, swimming, and pets within its boundaries by non-members.

The trails within the AMR are among the best maintained footpaths in the Adirondacks thanks to the efforts of the Adirondack Trail Improvement Society (ATIS), the AMR's trail-maintenance group. As you hike across AMR land, the markers are similar to the color-coded NYSDEC markers except that they have the ATIS logo on them.

At 0.4 mile, at the corner of the golf course, the route to Noonmark departs to the left. Continue on Ausable Road, heading northwest into the heart of the Ausable Club. The original clubhouse, which was first known as Beede House and then the Saint Huberts Inn, was built in the 1870s just after the Civil War ended, but it burned in 1890. The current sprawling white structure was built after the fire and is a National Historic Landmark. Many famous people, including author William James and psychiatrists Sigmund Freud and Carl Jung, spent time here.

Just before the clubhouse, at 0.6 mile, turn left between the tennis courts on Lake Road Way. At 0.8 mile the trailhead sits at the end of the pavement by the AMR gatehouse. After signing in turn right (north) on the narrow dirt road, following the yellow ATIS markers. You immediately pass through a multilegged junction. Continue straight, following the trail sign and the arrow, toward the sound of rushing water. About 50 feet later the trail comes to the Ausable River and bends to the left. A short way later it turns right, crossing the river on a long narrow bridge.

At 0.9 mile, at the far end of the bridge, lies the junction with the trail to Rooster Comb and an alternate route to Lower Wolfjaw Mountain. Head left (south) on the West River Trail, which is also a nature trail between here and the next bridge. Signs identify the different species of trees, such as hemlock, white ash, and beech. The trail is smooth and flat, a pretty woodland walk next to the river.

At 1.3 miles the nature trail ends at a four-way junction. A bridge crosses the river on your left. The lower trail to Cathedral Rocks departs to the right. Continue straight (south) on the West River Trail.

The trail rolls along parallel to the river, sometimes next to the water and sometimes a short distance from it. At 1.9 miles the trail climbs above the river to the second junction with the Cathedral Rocks Trail. Continue on the West River Trail.

At 2.0 miles the Canyon Bridge Trail departs to the left, over the river. Remain on the West River Trail, which climbs a short pitch and traverses a hillside above the water. After crossing a muddy area on puncheon and another climb, it reaches a plateau that's fairly high above the river, though the water roars loudly below.

The trail continues to head upward, though in waves, but you are not on a mountain yet. At 2.7 miles it turns left over a footbridge by a pretty cascade, which is the bottom of the much longer Wedgebrook Cascades, and comes to the junction with a trail from the Wolfjaws. You will close the loop here at the end of the day.

Continue south on the West River Trail, following the signs toward "Lower Lakes" and "Beaver Meadow Falls." The trail dips slightly and then crosses another muddy area on puncheon. The river is now a turbulent deluge crashing through a rocky gorge below you. The trail works its way back to the side of the river above the gorge and then bends right along a tributary stream to a bridge under Beaver Meadow Falls. At 3.4 miles, just past the bridge, turn right (west) onto the Gothics–Armstrong Trail (blue ATIS markers), climbing a ladder up some ledges.

The trail climbs very steeply above the falls to a rock perch by the stream, but then becomes a more reasonable ascent. At 3.6 miles the Lost Lookout Trail departs to your left. Continue straight (northwest) toward Gothics, following the stream.

The trail veers away from the stream and comes alongside a smaller stream on your left. At 3.8 miles you leave the AMR, crossing the boundary onto state land. The markers remain blue but now carry the NYSDEC logo. Follow the streamlet, continuing to make steady uphill progress. As the streamlet disappears, the climb takes you through a mixed forest of beech, maple, and hemlock. Soon you can glimpse humps of exposed rock through the trees, which is the north end of the Great Range, still high above you.

It's a stiff climb, which gets increasingly steeper and more eroded. As you make your way up the left side of a large cirque, entering the boreal forest, the soil is noticeably thinner, and the trail becomes rockier, like a streambed with rounded football-size rocks. This is a classic Adirondack climb, direct without switchbacks, and the section where you pay your dues on this route.

The trail eventually reaches the top of the cirque and bends right, easing somewhat before jogging left up a long stretch of low-angle slab. Soon the trees begin to shrink and thin out enough to see a mountain view, including the bald top of Noonmark close at the mouth of the ravine.

The path traverses a ridge protected by fir and spruce trees and then comes to a large glacial erratic (boulder) balanced on another rock on your right. The two boulders form a slanting shallow cave about 10 feet tall at its mouth. From here, there's more climbing, often up short rock chimneys.

As you approach Gothics col, you can see past Gothics deep into the High Peaks to your left. The uneven, rocky trail seems to hang on the side of the mountain. It drops and climbs as it traverses toward Gothics, whose great slides flow down the massive mountainside in front of you.

After a series of ladders down several sections of vertical bedrock, the trail reaches a junction at Gothics col at 5.4 miles. To bag Gothics, bear left. It's a ledgy, steep 0.6 mile to the summit (1.2 miles round-trip). To continue on the loop, bear right (northeast), toward Armstrong Mountain, now following yellow NYSDEC markers.

The climb continues upward from the col over slab and through krummholz to the high ridge that is part of the iconic view of the Great Range when you look at it from other peaks. Gothics towers behind you. You can also see Mount Marcy and Algonquin Peak to the west. The trail continues through high boreal, crossing several muddy areas. It's a nice break from the multiple rocky scrambles behind you, but the rock returns as you climb up Armstrong's summit cone. It's a quick ascent, reaching the summit at 5.8 miles.

Armstrong Mountain was named for an Adirondack pioneer named Thomas Armstrong. The summit of Armstrong is a broad flat rock at the top of a high cliff. It isn't a massive bald peak, but it's one of those places where you could linger on a sunny afternoon. The view to the south and west is endless but dominated by Gothics. Mount Colden crowns the ridge to the east. Look down to see the Johns Brook drainage, with Marcy and the MacIntyre Mountains beyond. Marcy Field is the large clearing to the northwest.

From the summit of Armstrong, continue northeast towards Upper Wolfjaw. The descent off the summit is slow-going over lengths of slab and ledge. There are a number of rock chimneys to down-climb, though a tall ladder helps you descend one particularly vertical cliff. Eventually, the terrain becomes less extreme, though you are still high in the mountains, with more rock slabs to descend and some impressive mud holes to cross.

The trail zigzags down the last drop into the col between Armstrong and Upper Wolfjaw. After crossing another large mud hole, it begins the ascent up Upper Wolfjaw. While the climb is more of the same—short rock walls and mud—it feels less

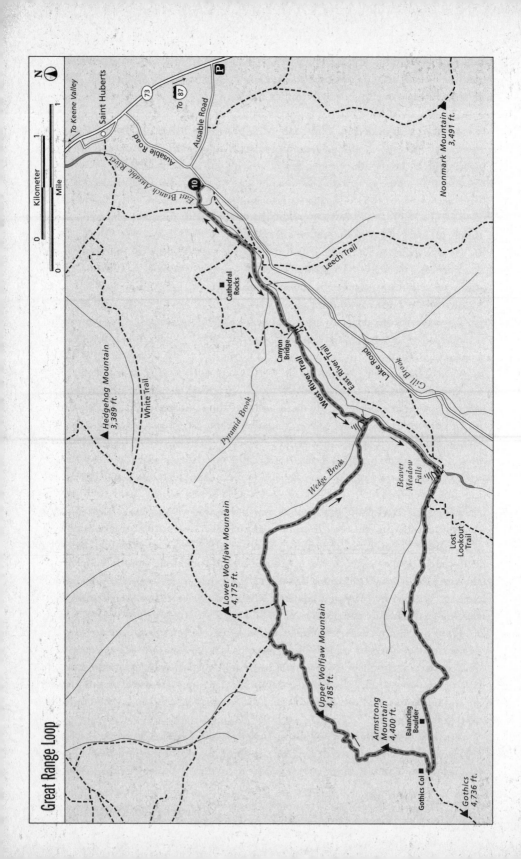

Great Range Loop

N

Kilometer
0   1

Mile
0   1

To Keene Valley
Saint Huberts
73
To 87
P
Ausable Road
East Branch Ausable River
Ausable Road
10
Noonmark Mountain
3,491 ft.
Leech Trail
Cathedral Rocks
Hedgehog Mountain
3,389 ft.
White Trail
Canyon Bridge
West River Trail
East River Trail
Lake Road
Gill Brook
Pyramid Brook
Wedge Brook
Beaver Meadow Falls
Lost Lookout Trail
Lower Wolfjaw Mountain
4,175 ft.
Upper Wolfjaw Mountain
4,185 ft.
Armstrong Mountain
4,400 ft.
Balancing Boulder
Gothics Col
Gothics
4,736 ft.

severe, perhaps because Upper Wolf-jaw is lower than Armstrong. At 6.4 miles a short, 20-yard spur departs to the left to the summit, a rock pinnacle surrounded by low trees, but with a nice view of Giant Mountain to the north, Big Slide to the east, and Armstrong to the southwest.

Return to the main trail and continue northeast toward Wolfjaw Notch. The trail descends gently and smoothly at first, but then reverts back to more rocky drop-offs, though nothing as extensive as earlier in the day. After passing a small clearing with a large boulder in it, the trail appears to split. Bear left around the boulder, continuing to descend. The rounded hump of Lower Wolfjaw is visible ahead through the trees.

At 7.1 miles, just as you feel like you are about to run into the side of Lower Wolfjaw, the trail comes to a T at Wolfjaw Notch. The left trail goes to Johns Brook Lodge. Take the right

Rock overhang beside trail

(east) trail, still following the yellow NYSDEC markers. After crossing a short mud pit, you immediately come to the junction with the upper trail to the summit of Lower Wolfjaw. To reach the summit, take the left fork (yellow markers). It is 1.0 mile round-trip.

To continue on the loop, go straight, following the blue NYSDEC markers under a rock wall and climbing moderately on a smooth path. As it levels off, on your right you can see the massive bare slabs and cliff that form the northeastern side of Upper Wolfjaw. At 7.3 miles the path comes to another T, this time with the lower trail to Lower Wolfjaw. Bear right (east) toward the West Brook Trail and Wedge Brook. The descent is rather steep and not very smooth, but at least there are no more rock chimneys to negotiate.

When the trail finally mellows at the bottom of the ravine, the hardwoods return and the descent mellows to a downhill saunter. At 8.5 miles it crosses back into the AMR and onto good footing.

After a long downhill stretch through the forest, the trail crosses a streamlet, flattens, and then comes to a brook and a pretty cascade. The trail bends to the right, parallel to the brook, which tumbles toward the Ausable River like an endless waterfall. The water is merely a ribbon most of the year, but it becomes a broad torrent during the spring. The brook pours into a pool at the base of a cliff called Wedge Brook Cascades.

At 8.8 miles you reach the junction with the West River Trail, closing the loop. Turn left and return to the trailhead via the West River Trail.

Miles and Directions

0.0 Start at the trailhead parking lot. Walk up the dirt road into the Ausable Club.

0.4 Continue up the dirt road, ignoring the trail to Noonmark, which departs to the left.

0.6 Turn left between the tennis courts on Lake Road Way.

0.8 Trailhead: Take the trail to the right, toward the river, then cross the river on a footbridge.

0.9 Turn left on the West River Trail on the far side of the bridge.

1.3 The lower Cathedral Rocks Trail departs to the right. Continue straight on the West River Trail.

1.9 At the junction with the upper Cathedral Rocks Trail, continue straight on the West River Trail.

2.0 At the junction with the trail to Canyon Bridge, continue straight on the West River Trail.

2.7 At the junction with the trail from Wolfjaw Notch, bear left (south), continuing on the West River Trail.

3.4 At the junction with the trail to Gothics col, turn right (northwest) toward Gothics col.

3.6 Lost Lookout Trail departs to the left. Continue straight on the Gothics col trail.

3.8 Cross the boundary onto state land.

5.1 Pass the balancing boulder.

5.4 GOTHICS COL! Turn right (northeast) toward Armstrong Mountain.

5.8 SUMMIT of Armstrong! Continue on trail toward Upper Wolfjaw.

6.4 SUMMIT of Upper Wolfjaw! Continue toward Lower Wolfjaw Mountain.

7.1 Turn right at Wolfjaw Notch, immediately passing the upper trail to Lower Wolfjaw.

7.3 Bear right through the junction with the lower trail to Lower Wolfjaw.

8.5 Cross the boundary onto AMR land.

8.8 Close the loop at the West River Trail. Turn left and retrace from here to the trailhead parking lot.

11.5 Arrive back at the trailhead parking lot.

11 Whiteface Mountain

A long forest walk past a large pond and along a substantial brook, and then a scenic climb on slab and rock to a historic observatory and interpretive center.

Nearest town: Lake Placid
Total distance: 11.4 miles, out and back
Highest point: 4,867 feet
Vertical gain: 3,198 feet
Approximate hiking time: 10 hours

Difficulty: Experts only
Canine compatibility: For experienced, fit hiking dogs only, due to length of hike and talus on upper mountain
Map: USGS Lake Placid Quad

Finding the trailhead: From the junction of NY 86 (Main Street) and NY 73 in Lake Placid, take NY 86 northeast toward Wilmington for 2.9 miles. Turn left at the NYSDEC sign for Connery Pond (dirt). Go 0.7 mile to the barrier, which is the trailhead. There are two small parking lots for hikers near the sign-in box, one on the left and one on the right. Trailhead: N44 18.527' / W73 56.189'

The Hike

The hike up Whiteface Mountain from the Lake Placid side is a long one. Two-thirds of the distance is a fairly flat approach, followed by a steep ascent up the southern side of the mountain. It's a full-day commitment, but it rewards with varied scenery and terrain along the way and arguably one of the best views of any mountain in the Adirondacks. The route passes a short spur to the shore of Lake Placid at Whiteface Landing. Some people take a motorboat the length of the lake to the landing and begin hiking from there. You'll also pass the Whiteface lean-to, which is a nice camping option if the mileage seems too long for a day hike.

Whiteface Mountain is the fifth-highest peak in the Adirondacks. It is a monadnock, 10 miles from any other 4,000-footer. The mountain is famous for its ski area, located on its eastern side, which was the site of the alpine skiing events during the 1980 Winter Olympics. The Whiteface Mountain Veterans Memorial Highway ascends from the north, stopping just shy of the summit. It is the only road to the top of a major mountain in the Adirondacks and is a popular tourist attraction from late May through mid-October. The summit "castle" houses a small interpretive center and museum as well as a scientific observatory. You won't be alone on this mountaintop on a fair-weather day, which is the only kind of day to do this hike. The upper mountain is mostly open rock and highly exposed. If the mountaintop is in the clouds, hikers can feel claustrophobic among the thick firs near tree line and disoriented on the open rock.

The trail begins on the continuation of the dirt road on the other side of a chain on a public right-of-way (red NYSDEC markers). The road immediately skirts a private camp on Connery Pond and then narrows to a footpath, which follows the

Hiker approaching summit observatory

western side of the pond. At 0.4 mile a second barrier marks the boundary of the MacKenzie Wilderness. Walk around it, continuing on the flat, smooth trail.

The path crosses a mossy streamlet and then begins a gradual climb on its long approach to the mountain. Though a footpath today, it is really an old woods road as evidenced by the intermittent culverts across the path. This section can be a tedious buggy slog, but by late September the bugs disappear and the forest ignites with color.

The route undulates through the woods on long, lazy inclines. At 2.4 miles you come to a T in a small clearing, which is the junction with the short spur to White-face Landing. Bear right (east) past a second sign-in box. The trail narrows, crowded by maple saplings on both sides, though it is still the woods road that you have followed from the trailhead.

At 3.0 miles the path bends sharply to the right just before crossing Whiteface Brook on a rerouted section of trail. Continue parallel to the brook, passing through a mud pit as you wind through the forest. Soon you come to a confluence of tributaries. Cross one of the two main branches of the brook on large rocks, and then a smaller streamlet on logs, following the left branch of the brook and heading northeast.

The trail makes a sharp right (south), away from the stream, and then arcs back toward it, reaching the Whiteface lean-to at 3.4 miles. From the lean-to, the trail bends to the east away from the brook, and then the real climb begins.

The ascent is moderate at first, loosely parallel to the brook, but it soon becomes more persistent. Conifers begin to dominate the forest mix as the trail reaches the top of a deep ravine above the brook, now a smaller stream. The trail becomes progressively rougher as you climb. Eventually the rocks become big and slick as you make your way through the boreal forest. Close to tree line, the fir trees thicken on both sides of you, creating an impenetrable corridor.

After climbing the low end of a cliff and the washout above it, it's a bit of a scramble over and around some small boulders and slab. The footing improves briefly, though the ascent remains steep, then the trail passes a curious hole, like a small vertical cave, formed by a big boulder. Watch the route, as branches of low fir trees obscure the path in places.

Soon you can see the sky through the trees and feel the elevation. After scrambling over and around more small boulders, the trail passes a large flat-sided rock, like a tilted a wall, and

Lower trail near Connery Pond

then bends east. At 5.3 miles the trees shrink and then give way briefly over a long length of slab. A view to the south appears behind you as you break into the krummholz. Follow the yellow paint as you climb up the talus slope.

Just below the summit a sign says "ORDA Ski Trails." Follow the arrow upward, reaching the summit at 5.7 miles. Whiteface has a substantial open rocky top. The observatory, nicknamed "Whiteface Castle," is ahead, just beyond a small viewing platform. The castle is 300 vertical feet above the end of the auto road. Granite removed during the construction of the road was used to build the castle. It was completed in 1935 under the administration of New York State Governor Franklin D. Roosevelt as part of a public works project that would later become the model for the New Deal initiative under his presidential administration during the Great Depression.

The view of the High Peaks from the viewing platform includes half of the 4,000-footers in the Adirondacks, including Giant, Noonmark, Dix, Nippletop, Gothics, Marcy, and Algonquin Mountains. You can also see Camel's Hump and Mount Mansfield to the east in Vermont and Montreal to the north. If you see a small brown bird flitting among the rocks, it might be a Bicknell's thrush, an endangered species known to reside here.

Return to the trailhead by the same route.

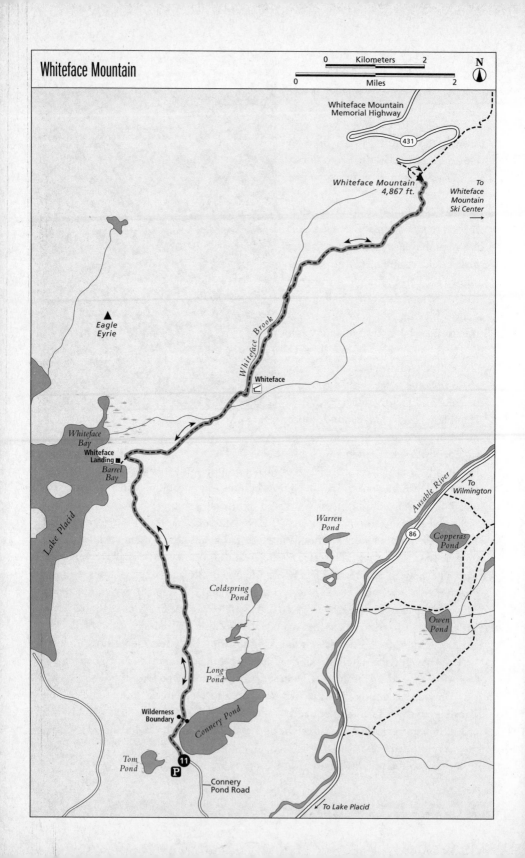

Whiteface Mountain

Kilometers
0   2

Miles
0   2

N

Whiteface Mountain
Memorial Highway

431

Whiteface Mountain
4,867 ft.

To
Whiteface
Mountain
Ski Center

Whiteface Brook

Eagle
Eyrie

Whiteface

Whiteface
Bay

Whiteface
Landing

Barrel
Bay

Ausable River

To
Wilmington

Lake Placid

Warren
Pond

86

Copperas
Pond

Coldspring
Pond

Owen
Pond

Long
Pond

Connery Pond

Wilderness
Boundary

Tom
Pond

11

P

Connery
Pond Road

To Lake Placid

Miles and Directions

0.0 Start at the trailhead by the sign-in box on Connery Pond Road. Head northwest on foot down the dirt road.

0.4 Walk around the gate that marks the boundary of the MacKenzie Wilderness.

2.4 Bear right (northeast) at the junction with the trail to Whiteface Landing.

3.0 Cross Whiteface Brook and continue to follow the brook.

3.4 Pass by the Whiteface lean-to and then begin climbing the southern side of the mountain.

5.3 Enter the krummholz zone and see the first clear view to the south. Continue up the talus slope.

5.7 SUMMIT! Return by the same route.

11.4 Arrive back at the trailhead.

12 Wright Peak

A lower, shorter alternative to nearby Algonquin Peak, but with equally stunning views in all directions.

Nearest town: Lake Placid
Total distance: 6.6 miles, out and back
Highest point: 4,580 feet
Vertical gain: 2,331 feet
Approximate hiking time: 6.5 hours

Difficulty: Strenuous
Canine compatibility: For experienced hiking dogs only due to smooth rock ledges at higher elevations.
Map: USGS Keene Valley Quad

Finding the trailhead: From Lake Placid, take NY 73 east toward Keene. About 1.2 miles past the Olympic ski jump complex, turn right (south) on Adirondack Loj Road. Go 4.7 miles to the end of the road and the sizable parking lot at Adirondak Loj. The trailhead is at the opposite side of the parking lot farthest to the right, directly in front of the information building. *Note:* There is a fee for parking here, which is discounted for members of the Adirondack Mountain Club. Trailhead: N44 10.978' / W73 57.765'

The Hike

Named for Silas Wright, who served as a U.S. senator from New York from 1833 to 1844, and then as governor of New York from 1844 to 1845, Wright Peak shares the same approach as Algonquin Peak and is the perfect alternative if you want a shorter

Trailhead by Adirondak Loj

hike both in terms of mileage and vertical climb, yet yearn for a 360-degree view from a majestic bald summit. That said, it is still a 4,000-footer, sixteenth highest among the Adirondack forty-six. It is the northernmost peak in the McIntyre Range and has a reputation as one of the windiest, so it still deserves respect.

From the trailhead, follow the blue NYSDEC markers into the woods on the smooth, wide path called the Van Hoevenberg Trail. This is the same trailhead for the hikes up Algonquin Peak and the Avalanche Lake–Mount Marcy Loop. The trail heads slightly downhill at first, crossing the Mr. Van Ski Trail at less than 0.1 mile. From there, the trail narrows briefly through a stand of young hemlocks, continuing its gentle descent.

At 0.4 mile the trail levels off over a small footbridge. It climbs three elongated steps and then crosses a long,

Approaching the summit of Wright Peak

highly constructed bridge through a wet area. The trail turns gently upward off the bridge over several log water bars, heading generally to the south. After passing a couple more ski trails, you reach the boundary into the High Peaks Wilderness.

At 0.9 mile the trail comes to a fork. The left path goes to Marcy Dam. Take the right (southwest) path toward Algonquin and Wright Peaks. The path soon becomes rockier and the climbing more noticeable.

At 1.3 miles the Whales Tail Ski Trail departs to the left. The ascent is steady now, coming alongside a seasonal stream. At 1.8 miles the trail turns 90 degrees right, crossing the stream at a yellow arrow, then curls back to its predominantly southwesterly direction. The trail is old, worn, and eroded now. A few well-placed stonelike steps aid the climb, which passes out of the mixed northern forest and into the lower boreal zone, mainly softwoods and paper birch.

After crossing a section of steep rock slab, the trail passes a spur to a primitive campsite on the left. The trail dips back to the stream and crosses under a 50-foot cascade at 2.3 miles. There is a nice pool at its base when the waterfall is running, though it might be just a small trickle down the rock face during a dry spell.

Shortly after the waterfall, the trail levels off through a muddy area. At 2.8 miles it bends sharply left up a short rock chimney and then crosses slab heading toward the

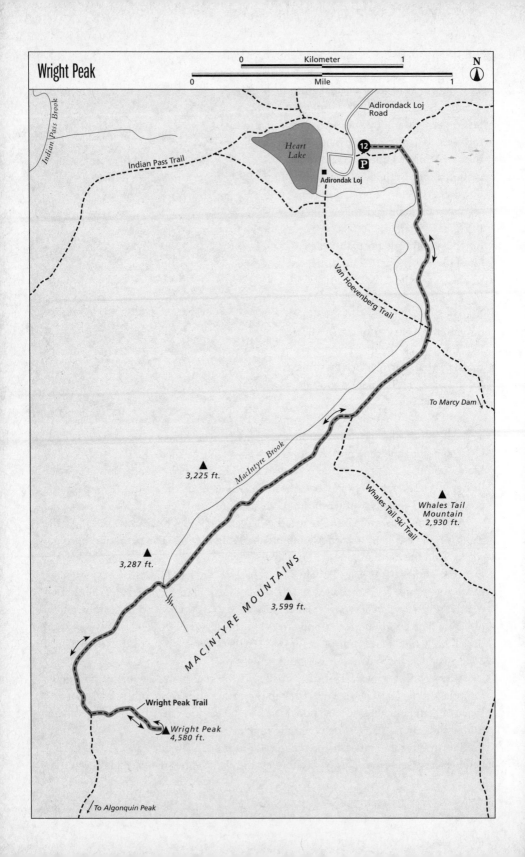

Wright Peak

0 Kilometer 1

0 Mile 1

N

Indian Pass Brook

Adirondack Loj Road

Heart Lake

Indian Pass Trail

P

Adirondak Loj

12

Van Hoevenberg Trail

To Marcy Dam

3,225 ft.

MacIntyre Brook

Whales Tail Ski Trail

Whales Tail Mountain 2,930 ft.

3,287 ft.

MACINTYRE MOUNTAINS

3,599 ft.

Wright Peak Trail

Wright Peak 4,580 ft.

To Algonquin Peak

distant hump of Algonquin. As the trees become shorter, you can glimpse neighboring peaks through the branches, but you'll want to pay attention to the route, which requires some low-angle friction climbing.

At 2.9 miles the Wright Peak Trail splits from the Algonquin Peak Trail. Turn left onto the Wright Peak Trail, continuing to follow the blue NYSDEC markers. There are more stretches of rock slab as you ascend into the krummholz, then a 10-foot rock wall blocks the path just as you clear tree line. The easiest route up the wall is on the left. From there, continue toward the summit following the rock cairns and painted blazes.

The steep final ascent on open rock takes you over a false summit and then arrives at the true summit at 3.3 miles. Algonquin Peak stands tall to your right (south) the entire way above tree line, a massive bald hump. The trail ends at the summit, where in 1962 a B-47 on a practice mission out of the former Plattsburgh Air Force Base crashed, killing all four aboard. For many years, hikers scavenged pieces of the plane, though little of it is apparent today. Rather than trampling the rare alpine sedges (grasslike flora) in search of a souvenir from the crash, pick a spot on the expansive open rock and enjoy the view of Mount Colden immediately to the southwest, with Mount Marcy just beyond. To the north, you can see Mount Jo above Heart Lake and Whiteface Mountain much farther away. Street and Nye Mountains lie nearby to the northwest, with many of the prominent western High Peaks beyond these two trailless 4,000-footers farther to the west.

Return to the trailhead by the same route.

Miles and Directions

0.0 Start at the trailhead. Follow the trail toward Marcy Dam.

0.1 Continue straight at the junction with the Mr. Van Ski Trail.

0.4 Cross a long, well-constructed footbridge over a wet area.

0.9 At the junction with the trail to Marcy Dam, bear right toward Algonquin and Wright Peaks.

1.8 Cross the stream and then follow the trail back to the southwest.

2.3 Pass by a 50-foot waterfall.

2.9 Turn left (east) on the Wright Peak Trail.

3.3 SUMMIT! Return by the same route.

6.6 Arrive back at the trailhead parking lot at Adirondak Loj.

High Peaks Region

Big Rewards under 4,000 Feet

While the High Peaks region of the Adirondacks is best known for its forty-six peaks over 4,000 feet in elevation, it also boasts numerous hikes with equally stunning views that do not surpass that lauded benchmark. In this section you will find twelve hikes of varying lengths and ability levels that are more modest in terms of vertical gain but superlative in enjoyment. Many offer a big reward for minimal effort and are thus perfect choices for a family outing. But don't expect solitude on the easier routes, as they attract many school groups and summer camps. Also be aware that a few of the routes are as challenging as the 4,000-footers either in terms of mileage or ruggedness of terrain. Always be prepared with proper footwear, clothing, food, water, and emergency items when attempting any of these day hikes, no matter how easy they may sound. There's a high chance of extreme weather in the High Peaks, no matter where you roam in this wilderness area.

◀ *View from a subpeak of Pitchoff Mountain into the heart of the High Peaks (Hike 23)*

persand Mountain

h, then a steep ascent to a broad open summit with a 360-degree view of the Saranac Lake chain of lakes to the north, the High Peaks to the south and east, and the Seward Range to the west.

Nearest town: Saranac Lake
Total distance: 4.8 miles, out and back
Highest point: 3,352 feet
Vertical gain: 1,779 feet
Approximate hiking time: 5 hours

Difficulty: Strenuous due to the vertical gain
Canine compatibility: Dog-friendly though small dogs may have difficulty on the steep rock on the upper mountain
Map: USGS Saranac Lake Quad

Finding the trailhead: From the junction of NY 3 and NY 86 in Saranac Lake, take NY 3 west for 8.2 miles. The trailhead is on the left (south) side of the road. The generous trailhead parking area is on the right (north) side of the road. Trailhead: N44 15.094' / W74 14.378'

The Hike

Located on the northwestern edge of the High Peaks region, Ampersand Mountain is believed to be named after nearby Ampersand Creek on its southern flank, which supposedly twists like an ampersand symbol (&), though Ampersand Lake, a private lake into which the creek flows, more closely resembles the symbol. The mountain is historically significant because it was the first mountain ever climbed by Bob Marshal,

Puncheon on the approach to Ampersand Mountain

the famous wilderness explorer and conservationist. He reached the summit in 1915 at age fifteen. Ten years later Marshal and his brother George were the first to reach the summits of all forty-six Adirondack peaks over 4,000 feet.

From the sign-in box next to NY 3, the path (red NYSDEC markers) is smooth and broad, through ferns and under maples, birches, and towering evergreens. The well-used but well-maintained route descends gently at first to a log bridge over a stream strewn with large mossy rocks, then heads toward the mountain on a long flat approach. It crosses several streamlets along the way, aided by intermittent footbridges and puncheon.

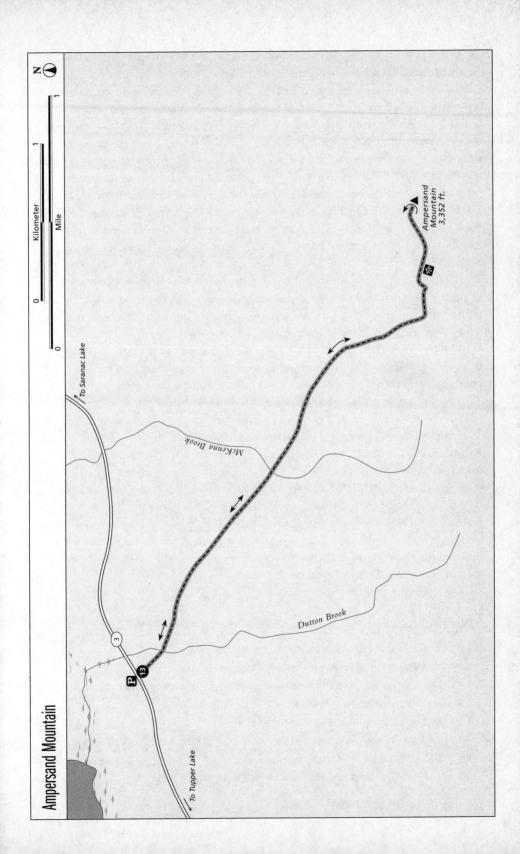

Ampersand Mountain

N

Kilometer
0   1

Mile
0   1

To Saranac Lake

McKenna Brook

Dutton Brook

Ampersand Mountain
3,352 ft.

3

13

P

To Tupper Lake

At 1.0 mile, after a long length of puncheon across a wet area, the path crosses yet another streamlet, which turns into McKenna Brook farther down the slope. Then, at 1.2 miles, the trail heads up several well-placed rocks and finally begins to ascend the mountain. Though the path becomes strewn with rocks, the footing remains good.

At 1.5 miles the trail bends 90 degrees right (south), crosses a streamlet, then continues to wind through the woods parallel to it. After climbing a series of large stepping stones, it leaves the wet area behind and wanders in a more easterly direction. Though the route gets steeper and rockier, the rocks are positioned like a long stone staircase.

At 1.9 miles the footing becomes rougher and more eroded, but more rock steps aid the steep climb. The trail passes under a mossy rock ledge, then ascends another rock stairwell as you enter the lower boreal zone. Hemlocks and birch now dominate the forest mix as the washed-out trail becomes a near vertical jumble of rocks and roots.

At 2.1 miles a view of the Saranac Lakes appears through the trees behind you as you scramble up a section of rock slab. Then the trail levels off, passing below a cone of open rock on your left, then under a huge boulder on the right. Yellow arrows point the way through this interesting narrow chasm. The boulders that form a wall next to the trail probably split apart during the last ice age.

The trail dips, then curves to the right (east). It seems to fork at a boulder, but follow the red markers, which lead you to the left. Soon the trail clears the trees onto open rock. Follow the yellow blazes to reach the summit at 2.4 miles.

The summit of Ampersand Mountain is technically below tree line. Most of the trees were cleared by W. W. Ely, who recorded the first ascent of the mountain in 1872, and then returned with four friends to build a lean-to there. The next year Verplanck Colvin cleared the rest of the trees to create a triangulation point during his Adirondack survey.

From 1920 through 1970 a 22-foot fire tower stood atop Ampersand. The plaque near the location of the fire tower is in memory of Walter Channing Rice, one of the early fire-watchers stationed there. Even though the fire tower is long gone, the view from atop Ampersand is one of the most striking in the Adirondacks for the contrast between the endless lakes of the Saint Regis Canoe Area to the north and the endless wilderness past the Seward Range to the south.

Return to the trailhead by the same route.

Miles and Directions

0.0 Start at the trailhead for Ampersand Mountain beside NY 3.

1.0 Cross a streamlet, which is really the top of McKenna Brook.

1.2 Ascend several well-placed rock steps, the beginning of the climb up the mountain.

1.5 Bend 90 degrees to the right and follow a streamlet as you climb.

1.9 Continue up a near-vertical washed-out area.

2.1 Check out the view of the Saranac Lakes while scrambling up a length of slab.

2.4 SUMMIT! Return by the same route.

4.8 Arrive back at the trailhead and cross the road to the parking area.

14 Baker Mountain

The consummate small mountain offers a big reward and a perfect kid hike to a view of the mountains and lakes around Saranac Lake, with the Great Range in the distance to the southeast.

Nearest town: Saranac Lake
Total distance: 1.6 miles, out and back
Highest point: 2,441 feet
Vertical gain: 843 feet

Approximate hiking time: 2.5 hours
Difficulty: Moderate due to vertical gain
Canine compatibility: Dog-friendly
Map: USGS Saranac Lake Quad

Finding the trailhead: From NY 3 (Bloomingdale Avenue) in Saranac Lake, turn southeast on Pine Street. Go 0.1 mile, then turn left (east) on Forest Hill Avenue, which goes around Moody Pond. Go 0.6 mile to the trailhead on the northeast side of the pond. Park in the shallow turnout on the pond side of the road, then cross the street to the trailhead. Trailhead: N44 19.891' / W74 06.961'

Descending through hardwoods on Baker Mountain

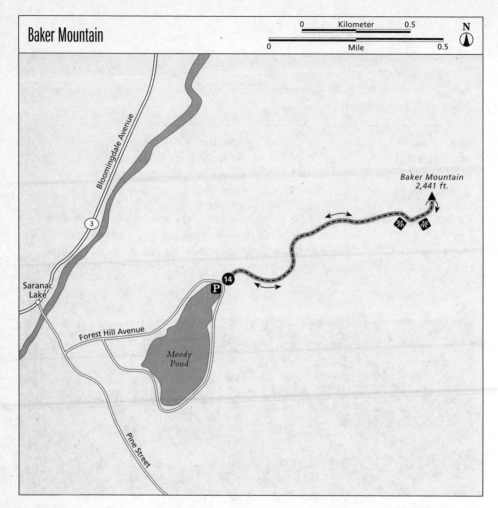

Baker Mountain

0　　　　Kilometer　　0.5

0　　　　Mile　　0.5

N

Bloomingdale Avenue

3

Baker Mountain
2,441 ft.

Saranac
Lake

14

P

Forest Hill Avenue

Moody
Pond

Pine Street

The Hike

From the sign-in box at the trailhead, the broad, obvious path (red NYSDEC markers) enters the woods and comes to a fork. An old trail up Baker Mountain is to
the left. Bear right (southeast) on the newer trail, which soon begins to climb up a
rock-strewn path. The trail is fairly steep at first, but the footing is good and it soon
moderates. You pass through a pretty hardwood forest filled with maples and poplars,
which glow red and yellow in late September and early October.

At 0.3 mile the trail reaches a plateau, where the walking gets easier on a gentle
incline. A few minutes later, it heads uphill again. Stone steps go up a ridge of rock in
the woods and then rock slab. As birch and pine start to take over, pine needles carpet
the trail around the rocks.

After several long sections of slab, you begin to glimpse the neighboring hills
and the village of Saranac Lake to your right (southwest). The many large rocks and

boulders along the trail are fun for kids to climb. At 0.6 mile the footing becomes a mosaic of roots and the trail braids often. Stay to the right, hugging the edge of the hillside, closest to the view.

At 0.7 mile the trail stops climbing and breaks out of the forest canopy onto a rocky outcropping laden with wild blueberries. There is an excellent view to the right (west) of Lower Saranac Lake. The round lake to the south with the island in the middle is Lake Kiwassa. Lake Flower is the lake in the middle of the village.

From here the hike passes a number of rocky perches en route to the summit. The best view is about 300 feet farther up the trail. McKenzie Pond lies below McKenzie Mountain to the southeast, with the heart of the High Peaks crowning the horizon.

At 0.8 mile the trail reaches the top of the mountain. The benchmark is on the broad knob of rock under a few scrubby pine trees and some raspberry bushes. The summit area is a web of unofficial trails. When it doubt, just head uphill and you'll get to the right place.

Return to the trailhead by the same route.

Miles and Directions

0.0 Start at the trailhead next to Moody Pond.

0.3 Traverse a small plateau and then continue climbing.

0.6 Stay to the right, hugging the side of the mountain nearest the view.

0.7 FIRST VIEW from a rocky outcropping! Continue to head uphill.

0.75 BEST VIEW from a rocky perch! Continue slightly farther to the summit.

0.8 SUMMIT! Find the benchmark in the bedrock below the scrubby pines. Return to the trailhead by the same route.

1.6 Arrive back at the trailhead.

15 Baxter Mountain

A local favorite to a nice view of many landmark mountains in the High Peaks region.

Nearest town: Keene
Total distance: 2.0 miles, out and back
Highest point: 2,341 feet
Vertical gain: 668 feet

Approximate hiking time: 2 hours
Difficulty: Moderate
Canine compatibility: Dog-friendly
Map: *USGS Keene Valley Quad*

Finding the trailhead: From the junction of NY 73 and NY 9N, follow NY 9N east up a steep hill toward Elizabethtown. About 2.1 miles from the junction, look for the trailhead on your right, about 50 yards past Hurricane Road, on the opposite side of the road. The sign is low and tucked into the trees. Park on the wide, grassy shoulder of the road. Trailhead: N44 13.253' / W73 44.971'

Author on the summit of Baxter Mountain

The Hike

There are three approaches up Baxter Mountain. This one (blue NYSDEC markers) is the shortest and easiest. The trail is smooth and flat as you enter the woods. It immediately passes through a power-line cut and then climbs easily through white birch, hemlock, and firs. It ascends some broad log steps as more hardwoods come into the mix, and then becomes steeper, though nothing harsh.

At 0.3 mile the trail flattens briefly, then bends sharply to the right (west) by a large hemlock partway up the next pitch. From here, you pass through a number of switchbacks on a newer section of trail as you ascend.

At 0.7 mile the path crosses a potentially muddy area on broad stones, then ascends more stones and roots. Soon it comes to the junction with the Beede Road Trail. Bear right (north), still following the blue markers.

After a couple more switchbacks past a low rock outcropping, the trail climbs to the west up some slab. At 0.9 mile it breaks free of the canopy at a rocky perch laden with wild blueberries. You can see the fire tower atop Hurricane Mountain to your left. Nippletop is to the right, with Giant Mountain in between.

From the perch, bear right (north), uphill, not along the rock cliff, leaving the view to your back and crossing a state wild forest boundary. You are now in the Giant Mountain Wilderness. Climb up a short, steep, rocky section, then cross some slab to find the northwest summit of the mountain, your destination for this hike, at 1.0 mile. It's a small knob of smooth rock surrounded by trees, but there is a nice ledge just below it with a beautiful view. Giant Mountain dominates the panorama to the south. Nippletop and a number of the other High Peaks lie to the southwest. Hurricane Mountain is to the east, easily identified by its fire tower.

Return to the trailhead by the same route.

Hiker on summit slab

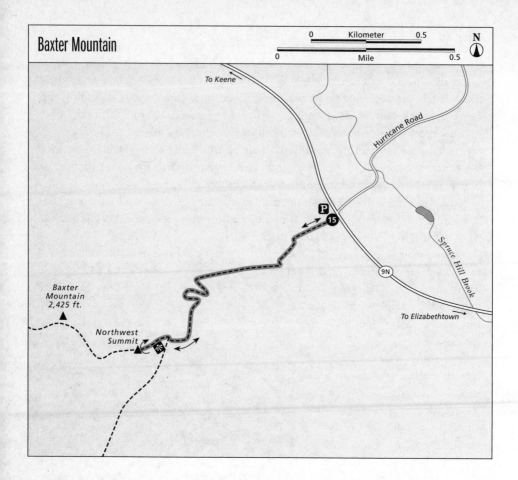

Baxter Mountain

Miles and Directions

0.0 Start at the trailhead on the side of NY 9N.

0.3 Pass a large hemlock and begin to ascend through a number of switchbacks.

0.7 Cross a muddy section on broad stones.

0.9 Enjoy the view and the blueberries from a rocky perch.

1.0 NORTHWEST SUMMIT! Return by the same route.

2.0 Arrive back at the trailhead.

16 Catamount Mountain

A minor peak with a major view of nearby Whiteface Mountain, and one of the longest, most fun scrambles over open rock in the Adirondack Park.

Nearest town: Wilmington
Total distance: 3.2 miles, out and back
Highest point: 3,173 feet
Vertical gain: 1,548 feet
Approximate hiking time: 4 hours

Difficulty: Strenuous due to vertical climb and extensive rocky scrambles
Canine compatibility: Not dog-friendly due to rock chimneys and large boulders
Map: USGS Wilmington Quad

Finding the trailhead: From the junction of NY 86 and Whiteface Memorial Highway in Wilmington, follow Memorial Highway (NY 431) for 2.8 miles. At the fork, bear right onto CR 18 (no sign) toward Franklin Falls. Go 3.0 miles, then turn right on Roseman Road (no sign, but it's the first right). Go 0.8 mile to a T, then turn right on Forestdale Road (no sign). The rocky peak beyond the fields on the left is Catamount Mountain. At 2.1 miles from the T, look for the trailhead on the left just after the fields. There is no NYSDEC sign, but a generous amount of red paint and surveyor's tape on the trees mark the start of the obvious path. Park in one of the small sandy pullouts on the side of the road or on the grassy shoulder. Trailhead: N44 26.576' / W73 52.790'

The Hike

There are five Catamount Mountains, plus one Catamount Peak and several more Catamount Hills and Knolls in New York State. This one is the highest. It's also arguably one of the most fun hikes in the Adirondacks. Often overlooked due to its short mileage and the fact that it's under 4,000 feet in elevation, Catamount is a favorite among regular hikers in the High Peaks region for its extensive open rock and ledgy scrambles. Don't let the low mileage fool you: It's a challenging hike that requires comfort on rock chimneys and other rocky ledges, boulders, and protrusions. Though it is considered subalpine, the extensive open rock feels like a long ridge above tree line.

Don't worry about meeting the mountain's namesake cat. Catamounts, also known as American panthers, cougars, mountain lions, and pumas, have not been officially recorded in the Adirondacks for over one hundred years. Biologists believe the catamount to be extinct in the region. On the other hand, there have been almost 700 rumored sightings since 1983 throughout the park. It's a topic of great debate, but as far as seeing a catamount on this trail, the odds are virtually zero.

The trail heads north into the woods through a corridor of spindly hemlock. From the sign-in box, the path is flat, winding into the forest. As you walk along the trail, note the yellow paint on the trees, which marks the edge of the hiker right-of-way. Pretty mosses grow in a patchwork of greens, pastel blues, and white to either side of the smooth, obvious route. The canopy is often open above you. At 0.3 mile the trail dips through a blueberry patch, then swings to the northeast briefly before bending back to the north. Maple, birch, and beech now dominate the forest mix.

View toward High Peaks from Catamount's Summit

Soon the trail begins to climb rather steeply and directly. Large and small rocks become strewn along the well-worn path. At the top of this first pitch, the trail bends east. In the fall the trunks of the many paper birches seem to glow white against the gold and orange foliage. You will likely flush a grouse while passing through this classic example of an upland wood.

At 0.7 mile the trail crosses a streamlet, which may have low or no flow in the fall. The climb resumes, soon becoming downright steep. A few minutes later it clamors up a large hump of rock and then more rock slab and boulders. You sense your elevation gain through the trees.

At 0.9 mile you get a two-breath reprieve as the trail bends left (north) again. You can glimpse the rocky summit to the left through the trees.

The trail seems to come to a T at the top of a rock outcropping. Bear right (southeast). Another rocky "mountaintop" appears above you, but this is a false summit. A few steps later you can see Whiteface Mountain from a small rock perch in the trees. From here the trail winds along a narrow outcropping, then breaks out onto a long, broad shoulder of the mountain. Small rock cairns mark the route.

At 1.1 miles the trail bends left (north) and opens onto rock again. It's a bit of a scramble, requiring some basic rock-climbing skills, for example, keeping three points of contact on the rock, to climb up several short, more technical sections. Follow the small rock piles as they wind up the face of the rock. There are many pronounced cracks in which to find good hand and toe holds.

At 1.3 miles the trail reaches a plateau among the scrub firs, stunted mountain ash, and blueberries. It traverses toward the peak, going up and down more easily over the boulders. Then it reenters the trees and begins a rocky, slabby ascent toward the true summit.

The last part of the climb goes over a patchwork of ledgy slab and trees. Keep following the small rock cairns, which are sometimes only two or three rocks in an

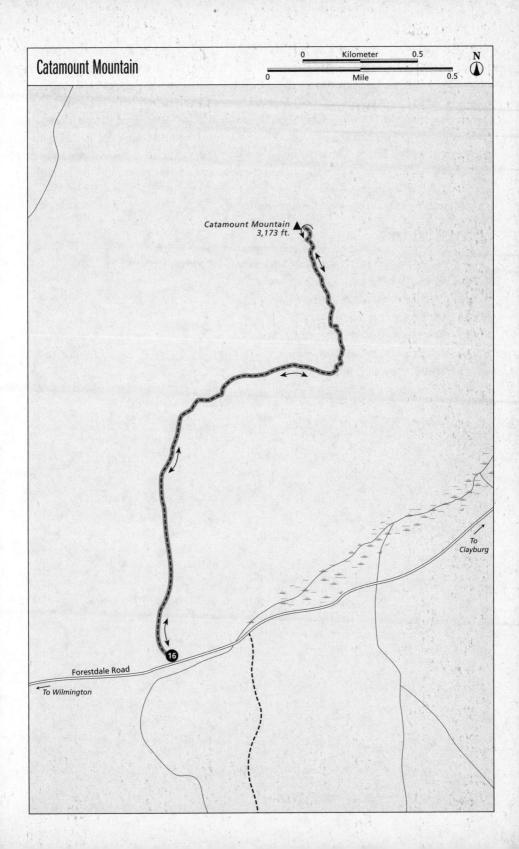

Catamount Mountain

Kilometer

Catamount Mountain
3,173 ft.

To Clayburg

16
Forestdale Road
To Wilmington

informal pile. At the top of a rocky knob, there is a nice view back toward the false summit and the omnipresent Whiteface Mountain to the south. The knob seems like a dead end due to the deep cleft in the rock. Bear right (east) to find the next cairn.

The route veers northeast just below the summit, then swings back onto the top of the mountain at 1.6 miles, where you'll find an almost-360-degree view. A clump of firs blocks a small part of the panorama to the northeast. Lake Champlain and the high ridge of the Green Mountains lie due east. Whiteface is to the south, with the rest of the 4,000-footers in the distance to the southwest. Silver Lake and Union Falls Pond lie below to the northwest.

Return to the trailhead by the same route.

Miles and Directions

0.0 Start at the opening in the trees marked with red paint and surveyor's tape.

0.3 Descend briefly through a blueberry patch.

0.7 Cross a streamlet, which may be dry.

0.9 Glimpse the rocky summit.

1.1 Climb a particularly difficult section of rock.

1.3 Traverse a plateau towards the summit.

1.6 SUMMIT! Return by the same route.

3.2 Arrive back at the trailhead.

17 Giant's Nubble via the Ridge Trail

A pleasant hike to a rocky lookout and a remote tarn on Giant Mountain, great for those who want a view but don't want to scale an entire 4,000-footer.

Nearest town: Saint Huberts
Total distance: 2.4 miles, out and back
Highest point: 2,743 feet
Vertical gain: 1,063 feet

Approximate hiking time: 3 hours
Difficulty: Moderate due to vertical climb
Canine compatibility: Dog-friendly
Map: *USGS Keene Valley Quad*

Finding the trailhead: From the junction of NY 73 and Ausable Road (the road to the Ausable Club) in Saint Huberts, head south on NY 73 for 2.0 miles, past the second entrance to Ausable Road and the parking area for the Roaring Brook Trail. The trailhead for the Ridge Trail is just past Chapel Pond on the left (north) side of the road. There is parking on both sides of the road.

If approaching from I-87, take exit 30, then take NY 73 and US 9 north for 2.1 miles. Where NY 73 and US 9 split, continue on NY 73 for another 3.0 miles. Trailhead: N44 08.318' / W73 44.597'

The Hike

Giant's Nubble is a knob of rock on the southern side of Giant Mountain, the tallest peak in the Giant Mountain Wilderness. There are two approaches to the Nubble, one from the Roaring Brook Trail and the other from the Ridge Trail, which are 1.3 miles apart on NY 73. If you have two cars, you can start at one end and hike to the other, which is about the same mileage as doing it as an out-and-back. It is not a good idea to walk beside NY 73, which winds through a narrow ravine between the two trailheads, with a guardrail on one side and a steep hillside on the other.

View just before reaching Giant's Nubble of the Great Range beyond Chapel Pond

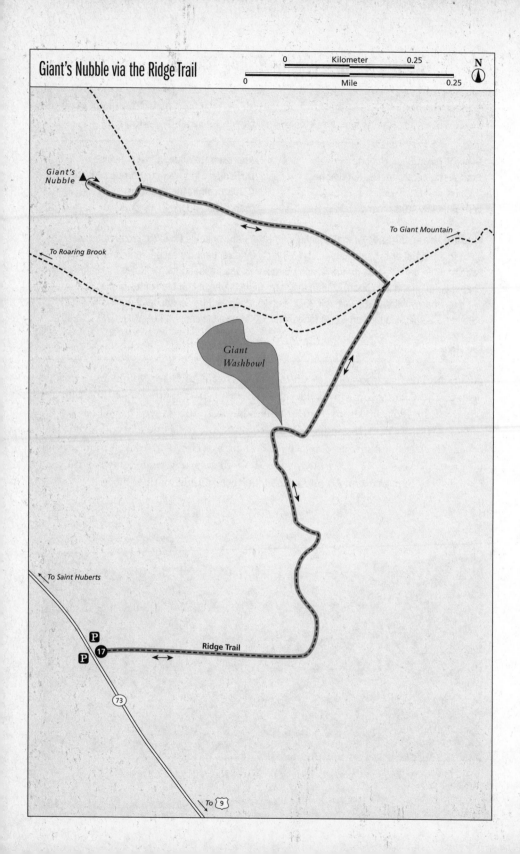

Giant's Nubble via the Ridge Trail

0   Kilometer   0.25
0   Mile   0.25

N

Giant's
Nubble

To Giant Mountain

To Roaring Brook

Giant
Washbowl

To Saint Huberts

P
17
P

Ridge Trail

73

To 9

The route described here is via the Ridge Trail, as it not only goes to the Nubble but also to Giant Washbowl, a serene mountain tarn that is the largest body of water in the Giant Mountain Wilderness.

From the trailhead, the path follows blue NYSDEC markers east into the woods over a couple of small footbridges to the sign-in box. From there it climbs moderately through a hardwood forest typical of the Adirondacks at lower elevations. In early July wild raspberries bloom profusely along the trail.

The path bends left over an unreliable streamlet and then angles to the northeast following the streambed. Though the trail is strewn with rocks and roots, the footing is generally good as you climb. Patches of wood sorrel blossoms brighten the ground here and there.

Soon the trail gets rockier and steeper. It crosses the streamlet again, angling up the slope. Everything around you seems green and lush. After several switchbacks and some stone steps up a particularly steep pitch, it comes alongside the streamlet again, and then crosses it. The slope eases a bit, crossing some sections of slab, heading north across a height of land. This is the top of the rock wall on the left side of the ravine above the trailhead. Once atop this plateau the road noise seems far below and quickly fades away.

At 0.5 mile there is a nice rock perch with a view of Chapel Pond below and the Great Range (Gothics, Armstrong, Upper Wolfjaw, and Lower Wolfjaw Mountains) to the west. From here the trail dips as it continues north back into the woods, away from Chapel Pond. Almost immediately, at 0.6 mile, it comes to Giant Washbowl. Nestled below a cliff, the Washbowl is a 4.2-acre pond that the state stocks with brook trout. Frogs hidden from view chirp among the water lilies that speckle the pond. It's a pleasant place to take a break if the rock perch you just passed is populated. There is a primitive campsite just beyond the pond on the right.

After taking a break to enjoy the Washbowl, continue a short way to the junction with the less-traveled trail to the Nubble at 0.8 mile. The trail climbs in spurts until it reaches Giant's Nubble, crossing sections of slab and several openings in the weathered trees.

At 1.2 miles the trail climbs an obvious rock highpoint, the Nubble! From the Nubble, Chapel Pond lies directly below you. Round Mountain is immediately across NY 73, forming the opposite side of the valley, with Noonmark just behind, but the eye is drawn to the Great Range, the string of 4,000-footers just to the right (northwest).

Return to the trailhead by the same route.

Miles and Directions

0.0 Start at the trailhead for the Ridge Trail up Giant Mountain.

0.5 Come to the first view of Chapel Pond from a rock perch.

0.6 GIANT WASHBOWL! Continue a short way farther on the Ridge Trail.

0.8 Turn left (west) on the trail to the Nubble.

1.2 GIANT'S NUBBLE! Return by the same route.

2.4 Arrive back at the trailhead.

18 Haystack Mountain (Ray Brook)

A pleasant hike to open ledges with a view of over two dozen of the High Peaks.

Nearest town: Ray Brook (between Saranac Lake and Lake Placid)
Total distance: 5.8 miles, out and back
Highest point: 2,864 feet
Vertical gain: 1,199 feet

Approximate hiking time: 6 hours
Difficulty: Moderate
Canine compatibility: Dog-friendly
Map: USGS McKenzie Mountain Quad

Finding the trailhead: From the junction of NY 3 and NY 86 in Saranac Lake, go 5.0 miles east on NY 86 toward Lake Placid. The trailhead is on the left (north) side of the road, 1.6 miles east of the NYSDEC office complex in Ray Brook. From Lake Placid, go 3.5 miles west on NY 86. Trailhead: N44 17.555' / W74 03.069'

The Hike

Not to be confused with the 4,960-foot giant, third highest in the Adirondacks, that is often paired with Mount Marcy by ambitious forty-sixers, this Haystack Mountain in the McKenzie Mountain Wilderness is a relatively easy climb to views of the 4,000-footers.

View from summit of Haystack Mountain toward Olympic Village

From the parking area, follow the blue NYSDEC markers into a grove of softwoods. The trail dips down over a muddy area then curves left (north). The footpath is soft at first over a mosaic of roots, but it's generally good, swinging northeast and traversing through a peaceful forest of birch, maple, and beech.

At 0.5 mile the path crosses a streamlet with a nice pool on your left below stepping stones. Then it bends to the left (northwest), traversing along the bottom of a hillside. It remains on the level, leaves the hillside, and passes through hemlocks before descending gently through a wet area on puncheon.

At 1.8 miles the trail comes alongside Little Ray Brook, a substantial stream, and bends to the northwest. The path parallels the brook along its east bank. You feel as if you're walking up a streambed as well, as the trail is now rockier and muddier in spots. Soon you are between the main brook and a

Trail through birch and conifers

tributary before crossing their confluence and climbing to higher, drier ground.

At 2.1 miles an old foundation lies on the right side of the trail, now reclaimed by the forest. Continue climbing comfortably, parallel to the stream, on smoother footing.

At 2.2 miles the trail forks. The trail to McKenzie Mountain departs to the right. Bear left (north) on the lower trail, continuing to follow the blue markers. The trail swings immediately back to the brook and then crosses it via a low dam.

From the dam, the climb gets steeper. It leaves the brook, heading north. After heading up one more steep section, you pass a rocky outcropping on your right in the woods. Paper birch become more and more prevalent in the forest mix. The trail feels more vertical here, due in part to the rocks and rubble on the trail.

At 2.8 miles the first view, from a small lookout, lies before you. You can see the former Olympic Village, now a prison, in the foreground and many of the High Peaks along the southern horizon, including Mount Marcy to the southwest.

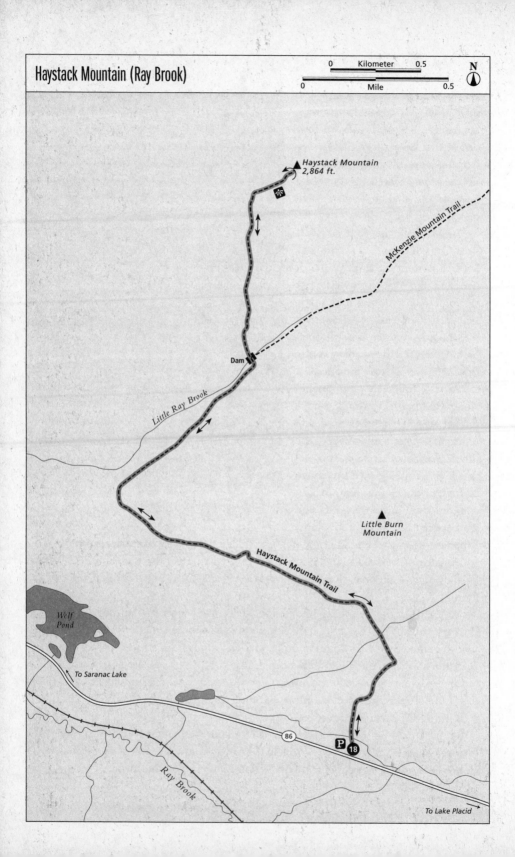

Haystack Mountain (Ray Brook)

0   Kilometer   0.5

0   Mile   0.5

N

Haystack Mountain
2,864 ft.

McKenzie Mountain Trail

Dam

Little Ray Brook

Little Burn
Mountain

Haystack Mountain Trail

Wolf
Pond

To Saranac Lake

86

P 18

Ray Brook

To Lake Placid

The trail continues to climb up slab and rocks. More views open up as the canopy breaks, and wild blueberries carpet either side of the trail. At 2.9 miles you know you're at the summit because an informal sign below blue and yellow discs says END OF TRAIL. The summit is a tilted expanse of slab with a patchwork of grasses, wildflowers, and low shrubs. It's a nice place to have a picnic or a nap in the sun, though the latter is unlikely considering the view. The panorama from the summit is less than 180 degrees, but it looks deep into the High Peaks.

Return to the trailhead by the same route.

Miles and Directions

0.0 Start at the trailhead beside NY 86.

0.5 Cross a streamlet with a nice pool on your left.

1.8 Climb parallel to Little Ray Brook.

2.1 Pass an old foundation in the forest.

2.2 Bear left onto the Haystack Mountain trail where it splits from the McKenzie Mountain trail.

2.8 Come to the first view from a rock perch.

2.9 SUMMIT! Return by the same route.

5.8 Arrive back at trailhead.

19 Hurricane Mountain

A fairly short but stout climb to an abandoned fire tower and one of the best views in the Adirondacks for a peak under 4,000 feet.

Nearest town: Elizabethtown
Total distance: 4.8 miles, out and back
Highest point: 3,678 feet
Vertical gain: 1,978 feet

Approximate hiking time: 5.5 hours
Difficulty: Strenuous due to vertical climb
Canine compatibility: Dog-friendly
Map: *USGS Elizabethtown Quad*

Finding the trailhead: From the junction of US 9 and NY 9N in Elizabethtown, go 6.6 miles north on NY 9N toward Keene. The trailhead is on the right (east) side of the road. There is no parking lot. Park on the wide dirt shoulder. From the junction of NY 9N and NY 73 southeast of Keene, go 3.6 miles south on NY 9N. Trailhead: N44 12.710' / W73 43.369'

The Hike

Although it is not a 4,000-footer, Hurricane Mountain is a big mountain that is visible from many of the eastern High Peaks. It is a recognizable landmark due to the fire tower on its bald summit, which continues to pierce the sky even though its useful life ended several decades ago.

Fire tower atop Hurricane Mountain

There are three approaches to the mountain, from the south, east, and west. The southern approach is the most popular and is described here. The route from the east was the original one used by the fire-watcher, but the road to it was closed to cars by the landowner. With the additional 1.2-mile walk up the road, which remains a public right-of-way for foot traffic, the eastern approach is now the same length as the southern approach but not as appealing due to the portion of the hike on the road. The western approach from Crow Clearing near Keene is longer—6.0 miles round-trip.

Enter the woods on log steps, following the red NYSDEC markers. It's a steady climb from the sign-in box under tall pines and striped maples on a wide, well-used trail that's strewn with rocks and roots. The trail is a designated birding site and is part of the Lake Champlain Birding Trail. The moun-

Puncheon through wetlands

tain is a known location for seeing bird species that inhabit the boreal forest, such as the Bicknell's thrush and the boreal chickadee.

The path levels off through a hemlock grove, then crosses a wet area on lengths of puncheon. At 0.6 mile a two-log bridge aids the crossing of a streamlet. From there, the trail continues along the left bank of the stream, still flat and well worn for a short way, then bends away to the north.

At 0.8 mile the trail crosses an open, marshy area on a long bog bridge, then heads around a denser portion of the marsh on more puncheon, soon coming to a stream (maybe a small trickle). It climbs beside the stream, then crosses it, continuing on the approach to the mountain over more bog bridges. The climb soon begins again, gently at first on good footing as you enter more hardwoods, and then more steeply with a lot of rubble underfoot.

At 1.5 miles the trail zigzags up lengths of slab, then mellows on a short eastward traverse before resuming an even steeper ascent. After a short but particularly vertical slope, it settles into a steady climb, offering a single reprieve as you walk across another long single log (bog bridge). A wild garden of purple asters frame the log to either side in September.

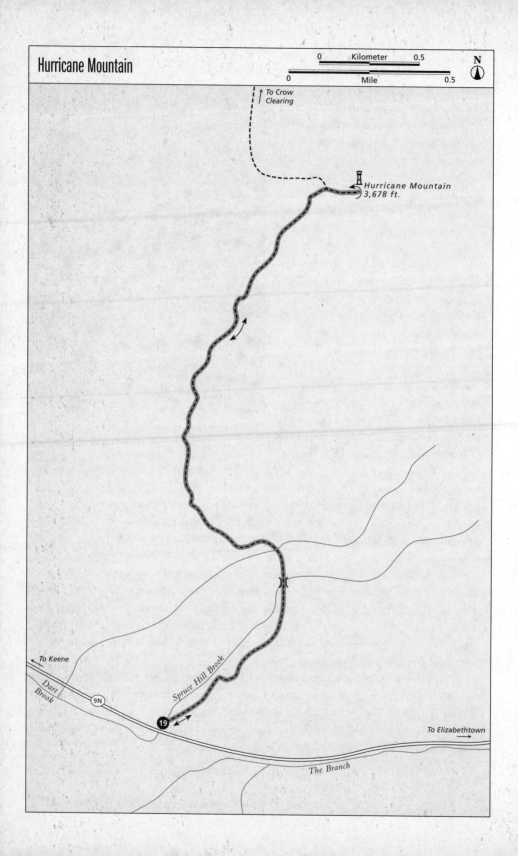

Hurricane Mountain

Kilometer

Mile

N

To Crow
Clearing

Hurricane Mountain
3,678 ft.

To Keene

Dart
Brook

9N

Spruce Hill Brook

19

To Elizabethtown

The Branch

The trail continues upward, resembling a dry streambed underfoot. It bends sharply left at a low rock outcropping, then bends right over the end of it, before continuing the long, steady climb up the washed-out path. At 2.3 miles it comes to the junction with the trail from Crow Clearing. Turn right (southeast), continuing to follow the red markers.

At 2.4 miles the trail breaks from the canopy on the summit, which was cleared by Verplanck Colvin during his Adirondack Survey. The fire tower is at the far end of the open rock. Through its rusty legs, you can see the length of Lake Champlain and the Green Mountains to the east. Most of the High Peaks are to the south. Mount Marcy stands tall on the horizon to the west.

Return to the trailhead by the same route.

Miles and Directions

0.0 Start at the trailhead beside NY 9N.

0.6 Cross a streamlet on a bridge.

0.8 Pass through a marsh on bog bridges.

1.5 Zigzag up rock slab.

2.3 Bear right at the junction with the trail from Crow Clearing, continuing toward the summit.

2.4 SUMMIT! Return by the same route.

4.8 Arrive back at the trailhead.

20 Mount Jo Loop

A short, kid-friendly hike along an interpretive trail to a big view of the High Peaks.

Nearest town: Lake Placid
Total distance: 1.9 miles, lollipop
Highest point: 2,876 feet
Vertical gain: 651 feet
Approximate hiking time: 2.5 hours

Difficulty: Easy
Canine compatibility: Dog-friendly. Dogs should be on leash.
Map: *USGS North Elba Quad*

Finding the trailhead: From Lake Placid, take NY 73 east toward Keene. About 1.2 miles past the Olympic ski jump complex, turn right (south) on Adirondack Loj Road. Go 4.7 miles to the end of the road and the sizable parking lot at Adirondak Loj. The trailhead is by the toll booth at the entrance to the parking lots. *Note:* There is a fee for parking here, which is discounted for members of the Adirondack Mountain Club. Trailhead: N44 11.039' / W73 57.885'

The Hike

Mount Jo is a small hike that delivers a close-in look at the biggest peaks in the Adirondacks. Its trailhead shares a parking lot with the trailheads to Mount Marcy, Algonquin, Wright, and a number of the other giants of the High Peaks. Originally called Bear Mountain, it was renamed in the 1870s for Josephine Schofield, fiancée of Henry Van Hoevenberg, the Adirondack guide who masterminded the original Adirondak Loj and who laid out many of the trails that begin here.

Schofield and Van Hoevenberg were engaged after camping with a group of friends by Upper Ausable Lake during the summer of 1877. Schofield's parents were adamantly opposed to the engagement. She died mysteriously before the marriage, and the heartbroken Van Hoevenberg named Mount Jo in her memory while building the home beside Heart Lake that they had planned to build together. However, instead of a modest home, he built an enormous log lodge, the original Adirondak Loj, considered the largest free-standing log structure in the country at the time.

In 1903 a forest fire burned the lodge and most of the surrounding forest. As with other bald peaks in the Adirondack Park that are technically below tree line, the summit of Mount Jo remains open because the soil quickly eroded away after the fire cleared the flora at this low but exposed point. Today the trail takes you through mature second-growth forest then ends at a fine viewpoint.

Mount Jo is popular among school groups and summer camps, so expect company at the summit. It follows an interpretive trail. You can buy an inexpensive guide to the interpretive trail at the nature museum, a small cabin near the edge of Heart Lake, a short way into the hike. There are two approaches to the summit, the Long Trail and the Short Trail, which combined make a nice loop as described here.

Heart Lake

The trailhead to Mount Jo also gives access to Rocky Falls, Indian Pass, and the Heart Lake Loop. It begins as a flat manicured path (red NYSDEC markers), passing several buildings tucked into the trees on the Adirondak Loj campus. At 0.2 mile it comes to a T near the edge of Heart Lake. The left path returns to Adirondak Loj. Turn right (northwest), passing the nature museum. In another 100 feet the trail to Rocky Falls and Indian Pass departs to the left. Turn right again, up a couple of rough stone steps and onto a "normal" footpath.

From the sign-in box, the well-used trail ascends steadily over rocks and roots, now following orange ADK markers. This is the nature trail, with numbered signposts along the way. At 0.4 mile the trail splits. The Long Trail to the left is 0.7 mile to the summit. The Short Trail to the right is 0.4 mile to the summit. You will close the loop here later. Turn right, following the Short Trail.

The Short Trail turns uphill, heading north and following a streamlet. It soon flattens across a muddy area. Many stepping stones help keep your feet dry. After crossing the streamlet the path turns upward again onto drier ground, though the footing is somewhat rougher. The trail weaves between boulders—glacial erratics that were deposited during the last ice age—and soon climbs beside a low cliff wall speckled with moss and lichen and discolored brown by minerals left behind by the constant drip of water.

At 0.6 mile an arrow painted on a wall of rock points the way to the left. The trail bends around the wall and continues its ascent, now rather vertical but aided by sections of stone steps. The climb eases briefly then continues upward on more steps angling along the hillside to the northwest. After yet another stone staircase, the trail pops onto open rock. You can see Algonquin Peak behind you before the trail bends left, entering a corridor of spruce and fir.

The trail soon passes a short spur on the right to a better lookout. Heart Lake lies below you. Mount Marcy is now visible to the southwest, with the Great Range to

Nature museum next to the trail to Mount Jo

the left and Avalanche Pass to the right of Marcy. From here, it's still uphill, but easier as you come to the upper junction with the Long Trail at 0.7 mile. Bear right, continuing uphill.

The path flattens as it reaches the summit plateau, then swings right (east) at the bottom of a rocky hump. This is not the summit. The trail crosses a muddy area, then dips over a two-log footbridge. After a couple of short, rocky scrambles, you arrive at the true summit at 0.8 mile.

The top of Mount Jo is a rock knob with a spectacular view. Algonquin looms above Heart Lake, with a string of the other High Peaks, including Cascade, Porter, Big Slide, Phelps, Basin, Marcy, Colden, Street, and Nye, among the impressive line of mountains before you. The view is not quite 360 degrees. To see the mountains to the north, mainly Whiteface, you need to walk among the trees in that direction.

To return to the trailhead, retrace back to the upper junction of the Long Trail and the Short Trail at 0.9 mile. Go straight (west), heading down the steeper route, though it is only steeper than the Short Trail for a short way and much less rocky. The Long Trail is mostly joint-friendly dirt, with some roots across the path. It becomes more rock-strewn and eventually rather eroded like a streambed but only for a short section.

At the bottom of the slope, the trail bends left (south) onto smooth, dry ground, passing under a 20-foot rock wall before coming to the junction with the Rock Garden Trail at 1.1 miles. Go straight (south) at the junction.

The trail passes through a muddy area, then continues downhill over some slab. It rolls gently up and down on a traverse to the east until you close the loop at the lower junction with the Short Trail at 1.5 miles. From here, retrace the path past Heart Lake and the nature museum, returning to the trailhead at 1.9 miles.

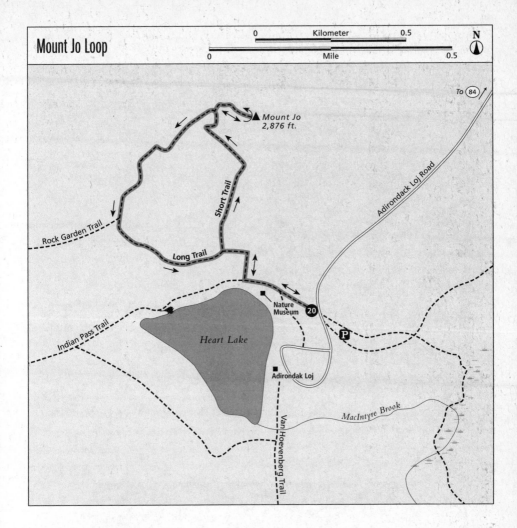

Mount Jo Loop

Mount Jo
2,876 ft.

To 84

Adirondack Loj Road

Short Trail

Rock Garden Trail

Long Trail

Indian Pass Trail

Nature
Museum

20

P

Heart Lake

Adirondak Loj

MacIntyre Brook

Van Hoevenberg Trail

Miles and Directions

0.0 Start at the trailhead by the toll booth at the entrance to the Adirondak Loj parking lots.

0.2 Turn right, passing the nature museum, then in another 100 feet turn right again up stone steps.

0.4 Turn right up on the Short Trail at the lower junction with the Long Trail.

0.6 Bear left at the arrow around the low stone wall.

0.7 Bear right at the upper junction with the Long Trail.

0.8 SUMMIT! Retrace back to the upper junction with the Long Trail.

0.9 Go straight at the upper junction with the Long Trail, following the Long Trail downhill.

1.1 Continue straight at the junction with the Rock Garden Trail.

1.5 Close the loop at the lower junction with the Short Trail.

1.9 Arrive back at the trailhead.

REGENERATION AFTER FIRE

As a result of forest fires and extensive logging during the early 1900s, much of the Adirondack wilderness is considered second-growth forest. The process of regeneration after a

forest fire is the reason why the species and size of trees along many of the trails in the Adirondacks exist today.

After a fire the scorched earth is a fertile ground for new plant life. In the Adirondacks typically berry, birch, spruce, fir, and maple seeds blow in or are deposited by birds, squirrels, and other small animals. Berry bushes and birch species are among the first plants to take hold. After fifteen to twenty years, fast-growing birches create a canopy under which shade-tolerant spruce and fir take root. About fifty years after a fire, the early birches die, exposing the underlying evergreens and young hardwoods to the

Birch trees

sun. A hundred years later the northern forest matures with the variety of trees that you see today along the hiking trails.

Wild blueberries

21 Noonmark Mountain–Round Mountain Loop

A long loop over two mountains with many views of the 4,000-footers from the open rock along much of the route.

Nearest town: Keene Valley
Total distance: 6.8 miles, loop
Highest point: 3,471 feet (summit of Noonmark)
Vertical gain: 2,953 feet

Approximate hiking time: 8 hours
Difficulty: Strenuous due to vertical gain
Canine compatibility: Not dog-friendly due to ladders and several rock chimneys
Map: USGS Keene Valley Quad

Finding the trailhead: From the bridge over Johns Brook in Keene Valley, follow NY 73 east toward Saint Huberts for 3.3 miles. Turn right on Ausable Road, the second entrance to the Ausable Club, just beyond the Roaring Brook Trailhead. The large parking lot for hikers is immediately on the left. This is the same parking lot for the Great Range (Gothics, Armstrong, Upper Wolfjaw, and Lower Wolfjaw). Parking is not permitted along Ausable Road. Trailhead parking: N44 08.978' / W73 46.055'

The Hike

There are several options for climbing Noonmark and Round Mountains, individually or together. The route described here is a big loop that goes over both peaks. Noonmark (elevation 3,471 feet) is the highpoint of the loop, both literally and figuratively. The mountain is due south of Keene Valley and marks the noon position of the sun, hence its name. It's a sturdy 2,177 feet of vertical in only 2.6 miles, but there is a lot to see along the way as you scramble up rocks and ladders. Round Mountain (elevation 3,084 feet) is an aptly named hump with many "view windows," each one better than the next.

From the hiker parking lot, continue up Ausable Road on foot. This dirt road is private but with a public right-of-way for hikers. At 0.1 mile a trail to Round Mountain departs to the left. You will close the loop here later. Continue to follow Ausable Road farther onto the club's grounds.

At 0.6 mile, at the corner of the golf course, the trailhead for the Noonmark Trail, also known as the Stimson Trail, is on your left. It is named for Henry Stimson, who created the route. Turn left onto the Stimson Trail, which is still a dirt road. After passing a couple of driveways, the road turns sharply uphill to the right. Continue straight, following the yellow markers and the TRAIL sign with an arrow pointing to the left.

Pass another house and then bear right at the arrow and the trail marker onto a footpath at 0.8 mile. The soft new trail traverses the side of a hill, soon meeting an older path. The route is wide and obvious with good footing. It provides a pleasant stroll through mature hemlocks with birch trees and other hardwoods in the airy forest mix.

Hiker departing Noonmark's summit

After crossing the boundary onto state land, the climbs becomes more obvious but is still moderate. A sizable stream (unreliable) lies below you on the left. At 1.1 miles you come to the junction with the Dix Trail, which is both to Dix Mountain and a second route to Round Mountain. Bear right, staying on the Stimson Trail, following the red markers.

The climb becomes steep and direct, but it is well maintained. At 1.5 miles the trail bends sharply right (north), up a stone staircase, allowing a brief respite from the persistent ascent. You feel closer to the sky, though you are still under the canopy. A couple of welcome switchbacks lie above the steps, and then the steady upward climb resumes.

At 1.7 miles the trail heads around the base of a rock outcropping, where you begin to see the next ridge of mountains to the northwest. It heads up the right side of the outcropping and then onto its top, where there's a beautiful view of Giant Mountain across the gap and many wild blueberries at your feet.

Above this first perch, the trail enters the boreal forest and becomes a patchwork of slab and ledge. The trees thin out as you leave the view of Giant Mountain behind. There are more large rocks to scramble up as you ascend the high shoulder of the mountain. At 2.0 miles a short spur to an awesome view of the Great Range is on your right. From here, the trail continues through the conifers and tons of blueberries.

At 2.2 miles you come to the first of two ladders, a short one up a half-buried boulder. The ladders are separated by a rock chimney and another great view of the Great Range, plus a look at the summit of Noonmark as you climb. The second ladder aids the ascent up a longer rock chimney. Finish the climb up this particularly vertical spot using the steps and crack in the rock.

The route is now more open in a subalpine zone with many lookouts as you scramble up more rock. At 2.6 miles the trail suddenly meets a 15-foot-high vertical wall. Head right to get on top of it, which is the summit of Noonmark. There is a 360-degree view, but you can't see it all at once due to a few low spruce trees. Nippletop, with its slides, lies to the southwest. Giant Mountain stands tall beyond Round Mountain, your next destination, to the northeast. Mount Marcy and the

Great Range lie to the west of the narrow valley that runs southwest from the Ausable Club.

To depart the summit toward Round Mountain, look for the orange disc with ROUTE 73 VIA ROUND POND handwritten on it. The official sign is 10 feet farther into the woods. The trail dives off the summit but soon descends at a more reasonable rate. There are nice views of the lower hills to the southeast as you cross sections of slab. This is called the Felix Adler Trail, though the sign denoting this is not at the summit. In the late 1800s and early 1900s, Adler spent summers in Saint Huberts in a house near the trailhead for this hike. He was an avid hiker and a popular lecturer and intellectual in his day, most known as the founder of the Ethical Culture Society, a nondenominational organization that believes in the separation of church and state and that human relationships, work, and common sense should guide society's ethical standards.

After descending several giant steps of rock and a short rock chimney, the trail reenters the hardwoods. The path is older here and washed out at first, but it soon becomes smooth, making the descent easier. After dropping over 1,000 feet into the narrow valley between Noonmark and Round Mountains, you come to a four-way junction at 3.5 miles. Turn left (north) on the Round Mountain/Dix Mountain Trail (yellow markers).

The author on the summit of Round Mountain with a view of the Great Range

The trail is smooth and flat, a nice break after the steep descent off Noonmark. Ferns fan out to each side as you pass a boggy old beaver pond. At 4.0 miles turn right (east) on the trail up Round Mountain (red markers). The climb resumes immediately through blueberries, spruce, and mountain ash. After passing an open rock with a limited view of Nippletop, the trail dips through a low ravine. The trail is now marked with both red NYSDEC discs and orange ATIS discs.

The trail winds steadily upward, soon crossing sections of slab. The trail angles generally to the east and is steep in places. When in doubt, look for the low cairns. The view gets better and better, with the Great Range to the right and Nippletop to the left of Noonmark.

At 4.7 miles the trail splits. At small sign on a birch tree gives two routes to Saint Huberts, the one you just came up and another one, which will be your way back. Walk straight past the sign over the broad reddish rock to find the summit marked by a low cairn. There is a 360-degree view from the top of Round Mountain. Giant Mountain is close by to the northeast. A stunning panorama lies in the opposite direction—a huge swath of the High Peaks, from Nippletop to the Great Range.

Retrace your steps back to the sign on the birch tree and take the right fork (also orange markers), heading across the open rock to the north. There are many picnic spots along this part of the summit ridge if the top is crowded.

As the trail drops down into the trees, it passes a pretty moss-covered boulder, which forms a wall beside the trail, then another steep descent begins. After the first pitch the trail rises to another view of Giant Mountain, then plunges downhill. The footing is basically smooth, a mix of dirt and slab, but there are just enough roots and irregularities to turn an ankle if you're not paying attention.

After passing through a cedar grove, the trail zigzags downward, periodically crossing more lengths of slab. There is a nice view of Whiteface through one break in the trees and another nice view of the Nubble in front of Giant Mountain's great cirque.

At 6.3 miles the trail reenters the hardwoods. It passes through a half-dozen large blowdowns, sawed apart to clear the trail. Then the descent mellows, traversing

Foam flower next to the trail

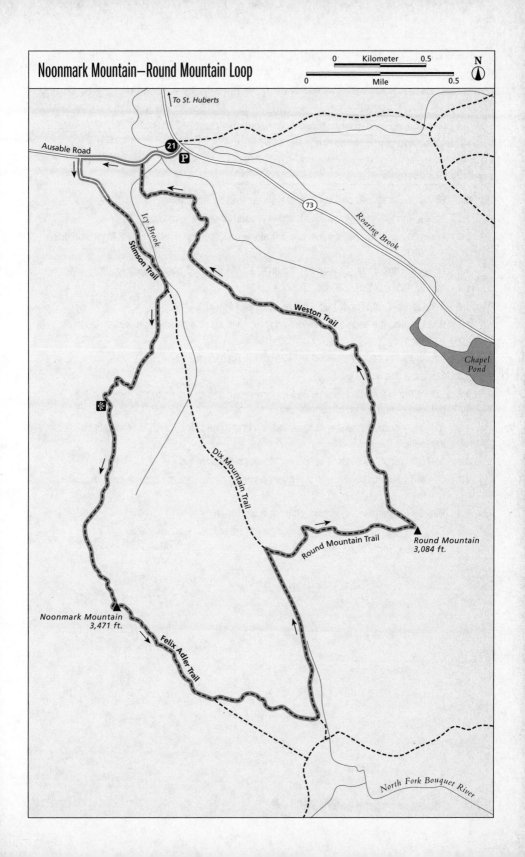

Noonmark Mountain–Round Mountain Loop

0 Kilometer 0.5

0 Mile 0.5

N

To St. Huberts

21

P

Ausable Road

73

Roaring Brook

Icy Brook

Stimson Trail

Weston Trail

Chapel Pond

Dix Mountain Trail

Round Mountain Trail

Round Mountain
3,084 ft.

Noonmark Mountain
3,471 ft.

Felix Adler Trail

North Fork Bouquet River

to the north, and even rises slightly at one point, a welcome change after the long aggressive descent.

The final descent comes in waves under tall hemlocks. As you cross the boundary onto Adirondack Preserve land, you can see NY 73 below through the trees. At 6.7 miles the trail ends at Ausable Club Road, closing the loop. Turn right, following the road back to the trailhead parking lot at 6.8 miles.

Miles and Directions

0.0 Start at the trailhead parking lot and walk up Ausable Road (dirt).

0.1 Pass a Round Mountain trailhead, where you will close the loop later.

0.6 At the corner of the golf course, turn left at the trailhead sign for Noonmark Mountain, also a dirt road.

0.8 Follow the arrow straight onto a footpath when the dirt road bends sharply right.

1.1 Turn right on the Stimson Trail.

1.5 Bend sharply right (north) up a stone staircase.

1.7 Head around the base of a rock outcropping, then up its right side to a view of Giant Mountain.

2.0 Take the short spur to an awesome view of the Great Range.

2.2 Climb the first of two ladders.

2.6 SUMMIT of Noonmark! Head past the handwritten disc to drop into the narrow valley between Noonmark and Round Mountains.

3.5 Turn left (north) at the four-way junction onto the Round Mountain/Dix Mountain Trail (yellow markers).

4.0 Turn right (east) on the trail up Round Mountain (red markers).

4.7 SUMMIT of Round! Bear right at the fork on the summit ridge to continue back to the trailhead.

6.3 Reenter the hardwoods, passing through a blowdown.

6.7 Close the loop at Ausable Road. Turn right toward the trailhead parking lot.

6.8 Arrive back at the parking lot.

22 Nun-da-ga-o Ridge–Weston Mountain–Lost Pond Loop

A varied hike along a rocky ridge, over a pleasant peak, and past a pretty pond, with many views along the way.

Nearest town: Keene
Total distance: 5.6 miles, loop
Highest point: 3,186 feet (summit of Weston Mountain)
Vertical gain: 1,403 feet

Approximate hiking time: 6 hours
Difficulty: Moderate
Canine compatibility: Dog-friendly
Map: USGS Jay Mountain Quad

Finding the trailhead: From NY 9N and NY 73 in Keene, go 2.2. miles east on Hurricane Road. Turn left on O'Toole Lane (dirt). Go 1.1 miles to the trailhead parking lot. Trailhead: N44 15.695' / W73 44.009'

The Hike

Then name "Nun-da-ga-o" is derived from the Onondagas, who called themselves "O-nun-da-ga-o-no" or "people on the hills." This wonderful ledgy ridge with many lookouts is also called the Soda Range on USGS maps. The ridge ends at Weston Mountain, the highest point of this hike. From the summit of Weston, it drops down to a small tarn, known as Lost Pond, and then closes the loop back at the trailhead. This hike is off the beaten path, but one you won't want to miss for the views and the solitude.

The trailhead, known as Crow Clearing, is also the start of the western approach to Hurricane Mountain and to two small nearby peaks called the Crows. Begin at the trailhead for Little Crow and Big Crow Mountains (red NYSDEC markers). After a short, flat approach, the trail climbs steadily and soon allows glimpses of the High Peaks to the west through the trees. At 0.1 mile it comes to the junction with

Girl by split boulder

Lost Pond

the trail to the Crows. Turn right (north). The narrow path is only lightly maintained, but the footing is fine as you traverse to the northwest.

Before long the trail dips and climbs through several softwood corridors, crossing lengths of slab. At 0.4 mile it gains the ridge and gives the first of many views of Hurricane Mountain with its fire tower, Giant Mountain behind Hurricane, and the Great Range across the valley to the south.

The trail reenters the woods, undulating up and down as it goes in and out of the trees, heading around the long, shallow bowl formed by the ridge. It bends east at the bottom of a rock cliff, then climbs up a shoulder of the cliff, continuing its moderate ascent through a classic boreal mix of firs, spruce, and paper birch.

At 1.5 miles, on one of the higher points of the ridge, the trail passes over a broad rock plateau, a great lunch spot, with over half of the 4,000-footers in the High Peaks in front of you, including Dix, Nippletop, Dial, Colvin, Blake, the Great Range, Big Slide, and Whiteface, as your eyes travel from east to west. Don't expect to set a speed record on this hike. There is too much to see!

Continue along the open ledge among the scattered firs, following the low cairns. The trail heads gradually downward for about 0.8 mile, still offering numerous views. At 2.3 miles the trail climbs again to another lookout and the longest length of open rock so far. Mount Weston lies directly ahead to the southeast.

After dropping into a wooded col between the main ridge and Weston Mountain, the trail climbs through a pretty birch forest, then heads up steeply through patches

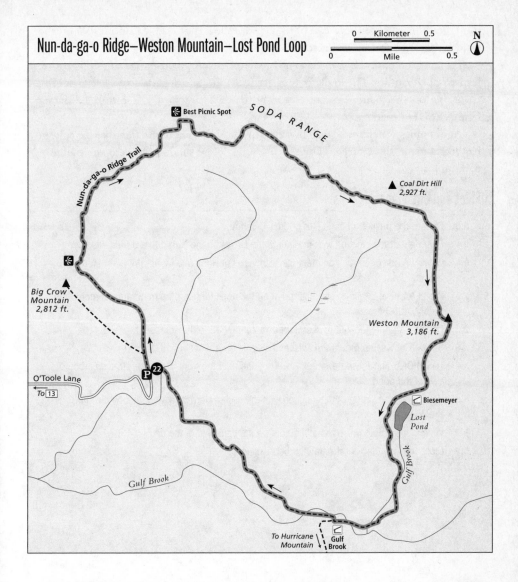

of wild raspberries, reaching the summit at 2.8 miles. Weston Mountain is also called Rocky Spar Peak. No surprise, given the slab and ledges near its summit. Lost Pond lies below to the southwest, your next destination.

It's a steep descent off the summit, passing through more birches, but after the initial drop the path becomes smoother and more joint-friendly. After a small rise, at 3.6 miles, you come to the Biesemeyer lean-to and a short spur to the marshy edge of Lost Pond directly behind the lean-to's fire pit. The lean-to would look to the pond except for the stand of trees blocking the view.

The trail crosses in front of the lean-to, then continues south, following yellow NYSDEC markers along the western edge of the pond, though a distance from the shoreline. Near the southern end of the pond, a short spur leads to a drier spot on the water's edge and a nice view across the pond.

From Lost Pond, the trail descends to Gulf Brook, then passes the Gulf Brook lean-to at 4.5 miles. The trail to Hurricane Mountain departs to the left (south). Continue on the gentle descent to the northwest, parallel to the brook, following blue NYSDEC markers.

At 5.0 miles watch for a small boulder on the right side of the trail that has split in half like a giant dinosaur egg. Then, at 5.6 miles, close the loop back at the trailhead parking lot.

Miles and Directions

0.0 Start at the trailhead parking lot at Crow Clearing.

0.1 Bear right at the junction with the trail to the Crows on the Nun-da-ga-o Ridge Trail.

0.4 Cross the first open rock on the ridge, with views of Hurricane Mountain, Giant Mountain, and the Great Range.

1.5 Pause (or have a picnic) at a high point on the ridge for a superb panorama of more than twenty 4,000-footers.

2.3 Climb to another lookout to see Mount Weston ahead to the southeast.

2.8 SUMMIT of Weston Mountain! Descend steeply toward Lost Pond.

3.6 LOST POND and Biesemeyer lean-to! Continue past the front of the lean-to along the west side of the pond.

4.5 Bear right (northwest) at the junction with the trail to Hurricane Mountain by the Gulf Brook lean-to.

5.0 Watch for the split-in-half small boulder on the right side of the trail.

5.6 Close the loop back at the trailhead parking lot.

23 Pitchoff Mountain

A point-to-point hike that climbs past a balancing boulder en route to the summit of a mountain, then descends over four subpeaks, each with a great view.

Nearest town: Lake Placid
Total distance: 4.4 miles, point to point
Highest point: 3,488 feet
Vertical gain: 1,413 feet

Approximate hiking time: 5 hours
Difficulty: Moderate
Canine compatibility: Dog-friendly
Map: USGS Keene Valley Quad

Finding the trailhead: From the junction of NY 73 and Old Military Road (by the fairgrounds in Lake Placid), go 8.4 miles on NY 73 east. Leave a car in the small parking lot across the road from the Pitchoff East trailhead, which is on the left (north) side of the road. Trailhead: N44 14.624' / W73 50.751'

Drive 2.7 miles back toward Lake Placid. Park in one of the three small lots by the Cascade Mountain trailhead just above Cascade Lake. Begin the hike at the trailhead for the Sentinel Range Wilderness, on the opposite (north) side of the road. Trailhead: N44 13.157' / W73 53.218'

The Hike

Pitchoff Mountain lies at the edge of the Sentinel Range Wilderness. It's a lovely hike that takes you through a patchwork of trees and shrubs, over ledges, and past

A patchwork of trees, shrubs, and open rock on Pitchoff Mountain

a gravity-defying rock. The hike up Pitchoff is much less crowded than Cascade Mountain across the ravine. While it doesn't have the cache of a 4,000-footer, you can see many of the major mountains in the High Peaks region from its multiple rock perches. Most people opt for a car drop at the far end of the ridge, though you can bike or walk the 2.7 miles between the trailheads, all uphill. Those who don't have transportation between the two trailheads can hike to Balanced Rock or the summit and then return by the same route, though you'll miss the four additional subpeaks, each with a unique eye-popping view.

Following the red NYSDEC markers, the hike leaves the side of NY 73 up a short, steep staircase. From the sign-in box, it's a moderate ascent up the hillside on an obvious footpath, though the path is not as wide or as eroded as other, more popular hikes in the region.

After a short, steep pitch, the trail levels off, then runs northeast, parallel to NY 73. You can glimpse Cascade Mountain and Cascade Lake through the trees to your right. At 0.5 mile a short spur on the right takes you to the first lookout, mainly an unobstructed view of Cascade Mountain and Lake, with Algonquin Peak poking up to the right.

At 0.7 mile there is a better view from another lookout, with Mounts Colden and Wright and the tip of Mount Marcy added to the mix. From here the trail turns uphill, scrambling over rocks in spots. It levels off again as it nears the edge of the long cliff line. Yellow coltsfoot and oxeye daisies bloom along the trail in late June.

After another downhill dip the trail turns away from Cascade Mountain and begins climbing among small boulders, then up an old short slide. As you enter the shrubs near the top of the slide, the trail comes to a T with an old route that is now blocked. Look back for a great view of Algonquin Peak.

The trail dips again, then climbs steadily and becomes more eroded, though nothing drastic. At 1.2 miles a sign that says merely "View" marks the short path to Balanced Rock. Turn right, crossing open bedrock toward Cascade Mountain. Blueberries, wild cranberries (lingonberries), wildflowers, and lichens color the cracks in the slab as you approach Balanced Rock at 1.3 miles. Beyond the rock, the view is a spectacular panorama, with the fire tower on Hurricane in the distance to the far left (southeast); the Olympic bobsled run to the far right; and Cascade, Big Slide, Marcy, Colden, and Algonquin filling most of the view in between. The summit of Pitchoff is now visible above you to the north.

Return to the junction and turn right on the main trail at 1.4 miles. The trail winds through boreal forest, crossing lengths of slab here and there. At one point it passes over the left shoulder of an enormous boulder with a yellow blaze on it.

Just below the summit, ferns fill the understory. The trail reaches the top of Pitchoff at 1.9 miles. The true summit is anticlimactic after the awesome views en route. The trail squeezes between two boulders in a stand of firs. You can see the Great Range if you get on top of the larger boulder. Instead, continue a short way along the summit ridge, descending slightly to a flat-top boulder by the edge of a cliff. From here the view is terrific and includes Giant Mountain, Hurricane, and the Great Range beyond Big Slide.

The trail traverses along the cliff edge through pencil-thin trees as it descends gently toward the first of Pitchoff's sub-peaks. When you reach subpeak 1 at 2.4 miles, you'll find the best view on this hike of Mounts Marcy and Colden.

At 2.5 miles the trail passes over sub-peak 2, where, for the first time, there is an excellent view of Whiteface to the north-west and the best view on this route of the Sentinel Range. This is a nice lunch spot if you arrive at Balanced Rock before you're hungry.

The trail bends left off of this subpeak, revealing a series of lower bumps below you. The trail drops down again. Lichens and mosses grow among the rocks, and wild blueberries are plentiful along this section of the trail.

Bunchberry flowers beside trail

At 2.8 miles you cross over subpeak 3, then head down a long smooth section of slab, which can be slick if wet. The trail continues to descend steeply through a tricky section next to a low rock wall. This is the most challenging part of the trail. At the bottom of another short rock chimney, bear left (northwest) where a rock wall blocks the path.

At 3.2 miles the trail crosses the lowest of the subpeaks, the only place on the hike with a 360-degree view. From this broad, open plateau, Giant Mountain is at its closest of the day. Cascade Mountain is now far to the right, and the view of Mounts Marcy and Colden will absolutely wow you!

From the last subpeak, the trail drops down, then crosses a muddy area before another sustained descent. The footing is rocky with many rollers and is washed out in places as you reenter the hardwoods. Eventually the slope eases, and the trail smoothes out, running parallel to a stream. At 3.8 miles the trail crosses the stream, then recrosses it by a mossy cascade. Emerge at the east trailhead at 4.4 miles.

Miles and Directions

0.0 Climb the stairs at the trailhead next to NY 73, across from the Cascade Mountain trailhead.

0.5 Take the short spur to the first lookout, mainly of Cascade Mountain and Cascade Lake.

0.7 Pass a second viewpoint, this time of Mounts Colden, Wright, and Marcy.

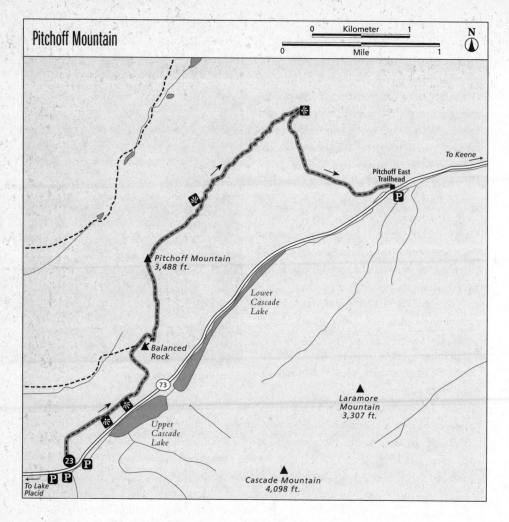

0   Kilometer   1

0   Mile   1

N

To Keene

Pitchoff East Trailhead P

▲ Pitchoff Mountain
3,488 ft.

Lower Cascade Lake

▲ Balanced Rock

73

▲ Laramore Mountain
3,307 ft.

Upper Cascade Lake

23 P

P P
To Lake Placid

▲ Cascade Mountain
4,098 ft.

1.2 Turn right following the view sign.

1.3 BALANCED ROCK! Retrace back to the main trail.

1.4 Turn right on the main trail and begin climbing toward the summit.

1.9 SUMMIT! Squeeze between two boulders, descending to another view.

2.4 SUBPEAK 1! Continue traversing the summit ridge.

2.5 SUBPEAK 2! Descend toward the next hump.

2.8 SUBPEAK 3! Descend the trickiest section of slab.

3.2 SUBPEAK 4! Reenter the hardwoods and descend beside a stream.

3.8 Cross the stream by a mossy cascade.

4.4 End at the east trailhead for Pitchoff Mountain.

24 Rooster Comb-Snow Mountain Loop

An enjoyable loop through pleasant woods to two excellent close-in views of the Adirondacks giants.

Nearest town: Keene Valley
Total distance: 5.8 miles, lollipop
Highest point: 2,592 feet (summit of Rooster Comb)
Vertical gain: 1,789 feet

Approximate hiking time: 6.5 hours
Difficulty: Strenuous due to vertical gain
Canine compatibility: Dog-friendly
Map: USGS Keene Valley Quad

Finding the trailhead: From the bridge over Johns Brook in Keene Valley, go 0.7 mile east on NY 73. The trailhead and substantial parking lot is on the right (west) side of the road at the end of the village. Trailhead: N44 11.124' / W73 47.226'

The Hike

Rooster Comb and Snow Mountain are lesser peaks compared to their 4,000-foot neighbors, but both offer spectacular close-up views of those neighbors, particularly from the summit of Rooster Comb. The hike described here takes you over both peaks, but you can opt out of Snow Mountain and just hike Rooster Comb as a loop (4.6 miles), or you can hike Rooster Comb out and back the same way (4.3 miles). Snow Mountain adds an extra mile to the route, but it's an easy mile, and once you're at the junction, the temptation is difficult to resist. And from Snow Mountain, you get a very nice view of Rooster Comb!

From the parking area, follow the yellow NYSDEC markers over a well-constructed footbridge across a boggy backwater to the sign-in box. The smooth, obvious trail, adjacent to a school, runs alongside the marsh and soon comes to a T. Turn left (southeast), following the arrow. After passing a bench it heads along the edge of a pond, which is part of the school's nature trail. At the junction at the southwest corner of the pond by a half-buried stone foundation, continue straight, heading deeper into the forest.

The trail soon bends right, crossing another low bridge over mud and a seasonal streamlet. It winds through a stand of tall hemlocks, crossing a state wilderness boundary, and then begins to climb, aided by several sets of wooden steps. The ascent is steady under towering conifers with little undergrowth. The trees seem like random pillars holding up the sky.

At 0.5 mile the trees become thicker with more undergrowth, and hardwoods enter the forest mix. The trail comes to a junction with the trail from Snow Mountain, where you will close the loop later. Bear right (straight), continuing to the southwest.

Tree roots growing over a large boulder

The steady climb levels off on a narrow woods road. The footing is nice—smooth dirt—and noticeably wider than a footpath. At 1.1 miles the trail turns 90 degrees left, leaving the woods road where logs and sticks block the way. It heads upward on the usual mix of scattered rocks and roots, though nothing too extreme.

After a half-dozen stone steps, the path passes a large boulder hugged by a web of thick tree roots. Many years ago a tree germinated atop the rock. It now reaches down around it to take hold of the ground. A few minutes later the trail crosses a stream, which could be only a small trickle after a dry spell, and bends to the right (west). Then it swings left (south) and eases, traversing through dense maples and beeches, as it continues upward on a moderate grade.

At 1.6 miles the Hedgehog Mountain Trail departs to the left. This is also the trail to Snow Mountain, which you will take later. Bear right (straight) uphill, now following the blue NYSDEC markers. The path goes around an enormous glacial erratic, then dips and traverses to the northeast. It passes under a 25-foot-high rock wall, then climbs some rock steps by another rock outcropping. After a couple of switchbacks, you start to feel the elevation gain as you glimpse a nearby ridge through the trees.

At 1.8 miles the trail reaches a T. Bear right (northeast) toward Valley View Ledge on a smooth descent, reaching the ledge at 1.9 miles. The view of Keene Valley and Marcy Field is quite pleasing. You can also see the fire tower atop Hurricane Mountain to the east across the valley. The ledges of The Brothers and the hulk of Big Slide dominate the view to the north.

Retrace your steps back to the main trail, bearing right (west), uphill, to continue to Rooster Comb's summit. The final approach to the summit is through classic boreal forest as evidenced by the low spindly conifers and birches. The trail traverses to the south, then bends sharply right, up a short but steep bit of slab. It continues to

Pond near the trailhead for Rooster Comb and Snow Mountains

climb more persistently below some ledges, then turns sharply right again up a steep wood staircase.

After a fun scramble up another ledgy area, you get a great view to the east into Giant's huge cirque just beyond Round Mountain. NY 73 winds past Chapel Pond along the valley floor like a gray ribbon below you.

After a short eroded section and several long lengths of slab, you come to the summit area at 2.2 miles. Head southwest to the open ledge and an awesome view of Giant to the east, Noonmark to the south, and Mount Marcy to the southwest. It's not a 360-degree view, but the close proximity of these big peaks more than makes up for the partial panorama.

Retrace back to the junction with the spur to Valley View Ledge at 2.4 miles. Turn right, descending to the junction with the trail to Snow Mountain/Hedgehog Mountain at 2.6 miles. Bear right toward Snow Mountain. About 10 yards later the trail to Hedgehog splits from the trail to Snow. Bear left, heading downhill. The narrow trail (blue markers) is easy to follow and continues to descend steadily. You might spy a whitetail deer or flush a grouse as you walk along this lesser-used path through a peaceful upland forest.

The trail comes alongside a streamlet, which grows to a bigger stream as it descends the shallow drainage. At 3.0 miles, at the junction with a trail to Saint Huberts, turn right (southwest), still following the blue markers, crossing the stream. The descent continues, though shallower, through conifers and crosses a couple more streams (unreliable) on a traverse to the southeast.

At 3.3 miles the trail to the summit of Snow Mountain splits from another route to Saint Huberts. Bear left (northeast) for the short climb up the cone of Snow Mountain, following the yellow markers. The trail remains level for a short way, then climbs steadily up a somewhat eroded trail. It turns steeper still as it leaves the canopy for a short time, but there are many natural steps in the rock.

At 3.6 miles the trail opens onto a ledge. It's a short traverse to the summit, which is a patchwork of scrub trees and rock perches, each with a different perspective of Rooster Comb to the northwest and Nippletop to the south. Snow Mountain is not a premier destination in its own right given the nearby bald peaks, but it is a nice addition to the Rooster Comb loop with good views nonetheless.

From the summit, retrace, bearing right at the junction with the trail to Saint Huberts at the bottom of the summit cone. Continue to retrace, heading back toward Rooster Comb. At 4.1 miles, at the next junction, turn right (northeast), heading downhill toward NY 73. The trail (red markers) descends steadily through a forest dominated by maple and birch coming to a stream on your right.

The path gradually veers away from the stream on its long, long descent. At 4.8 miles it levels off and bends to the north, climbing gently past the original trail, which was abandoned in 1998 because it passed through private property.

The route continues casually downhill. After a long traverse, close the loop at 5.3 miles. Bear right, following the yellow markers, and arrive back at the trailhead at 5.8 miles.

Miles and Directions

0.0 Start at the trailhead beside NY 73 at the edge of Keene.

0.5 Bear right at the junction with the trail from Snow Mountain, heading uphill toward Rooster Comb. Close the loop here later.

1.1 Turn 90 degrees left, leaving the woods road.

1.6 Bear right at the upper junction with the trail to Snow Mountain, heading toward Rooster Comb.

1.8 Turn right toward Valley View Ledge.

1.9 VALLEY VIEW LEDGE! Retrace to the trail junction and continue straight (southwest) toward the summit.

2.2 SUMMIT of Rooster Comb! Retrace to the junction.

2.4 Turn right and descend from the summit ridge.

2.6 Bear right toward Snow Mountain/Hedgehog Mountain at the junction, then bear left 10 yards later when the trail splits, heading downhill.

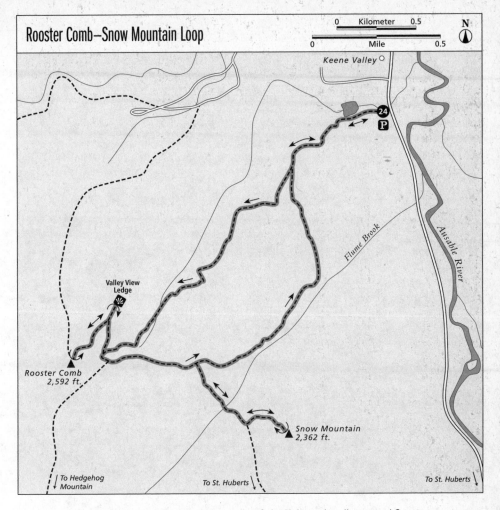

Keene Valley

Flume Brook

Ausable River

Valley View
Ledge

Rooster Comb
2,592 ft.

Snow Mountain
2,362 ft.

To Hedgehog
Mountain

To St. Huberts

To St. Huberts

3.0 Bear right at the next junction with a trail to Saint Huberts, heading toward Snow Mountain.

3.3 Bear left and climb the summit cone of Snow Mountain.

3.6 SUMMIT of Snow Mountain! Retrace down the summit cone.

4.1 Turn right (downhill) at the junction with the trail from Rooster Comb.

4.8 Bend north past an abandoned trail.

5.3 Close the loop and bear right, retracing to the trailhead.

5.8 Arrive back at the trailhead and parking area.

Eastern
Adirondacks

The eastern Adirondacks are much more than the popular Lake George area. They encompass the entire eastern edge of the Adirondack Park, a long narrow swath from Ausable Chasm south along Lake Champlain to Fort Ticonderoga and then along NY 22 south to Whitehall on the Vermont border. From there, the region zigzags west below the southern tip of Lake George, then continues back to Ausable Chasm along US 9. While Lake George is certainly a focal point of the region, mainly due to the concentration of visitors there, there are many acres of designated wilderness and wild forest with scenic mountaintops and pristine bodies of water to explore.

The eastern Adirondacks have one potential hazard unique to the region: rattlesnakes. The rattlers endemic to the region are smaller than their western cousins but still venomous. Called "timber rattlers," they are a threatened species and rarely seen by hikers, but you should be aware of their existence particularly if you are hiking in the Tongue Mountain Range (Hike 29).

Because I-87 runs the length of the region parallel to US 9, the trailheads in the eastern Adirondacks are among the most accessible in the Adirondack Park, yet these hikes deserve the same respect as more remote regions. Always wear appropriate clothing and footwear and bring gear, food, and water for the backcountry. Don't forget the rain gear and bug spray!

◀ *View of Whiteface in distance from Poke-O-Moonshine (Hike 28)*

ck Mountain

hike to the highest mountain and some of the best views in the Lake George a...

Nearest town: Whitehall
Total distance: 5.2 miles, out and back
Highest point: 2,650 feet
Vertical gain: 1,160 feet

Approximate hiking time: 4 hours
Difficulty: Moderate
Canine compatibility: Dog-friendly
Map: USGS Shelving Rock Quad

Finding the trailhead: In Whitehall at the junction of NY 22 and US 4, go north on NY 22 for 7.0 miles. Turn left on CR 6 at the HULETTS LANDING sign. Go 2.7 miles, crossing into Lake George Park, then turn left on Pike Brook Road. The trailhead and parking lot are 8.0 miles farther on the right (west). From Ticonderoga, take NY 22 south for 8.4 miles then turn right on CR 6. Trailhead: N43 36.705' / W73 29.601'

The Hike

Black Mountain is the highest peak with a trail in the Lake George area. It crowns the eastern shore of the lake at its halfway point. There are two trails to its summit, one from the shore of the lake, requiring a boat, and the other one from Pike Brook Road, which is described here. This one is longer but climbs less vertically.

Unlike many of the prominent peaks in the Adirondack Park, Black Mountain is not named for a person. In the late 1800s a Professor J. Geugot from Princeton University dubbed the mountain "Black" because of its dark appearance due to the predominance of evergreens on its upper slopes.

From the trailhead, head up the old fire road, following the red NYSDEC markers and the orange snowmobile markers. Black Mountain is in the Lake George Wild Forest. In the Adirondacks the difference between trails in a designated "wilderness" versus a "wild forest" is that horses, mountain bikes, and snowmobiles are allowed on trails in a wild forest. That said, horses and mountain bikes are not allowed on Black Mountain, and snowmobiles only share the flat approach to the peak.

At 0.2 mile the fire road comes to a blocked road on your right. Follow the arrow and the FOOT TRAIL sign straight ahead to the west.

At 0.6 mile bear right at another sign, avoiding a camp and a gate. The route is still level, though more eroded, with large cobblestone-like rocks underfoot. It seems more a wide footpath as you traverse through a mixed northern forest of beech, birch, and hemlock.

At 1.0 mile the Lapland Pond Trail departs to your left (south). Continue straight (west) on the eroded roadlike path, now crossing intermittent lengths of slab.

At 1.4 miles the trail crosses a stream, which can be wet during the springtime. It turns 90 degrees to the north, becoming even more eroded, as it begins to climb gen-

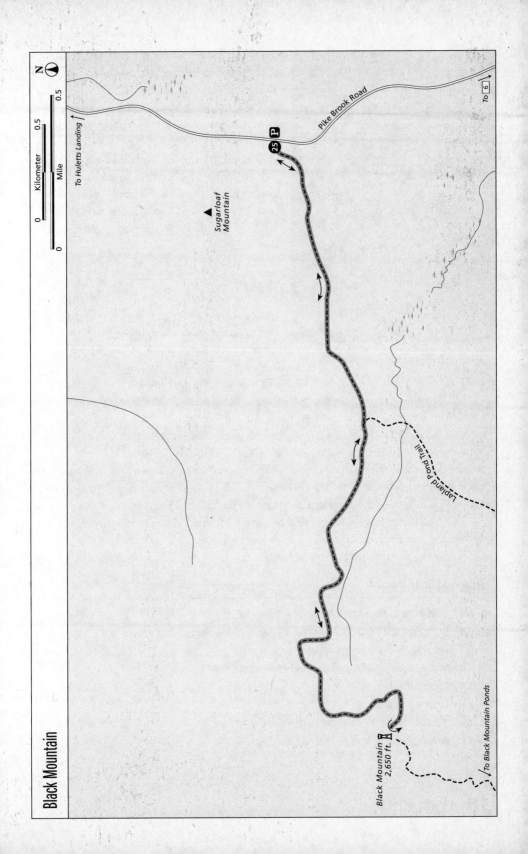

Black Mountain

N

0   0.5   Kilometer   0.5
0   Mile

To Huletts Landing

Pike Brook Road

To 6

25 P

▲ *Sugarloaf Mountain*

Lapland Pond Trail

Black Mountain 2,650 ft.

To Black Mountain Ponds

View of Lake George from Black Mountain

tly. A few minutes later it bends left (northwest) and climbs next to a seasonal stream, ascending more aggressively now.

At 2.1 miles the ascent eases, and the footing becomes smoother as you cross a mud hole. Grass grows along the slab. The climb is easier along this high plateau, but soon it tilts upward again, bending to the southwest after passing through a couple of switchbacks. There are still deciduous trees in the mix, though they are shrinking and getting thinner.

As you climb into a glade of tall hemlocks, look back for a glimpse of the High Peaks to the north. The trail levels off, passing among a lawn of ferns. It dips briefly, passing an impressive glacial erratic on your left. The footing becomes rocky again as you wind up the slope, eventually climbing over a ledge just below the boreal zone.

At 2.6 miles the trail breaks out of the canopy onto a sizable rocky perch just below the summit. This is the best place for a picnic, with striking views of Lake George below to the north and the Green Mountains of Vermont to the east. Huletts Landing is the grassy peninsula on the east side of the lake. Sabbath Day Point is on the opposite shore. The footings of the old fire tower are here. The tower was manned until 1988 and was the only fire tower in the Adirondacks with a light on its cabin. Like a lighthouse in the sky, it warned pilots of the summit at night.

The true summit is marked with a cement block and a metal pipe above a search-and-rescue communication tower, which blocks the view.

Return to the trailhead by the same route.

Miles and Directions

0.0 Start at the trailhead on Pike Brook Road.

0.2 Go straight, following the arrow and sign, ignoring the blocked road on your right.

0.6 Bear right at another sign, avoiding a camp and a gate.

1.0 Continue straight at the junction with the Lapland Pond Trail.

1.4 Cross a stream.

2.1 Cross a mud hole.

2.6 SUMMIT! Return by the same route.

5.2 Arrive back at the trailhead parking lot.

26 Buck Mountain

An invigorating hike to a terrific view of Lake George and the distant High Peaks.

Nearest town: Pilot Knob
Total distance: 5.8 miles, out and back
Highest point: 2,334 feet
Vertical gain: 1,980 feet
Approximate hiking time: 5 hours

Difficulty: Strenuous due to vertical climb
Canine compatibility: Dog-friendly, except for weekend crowds
Map: USGS Bolton Landing Quad

Finding the trailhead: Take exit 21 from north or south—Lake Luzerne/Prospect Mountain/ Hadley/9N—off I-87. At the end of the ramp turn onto NY 9N north. Go 0.2 mile, then turn left on NY 9N north/9L/9. At the next light, turn right and go 7.3 miles on NY 9L through Cleverdale. Turn left at the sign for Pilot Knob onto Pilot Knob Road, which is also NY 32. The trailhead and parking lot are 3.3 miles ahead on the right. Trailhead: N43 30.561' / W73 37.818'

The Hike

Buck Mountain sits on a piece of land within the Lake George Wild Forest just below the skinny southern end of Lake Champlain on the shore of Lake George. It's

View of Lake George from the summit of Black Mountain

a relatively easy hike despite the nearly 2,000 feet of vertical gain because the climb comes in waves, up short, steep pitches with generous mellow sections in between. It's special for the view of Lake George. There are two approaches to the mountain, one from the east and this one, from the west near the shore of the lake. This one is the more popular because of its pleasing views of the lake along the way.

Following the yellow NYSDEC markers, walk around the gate by the sign-in box, which is meant to keep motorized vehicles off the hiking route, which begins as a smooth, wide, flat woods road. After crossing another woods road, the trail comes to a fork at 0.3 mile. The right fork goes to Inman Pond via the Hogtown Trail. Bear left (northeast), continuing toward Buck Mountain.

The old rock-strewn road climbs gradually, following a tributary of Butternut Brook on your left. It bends left (north), crossing the stream, then winds up through a stand of tall conifers. After a steep section it levels off again. Many large rocks and boulders are scattered in the woods on the hillside to your left.

After a cube-shaped glacial erratic beside the trail, the path passes an old stone wall similar to the mortar-less stone piles through the woods of New England. It crosses a stream, then climbs beside it. After a pretty cascade you come over a rise to a junction with another trail to Inman Pond at 1.1 miles. Turn left (northeast), continuing to follow the yellow markers.

At 1.5 miles the trail comes to a stream. Do not cross here. Head slightly right over a smooth rock outcropping, keeping the stream on your left. The trail bends right, parallel to the stream. At the next level area, cross the stream following a tributary (maybe dry), heading east. Watch for a double marker and the TRAIL sign with an arrow pointing the way on a recently relocated section of trail. Cross the streamlet, continuing uphill.

The trail soon turns uphill dramatically, climbing up a rocky, washed-out pitch, "the Stairmaster portion of the climb," as one hiker described it. As the pitch mellows, you feel more sun above you and more ledge underfoot.

At 2.6 miles the trail emerges onto open slab with expansive views of the southern end of Lake George. From here, the trail goes in and out of the trees. Follow the cairns and yellow paint to stay on the trail. *Note:* This section of trail is laden with both wild blueberries and a bluish berry on a taller bush. The blueberries are edible, but the other berries are not.

About 200 feet below the summit, the trail drops down a small ledge to the junction with the trail from Shelving Rock Road. Continue straight (north), following the sign for the summit. After scrambling up more slab, you arrive at the broad, bare summit at 2.9 miles.

Bear right on the summit slab for an excellent view of the Tongue Mountain Range and the north end of Lake George. From the main summit hump, you look directly across the lake at the Sagamore Hotel, with the High Peaks on the northwestern horizon. The ski trails on Gore Mountain are also visible to the west.

Return to the trailhead by the same route.

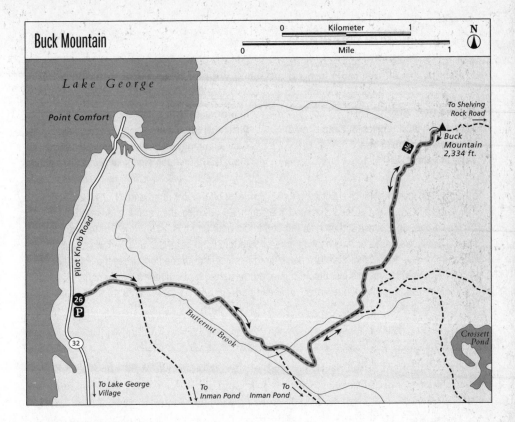

Miles and Directions

0.0 Walk around the gate by the sign-in box.

0.3 Bear left at the fork with the Hogtown Trail, continuing toward Buck Mountain.

1.1 Turn left at the second junction with a trail to Inman Pond.

1.5 Come alongside a stream, but wait until the next rise to cross it.

2.6 Emerge on open slab with a view of Tongue Mountain and the northern end of Lake George.

2.85 Continue straight at the junction with the trail from Shelving Rock Road.

2.9 SUMMIT! Return by the same route.

5.8 Arrive back at the trailhead and parking lot.

27 Pharaoh Mountain

A woodland walk to a multi-topped mountain with excellent views in all directions.

Nearest town: Schroon Lake
Total distance: 6.8 miles, out and back
Highest point: 2,533 feet
Vertical gain: 1,458 feet

Approximate hiking time: 6 hours
Difficulty: Strenuous
Canine compatibility: Dog-friendly
Map: USGS Pharaoh Mountain Quad

Finding the trailhead: Take exit 22 off I-87. Turn east off the exit ramp onto NY 74. Go about 100 yards and turn right at the light onto US 9 south. Go 0.6 mile, then turn left (east) on Alder Meadow Road. Go 2.1 miles, then bear left at the fork onto Crane Pond Road, which turns to dirt after 0.7 mile. Go past a sizable parking area on your left. From here, the road narrows and is unmaintained, so four-wheel drive is a must. From the fork onto Crane Pond Road, go 3.1 miles. Park under the tall hemlocks just before the road drops steeply to a flooded beaver pond. (The road continues but is likely underwater.) Trailhead parking: N43 51.204' / W73 40.055' (parking before flooded area)

The Hike

Pharaoh Mountain is the namesake peak of the Pharaoh Lake Wilderness, a 45,883-acre wilderness area between Schroon Lake and Ticonderoga. It's also the highest peak in the area and a worthy hike for its various views. There are several rock knobs on the summit. By walking from knob to knob, you get a spectacular view in every direction.

From the parking area before the flooded part of the road, look to the left side of the beaver pond, where a sign says "Trail." This short detour takes you around the flooded area without getting your feet wet. Follow the yellow NYSDEC markers on this detour back to Crane Pond Road on the far side of the flood, and continue on the road past the junction with the Blue Hill Trail, which departs to the left at 0.2 mile.

At 0.4 mile the dirt road ends at Crane Pond and the real trailhead for Pharaoh Mountain. Turn right at the last small parking lot, following the red NYSDEC markers. A well-constructed footbridge at the outlet of the pond leads to a woods road. Walk under the tall conifers to reach the sign-in box.

At 1.2 miles the trail comes to the junction with the Long Swing Trail to Glidden Marsh. Turn right, staying on the Pharaoh Mountain Trail, now a footpath, passing through a mixed forest, where the foliage has a golden glow in autumn. The trail comes alongside the northwestern corner of Glidden Marsh on your left. Glidden Marsh is an open body of water that seems a pond rather than a marsh from the trail, which follows its western side. After passing through another grove of mature conifers, it crosses a short bog bridge as you leave the southern end of the marsh, winding deeper into the woods and beginning to climb.

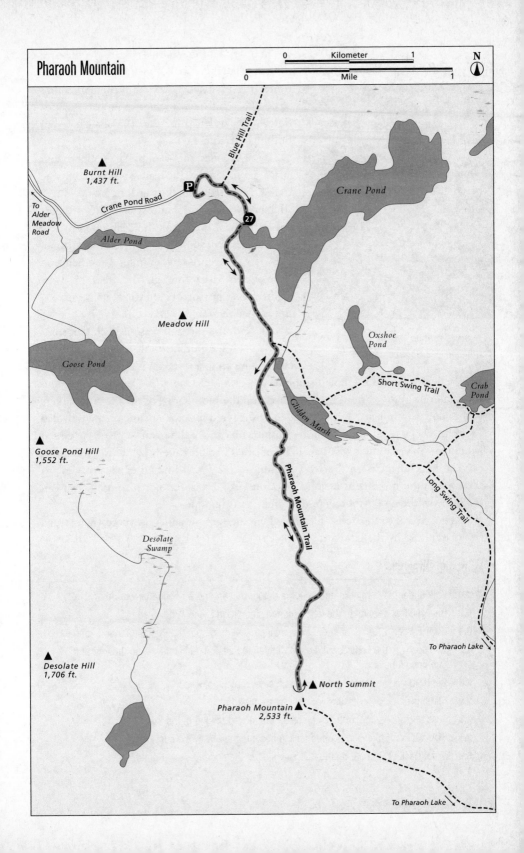

Pharaoh Mountain

0   Kilometer   1

0   Mile   1

N

Blue Hill Trail

Burnt Hill
1,437 ft.

Crane Pond

P

Crane Pond Road

27

To
Alder
Meadow
Road

Alder Pond

Meadow Hill

Oxshoe
Pond

Short Swing Trail

Crab
Pond

Goose Pond

Glidden Marsh

Goose Pond Hill
1,552 ft.

Long Swing Trail

Desolate
Swamp

Pharaoh Mountain Trail

Desolate Hill
1,706 ft.

▲ **North Summit**

To Pharaoh Lake

Pharaoh Mountain ▲
2,533 ft.

To Pharaoh Lake

Beaver Pond on the approach to Pharaoh Mountain

At 2.0 miles the trail makes a 90-degree turn to the right, where sticks block the older straight route. It levels briefly after the turn, then climbs again. The trail gets rockier as it gets steeper. Soon roots and slab increase the challenge, but nothing extreme.

By 2.9 miles the canopy feels closer and airier as you sense the gain in elevation. The trail is worn to bedrock over longer and longer stretches, which can be mossy and slick if wet. It passes below a broad side-hill slab on your left, with a view through the trees to the north of the Dix Range. A few minutes later Schroon Lake looms large through the trees on your right (west), just before the first open view in the same direction.

At 3.3 miles the trail passes a rock that splits off the main summitlike knob, forming a narrow chasm. The knob above you is the north summit. The trail arcs around the north summit to a grassy plateau at 3.4 miles, where herd paths fan out to the various rock perches atop the mountain. Follow the red markers to the south summit first, which is the most sheltered spot for a picnic on a windy day. From the rocky perch on the south summit, you can see the main ridge of the Green Mountains in Vermont across Lake Champlain. Pharaoh Lake is below to the south.

The benchmark is on the west summit, where you'll find an expansive view to the west to the mountains beyond Schroon Lake. From the north summit, you can see many of the 4,000-footers in the High Peaks region.

Retrace back to the grassy plateau where the summit paths converge, then return to the trailhead by the same route.

Miles and Directions

0.0 Park under tall hemlocks and take the detour trail around a flooded beaver pond.

0.2 Blue Hill Trail departs to the left. Continue straight on Crane Pond Road.

0.4 CRANE POND! Turn right at the last small parking area onto the Pharaoh Mountain Trail.

1.2 Junction with the Long Swing Trail to Glidden Marsh. Turn right, staying on the Pharaoh Mountain Trail.

2.0 Bend 90 degrees to the right, where an older route is blocked.

2.9 Climb over rocks, roots, and long stretches of bedrock.

3.3 Pass a rock chasm formed by a split in the rock to the left of the trail.

3.4 SUMMIT! Visit the various open rock knobs, then return by the same route.

6.8 Arrive back at your car on the opposite side of the flooded beaver pond.

28 Poke-O-Moonshine

Short, steep hike along a nature trail to a fantastic view from a fire tower across Lake Champlain and into the High Peaks region from the top of a landmark 1,000-foot cliff.

Nearest town: Keeseville
Total distance: 2.4 miles, out and back
Highest point: 2,180 feet
Vertical gain: 1,262 feet
Approximate hiking time: 2.5 hours

Difficulty: Moderate
Canine compatibility: Dog-friendly. Dogs must be on leash.
Map: USGS Clintonville Quad

Finding the trailhead: From the junction of Deerhead Road (NY 14) and US 9 about 6.5 miles north of Lewis, head north on US 9 for 5.4 miles. The parking area and trailhead are at the Poke-O-Moonshine campground on the left (west) side of the road. If approaching from Keeseville, at the junction of US 9 and NY 22, take US 9 south for 2.9 miles. Park at the campground, which is no longer in operation. Trailhead: N44 24.202' / W73 30.148'

The Hike

Poke-O-Moonshine is an anglicized version of two Algonquin words, "pohqui," which means "broken," and "moosie," which means "smooth." It is an apt description of the well-used rock-strewn trail to the top of this famous cliff, a wall of granite gneiss that rises 1,000 feet from the valley floor. It is a popular spot for rock climbing, though some of the routes may be closed if peregrine falcons are nesting. Day hikers miss the vertical ascent up the cliff, but the trail feels almost as vertical. It's worth the short effort for the long 360-degree views from the fire tower on top.

From the toll booth at the entrance to the Poke-O-Moonshine Campground, turn left (southwest) down the dirt road with a grassy middle that runs parallel to US 9. The road passes a number of campsites, coming to the trailhead at 0.1 mile. At the trailhead, turn 90 degrees right (west) and enter the woods following the red NYS-DEC markers. The NYSDEC, Friends of Poke-O-Moonshine, and other volunteers turned the route to the top of mountain into an interpretive trail in 2000. Numbers on stakes along the trail point out various examples of natural history, geology, trail work, and flora. (Brochures are available at the sign-in box at the trailhead.)

The trail climbs steeply, passing several large glacial erratics. Whitewood asters bloom at the foot of maples, beech, and birches, the dominant trees in the forest mix. A number of stone water bars and other well-placed rocks help keep the trail in shape.

At 0.4 mile the trail comes to a 40-foot rock wall. It bends left (south) along the base of the wall, still climbing. The footing becomes rockier as the path turns right over

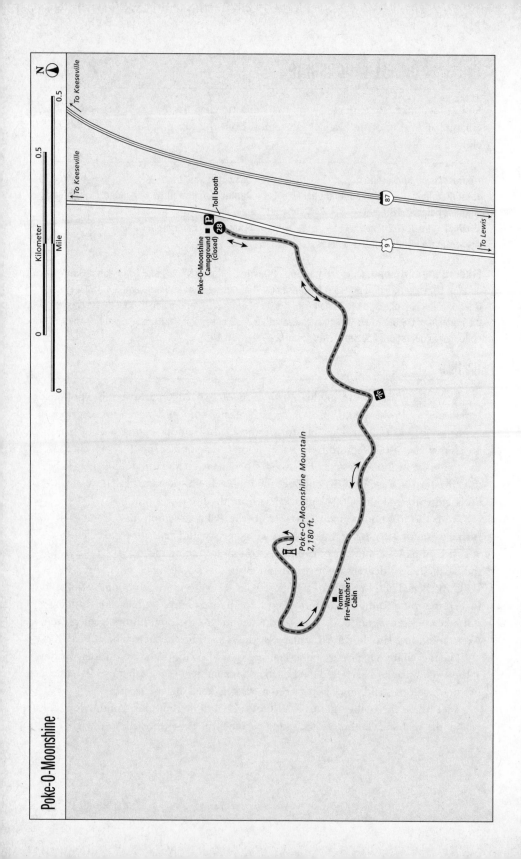

Poke-O-Moonshine

the top of the wall to a lookout. The view is mainly down I-87 except for one break in the far ridge, where you can see the Green Mountains in Vermont to the east.

The trail heads west, away from the cliff, and mellows on good footing. A few minutes later the climb resumes and the trail becomes rougher, like a narrow, dry streambed. The footing improves again as you come alongside a streamlet, then it flattens as you cross a muddy area on stepping stones. Ferns cover the ground to the left, and another huge boulder lies to your right.

At 0.8 mile, at the other end of the mud, the trail comes to the chimney and foundation of the old fire-watcher's cabin. Turn right (north) at the cabin remains, continuing uphill. The path soon

Chimney from the former fire-watcher's cabin on Poke-O-Moonshine

flattens again, passing another lookout on your left, where you see Whiteface Mountain to the northwest and other High Peaks to the west.

The narrow trail is smooth and easygoing, basically along the edge of a cliff but with a row of trees as a buffer. Clintonia and bunchberries bloom along the edges of the trail, signaling your elevation gain. Then, as you climb more steeply again, tall pines work their way into the forest mix and the canopy becomes more open.

At 1.0 mile the trail bends right (southeast) and flattens one more time, almost doubling back on a high shoulder of the mountain. After passing through a grove of spindly striped maple and then climbing up a short bit of slab, the fire tower lies ahead at 1.2 miles.

The original fire tower atop Poke-O-Moonshine was built in 1912 with a wood cabin on top. The metal one that exists today was installed in 1916. It became a National Historic Landmark in 2001. It is not particularly high and the cabin is likely locked, but the view is terrific nonetheless. Lake Champlain takes up the entire eastern panorama, with Camel's Hump the dominant mountain beyond in the Green Mountains. The Adirondack High Peaks are equally spectacular to the northwest.

Return to the trailhead by the same route.

Miles and Directions

0.0   From the toll booth at the entrance to the Poke-O-Moonshine Campground, follow the dirt and grass road southwest, parallel to US 9.

0.1   Turn 90 degrees right at the trailhead sign and begin climbing up the interpretive trail.

0.4   Bear left at a 40-foot rock wall, climbing to the top of the wall for a view of the I-87 corridor.

0.8   Pass the remains of the old fire-watcher's cabin.

1.0   Double back on a high shoulder of the mountain.

1.2   FIRE TOWER! Return by the same route.

2.4   Arrive back at the toll booth at the entrance to the campground.

29 Tongue Mountain Loop

An overnighter along the shore of Lake George, then a climb over three mountains on a ledgy ridge with many grand views of the lake, unusual flora, and the chance to spot an Adirondack rattlesnake.

Nearest town: Bolton Landing
Total distance: 12.1 miles, loop
Highest point: 1,756 feet (summit of French Point Mountain)
Vertical gain: 2,081 feet (total for 3 summits)

Approximate hiking time: 2 days/1 night
Difficulty: Strenuous
Canine compatibility: Not dog-friendly due to ledgy terrain with ladder and rattlesnakes
Map: USGS Shelving Rock Quad

Finding the trailhead: From the junction of NY 9N and Sagamore Drive in Bolton Landing, take NY 9N north for 6.2 miles. The trailhead, called Clay Meadow, is on the right, with parking about 100 yards farther, also on the right, next to a small pond. Trailhead: N43 37.727' / W73 36.497'

The Hike

The Tongue Mountain Range in the Lake George Wild Forest is literally a long tongue of land that juts into Lake George from its western shore, creating a fjord called Northwest Bay. There are five distinct peaks along the high ridge of the range—Brown Mountain, Five-Mile Mountain, Fifth Peak, French Point Mountain, and First Peak, from north to south—and several hiking options. Many people opt for the short hike to Deer Leap, a rock cliff that drops to the lake at the northernmost end of the range. Tongue Mountain Trail traverses the entire 7.0-mile range from north to south, and Five-Mile Mountain Trail cuts across the range at its middle, from east to west. Both of these options require a boat at one end or an out-and-back journey. The hike described here is the only loop. Though it can be done as a long day hike, it's more fun to break it up into two days, the first a nice stroll along the western shoreline of the peninsula, and the second a challenging scramble over three of the five mountains. They may be only half the height of the High Peaks, but the views from atop First Peak, French Point Mountain, and Fifth Peak are unequaled in the Adirondacks.

Day One

The wide sandy path enters the woods following the blue NYSDEC markers. It heads downhill under the tall pines to a highly constructed bridge just beyond a clearing of pickerel grass, then it turns slightly uphill through acres of ferns.

At 0.3 mile you come to the junction with the Five-Mile Mountain Trail, where you will close the loop tomorrow. Turn right (south), continuing on the flat path, soon crossing a streamlet on a footbridge.

The trail climbs a rise where you can see Northwest Bay narrowing toward its riverlike end. The path climbs farther and is more eroded, like a streambed, heading

View of Lake George from First Peak

deeper into the woods. It crests a hump and then descends, passing a fire ring at 1.3 miles as you head toward the water's edge.

After traversing under a low ridge of rock, the trail comes to another fire ring at 1.9 miles, a nice spot for lunch. A few minutes later you cross another footbridge and then head uphill again, rolling along above the shoreline.

At 2.4 miles the path passes through a grassy clearing just beyond a small spit of land called Bear Point. It hugs the shoreline most of the remaining distance to Montcalm Point at the end of the peninsula.

At 2.9 miles the trail comes to a more elaborate fire pit. A pretty cascade blocks the path just beyond the fire pit. Turn left, up the short rise, for an easier crossing above the waterfall.

At 3.8 miles at a swampy inlet, the path makes a 90-degree turn to the right (northwest) over a streamlet. Cross the streamlet on large rocks, then continue through a swamp, breaking out of the trees into a boggy area covered with grass and reeds.

At 4.2 miles the trail hangs over the water about 10 feet above it, then bends left away from the water up a rise. At 4.6 miles you come to another bucolic lakeside campsite with an unofficial fire ring. The trail swings away from the water over roots and mud, avoiding a private camp, as it comes to the junction with the French Point Mountain Trail. Go straight until you reach Montcalm Point at 5.0 miles.

Montcalm Point is named for Marquis Louis-Joseph de Montcalm, who commanded the French forces in North America during the French and Indian War and won an important victory at nearby Fort Carillon (now Fort Ticonderoga). Montcalm Point is an airy wooded spit of land where you'll find many spots to pitch a tent. The only downside is the boat traffic. Be sure to set up camp at least 150 feet from the edge of the lake and from the trail.

Day Two

The next morning retrace back to the junction with the French Point Mountain Trail. Bear right, heading toward First Peak, still following blue NYSDEC markers. *Note:* The trail is also called First Peak Trail on one sign.

The trail is flat briefly, then starts to climb up a rocky slope. At the top of the first grassy knoll, you get a nice view of the lake through the trees. Don't dally long. There are many better views to come.

The trail drops down a short, steep pitch to an unmarked junction. To the southeast you can see the lake and Shelving Rock Mountain through the trees from a lookout. The main trail heads generally northeast, now with many excellent views of the lake on your right. It levels off on a plateau through a grassy open forest, where there are more views to take in when you're not looking down to pick wild blueberries.

After another steep slope, the trail climbs more steadily over grass and slab. At 5.9 miles the trail appears to go up another very long, steep pitch, but it bends right (northeast) about halfway up the slope, continuing to ascend at an angle. A pronounced crack aids the climb up a rock chimney at the top of the slope, then the path mellows, passing a sizable overlook before traversing a high shoulder of the mountain. A breeze cools you and the everexpanding views cheer you greatly after the effort of the climb.

Continue on the steady ascent, climbing through patches of prickly juniper bushes while taking in the many breathtaking views of the lake, especially to the south. The trail bends away from the ledge, cresting a false summit at 6.2

Shag bark hickory on the Tongue Mountain Loop

miles. It dips through a narrow saddle, then continues to climb through open, ledgy woodland. The trees here are different than other parts of the Adirondacks, with many chokecherry and unusual shag bark hickory trees scattered around the mountainside.

The trail angles back to the northeast and breaks out of the forest, where there's a view of the many islands below and Erebus Mountain across the water. At 6.8 miles you reach the top of First Peak and the first view of the entire length of Lake George from north to south. The official summit is actually a few steps farther into the woods, then it's a long, smooth descent into denser forest, where a streamlet marks the col between First Peak and French Point Mountain at 7.3 miles. The path turns to rocky rubble and becomes steep again as you climb out of the col, but it soon eases as you reenter an airy grassy woodland.

The trail bends northwest and flattens, crossing under a ledgy area still in the trees and then a rock moraine. It heads up the left side of the rock pile at an angle. After another stiff pitch it reaches a knoll laden with wild blueberries and a view of Black Mountain to the west. No rest for the weary! The trail keeps going up, over slab and ledge, but the footing is generally good.

The route levels off briefly as you pass a small pool on your left, then it climbs again, soon emerging onto a rocky cliff line, which it follows. The view is oriented toward the north now, though you can still see the entire north–south length of the lake. This is a nice spot for lunch, or you can wait a few minutes until you reach the top of French Point Mountain, at 7.6 miles, the highest point of the hike.

From French Point Mountain, the trail begins a long downward roll until it reaches a cliffy area. It traverses under a ledge, then turns left up through the rock. At the next rock wall, turn left again, heading upward, then turn right, climbing over the ledge at a natural break in the rock.

The climb continues through tall pines and well-spaced blueberry bushes on a slabby, ledgy trail, with glimpses of the lake and the ridge to the right (east). After cresting a subpeak the trail descends again to the base of another rock pile below a ledge. An arrow on a tree directs you left (northwest) around the cliff and then up its left side. The forest is more Adirondack-like here, with lots of hemlock and maple in the mix.

After a couple more steep scrambles, look back to see the two peaks you just climbed. The trail mellows as you reach the summit plateau of Fifth Peak at 9.6 miles, where you'll find another rocky ledge and a view of the lake to the west.

The trail descends to another cliff wall by a small murky pool. Turn left, continuing to a junction at 9.9 miles. The sign gives mileage and directions to the Fifth Peak lean-to and from French Point Mountain and Point of Tongue (Montcalm Point). Bear left (northeast), heading downhill. It's a relatively smooth, steady descent to a small flat spot and a sharp left turn, then the trail climbs and arcs back to the right.

The trail becomes wider and the downhill walking becomes easier as you near the next junction at 10.4 miles. Turn left (west) on the trail to Clay Meadow, continuing to descend on an easy grade through a mixed northern forest.

The trail eventually heads through a couple of switchbacks and some rougher, steeper sections, coming to a wide, well-constructed bridge. The path is smoother on the other side and turns into an old woods road. It passes through a blowdown, where mossy, decaying trees were sawed apart long ago to clear the path.

The downhill seems to go on and on, following a stream on your left. At 11.7 miles you reach the junction with the Montcalm Point Trail, closing the loop. Arrive back at the trailhead at 12.1 miles.

Miles and Directions

Day One

0.0 Begin at the trailhead called Clay Meadow.

0.3 At the junction with the Five-Mile Mountain Trail, turn right (south), continuing on the flat path, soon crossing a streamlet on a footbridge.

1.3 Pass a fire ring as you descend toward the water's edge.

1.9 Come to another fire ring—a nice lunch spot.

2.4 Pass through a grassy clearing just beyond Bear Point.

2.9 Come to a fire pit, then climb a short rise to cross at the top of a cascade.

3.8 Turn 90 degrees to the right (northwest), over a streamlet.

4.2 Follow the hanging trail over water, then up a rise.

4.6 Pass another bucolic lakeside campsite with an unofficial fire ring.

4.9 At the junction with the trail to French Point Mountain, continue straight toward Montcalm Point (aka Point of Tongue).

5.0 MONTCALM POINT! Camp here.

Day Two

5.1 Retrace back to the junction with the French Point Mountain Trail and bear right, heading toward First Peak.

5.9 Bend right (northeast) about halfway up a steep slope, continuing to ascend at an angle.

6.2 Head over a false summit.

6.8 FIRST PEAK! Take in the view of the entire length of Lake George, then descend to a col.

7.3 Arrive at the col between First Peak and French Point Mountain, climbing out of the col on a steep rocky path.

7.6 FRENCH POINT MOUNTAIN! Begin a long downhill traverse.

9.6 FIFTH PEAK! Descend another cliff to a small murky pool and turn left.

9.9 At the junction with the trail to the Fifth Peak lean-to, bear left (northeast), heading downhill.

10.4 Turn left (west) at the junction with the trail to Clay Meadow, continuing to descend.

11.7 Close the loop at the junction with the Montcalm Point Trail, retracing back to the trailhead.

12.1 Arrive back at the trailhead.

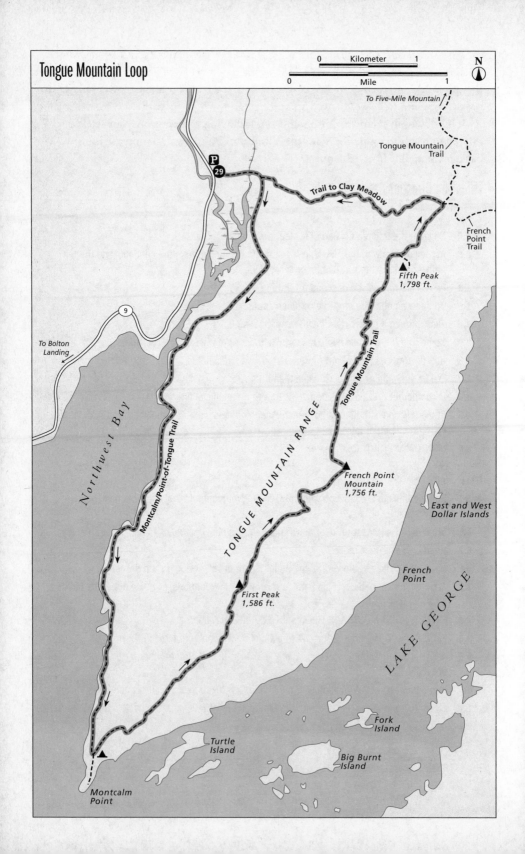

Tongue Mountain Loop

0   Kilometer   1

0   Mile   1

N

To Five-Mile Mountain

Tongue Mountain
Trail

P
29

Trail to Clay Meadow

French
Point
Trail

Fifth Peak
1,798 ft.

9

To Bolton
Landing

Montcalm/Point-of-Tongue Trail

Northwest Bay

TONGUE MOUNTAIN RANGE

Tongue Mountain Trail

French Point
Mountain
1,756 ft.

East and West
Dollar Islands

French
Point

First Peak
1,586 ft.

LAKE GEORGE

Fork
Island

Turtle
Island

Big Burnt
Island

Montcalm
Point

RATTLESNAKES IN THE ADIRONDACKS

The only poisonous snake in the Adirondacks is the timber rattler *(Crotalus horridus)*. Also called a canebrake rattlesnake or a banded rattlesnake, the timber rattler was the snake on the first flag of the Continental navy during the American Revolution—not surprising, as several important battles played out around Lake Champlain and Lake George, where this snake was common. But no longer! Today this shy reptile is considered a threatened species. In the Adirondack Park, the northern tip of its range, it inhabits a few isolated spots around Lake George, particularly the Tongue Mountain Range (see Hike 29) and on Split Rock Mountain near Lake Champlain.

Timber rattlesnake

Smaller than its western cousins, the average timber rattlesnake grows from 3 to 4.5 feet long and can be rather stout in diameter—over 4 inches wide. Its head is triangular, and its body coloring can vary from pale yellow to blackish, but always with multiple dark bands along the length of its body. These snakes are well camouflaged, making them difficult to spot unless you hear their warning rattle. They feed on small mammals, birds, amphibians, and other snakes, but they will bite a hiker if he or she gets too close, and their venom can kill you if left untreated.

While the odds of spotting a timber rattlesnake are low, hikers should take basic precautions when hiking around the Lake George area. During the summer rattlers warm themselves on sunny ledges, so it's best to look before you reach for a rocky handhold. Their dens tend to be inside old logs or similar places on the forest floor, where they hibernate during the winter, so avoid reaching inside moist stumps or fallen wood. If you hear or see a rattlesnake, give it a wide birth. Rattlers are said to reach up to half the length of their body when striking, but that doesn't include a quick slither closer beforehand.

Southern Adirondacks

The Southern Adirondacks encompass the section of the Adirondack Park south of US 8 between Prospect and Speculator, plus the land in the southern half of the Wilcox Lake Wild Forest between Speculator and Lake George Village. It is the region of the park closest to large population centers, particularly Albany, the state capital, yet the trails are not crowded, especially midweek.

There are only a handful of mountains over 3,000 feet (barely) in the southern Adirondacks, and most of these are tree-covered and trail-less. Hikers who wish to bag major peaks or embark on multiday high-mileage backpacking trips should head farther north. The southern region is better characterized by braided rivers and creeks that wind their way between the lakes and ponds that dot the hilly countryside. The Silver Lake Wilderness is the only designated wilderness area in the region. Most of the backcountry is contained in Ferris Lake Wild Forest, Shaker Mountain Wild Forest, and Wilcox Wild Forest.

Because the topography of the southern Adirondacks is gentler than in the heart of the Adirondack Park, the hikes here are particularly nice for families who are either new to hiking or who don't want to make a full day of it. The four routes described in this chapter are among the classics of the region. Each offers a beautiful view at the end of a pleasant woodland walk with just enough topography to keep things interesting.

◀ *Fire tower poking above the trees on Hadley Mountain (Hike 32)*

30 Crane Mountain–Crane Pond Loop

A fun climb up rocks, slab, and a couple of ladders to an eye-popping view of the region, then a gentle descent to a small remote pond.

Nearest town: Thurman
Total distance: 2.6 miles, lollipop
Highest point: 2,851 feet
Vertical gain: 1,165 feet
Approximate hiking time: 3 hours

Difficulty: Moderate
Canine compatibility: Not dog-friendly due to ladders near summit
Map: USGS *Johnsburg Quad*

Finding the trailhead: At the junction of US 9 and NY 418 in Warrensburg, go 3.6 miles west on NY 418 toward Thurman. At a cluster of signs on the right, turn right (northwest) on Athol Road (no sign), following the signs toward the town hall and Veteran's Field. Go 1.1 miles to a T. Turn right (northeast) at the T onto Cameron Road. Go 0.9 mile, then bear right (north) on Glen/Athol Road. Go 1.4 miles, then turn left on Valley Road. Go 4.6 miles, then turn left on Garnet Lake Road South. Go 1.3 miles, then turn right on Ski Hi Road (dirt). Go 1.9 miles. The road narrows at the top of a hill as it crosses onto forest preserve land and ends at the trailhead parking area. There is no trailhead sign, but the path is obvious at the end of the parking area. Trailhead: N43 32.239' / W73 58.034'

The Hike

The hardest part of this hike is finding the trailhead, but once there you'll enjoy the short, interesting climb to the summit of Crane Mountain and the pleasant walk to the pond of the same name. This hike is a lollipop, meaning you begin and end on the same trail, but make a loop over the mountaintop, then down to the pond on a high shelf of the mountain, before rejoining the trail you started on.

There are two stories behind the name of the mountain and the pond, one crediting a pair of cranes that were rumored to have nested on the pond in the previous century, the other crediting a state surveyor with the last name of Crane who marked a 55-mile line that ran over the mountaintop.

Two trails depart from the sign-in box, one to Putnam Farm Junction/Crane Pond and the other to Crane Mountain/Crane Pond. *Note:* The actual name of the pond is "Crane Mountain Pond," though the sign says only CRANE POND. Bear right (north), following the red NYSDEC markers toward Crane Mountain. The well-worn trail tilts upward over rocks and roots through a dense hardwood forest of maple, birch, and beech. The footing soon becomes a jumble of rocks as you quickly gain elevation.

You can see the neighboring hills through the trees where the trail bends left (northwest) at the base of a sizable rock face. The jumble of rocks becomes more vertical as you climb up the broad rocky slope, similar to ascending an old slide, but more stable.

View to southwest from a rock perch on Crane Mountain

At 0.4 mile, at the top of the talus, a yellow arrow points to the right up a section of smooth slab, a low-angle friction climb. At the top of the slab, there is a short spur trail to a lookout to the northwest over blueberry bushes. Crane Mountain is a wild-blueberry bonanza in July.

Above the slab, the forest transitions to birch and softwoods, and the trail changes to roots rather than rocks underfoot. It parallels a ledge, passing a few other spots where you can poke through to get a view. Then the trail breaks out onto an expanse of slab, part of the patchwork of rock that you can see from the road as you approach the mountain.

Head straight up the slab to the junction where the Summit Trail and the Pond Trail split at 0.5 mile. Bear right (northeast) on the Summit Trail. The path dips, then heads up another short, steep, eroded jumble of rocks and roots before reaching better footing.

At 0.6 mile a short ladder aids the ascent up a short rock wall, then the trail flattens through a grove of hemlocks as it bends to the east.

At 0.9 mile the trail swings back to the north up another washout, then climbs more rubble to a second, longer ladder. Above the ladder there is an excellent view from a rocky perch to the southwest. Wildlands sprawl before you as far as you can see! From here, the trail winds up a few more steps, arriving at the summit at 1.0 mile.

The footings of an old fire tower are embedded in the rock on the summit, but there is no need for a tower to take in the incredible view. The mountains along Lake

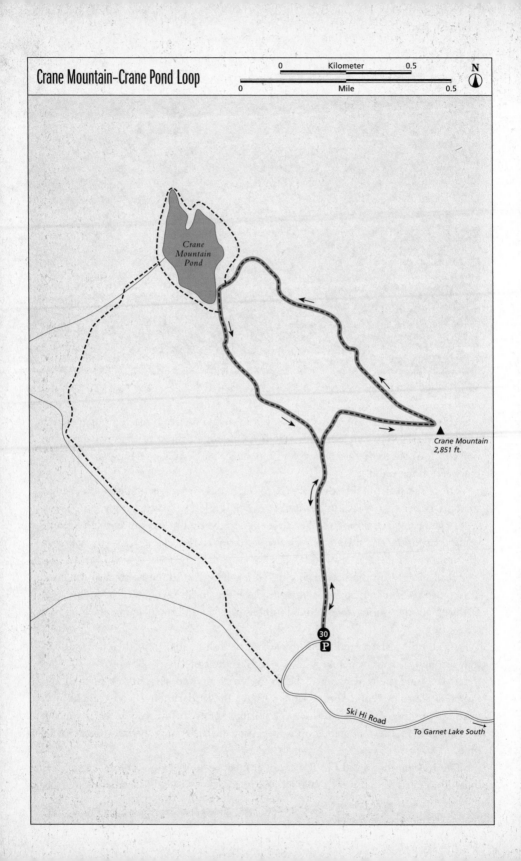

Crane
Mountain
Pond

Crane Mountain
2,851 ft.

30
P

Ski Hi Road

To Garnet Lake South

Kilometer
0   0.5

Mile
0   0.5

N

George and the Green Mountains of Vermont beyond lie to the east. Moose Mountain and Baldhead dominate the view to the south, and Blue Mountain stands guard on the far shore of Garnet Lake to the southwest.

From the summit, head north on the elongated summit ledge, which narrows to a footpath. The path begins with a gentle downhill traverse, then descends more deliberately. The trail is well used but less rocky than on the way up. It levels off as you reenter the hardwoods, becoming narrower and smoother. At 1.5 miles it passes through a short muddy stretch just before arriving at the eastern side of Crane Mountain Pond. Look for a short spur on your right for a peek across the fourteen-acre pond.

The trail bends to the west, following a yellow arrow and heading along the southern shore of the pond. You can see a nice beach and campsite across the water. If you have the time, the beach is a pleasant spot for a swim. You may see anglers casting for brook trout from the shore or from float tubes in the water.

At 1.6 miles, at the southwest corner of the pond, the trail splits. The right fork takes you to the beach and campsite. Bear left (southeast), away from the pond, heading back into the woods on the Pond Trail (no sign).

The trail climbs moderately on a dry streambed, then smoothes out. It crosses a length of puncheon through a hemlock grove, traversing a shoulder of the mountain, then, at 2.1 miles, you reach the junction with the Summit Trail, closing the loop. Bear right, retracing the last half mile down the rocky hillside, returning to the trailhead at 2.6 miles.

Miles and Directions

0.0 At the trailhead take the right trail toward Crane Mountain/Crane Pond.

0.5 Turn right where the Pond Trail and the Summit Trail split, following the Summit Trail.

0.6 Climb a ladder up a short rock wall.

0.9 Climb another, longer ladder.

1.0 SUMMIT! Head north along the summit ridge to descend toward the pond.

1.5 POND! Take the short spur trail for a view across the pond, then head along the southern shore of the pond.

1.6 Bear left at the fork on the Pond Trail (no sign), heading away from the pond into the woods.

2.1 Close the loop at the junction with the Summit Trail. Turn right and retrace back to the trailhead.

2.6 Arrive back at the trailhead and parking area.

31 Echo Cliff

A short, steep ascent to a cliff-top view of Piseco Lake and the Silver Lake Wilderness.

Nearest town: Piseco
Total distance: 1.6 miles, out and back
Highest point: 2,435 feet
Vertical gain: 651 feet
Approximate hiking time: 2 hours

Difficulty: Moderate
Canine compatibility: Dog-friendly. Dogs should be on leash around cliff.
Map: USGS Piseco Lake Quad

Finding the trailhead: From US 8 at the southwestern corner of Piseco Lake, turn north on West Shore Road. *Note:* The road sign may be missing, but follow the brown and gold NYSDEC sign at the turn that says POINT COMFORT, LITTLE SAND POINT, POPLAR POINT, PISECO VILLAGE. Go 2.5 miles to the trailhead for "Panther Mountain" on the left (west) side of the road. Trailhead parking is a turnout on the right (east) side of the road, across from the trailhead. Trailhead: N43 24.683' / W74 33.448'

The Hike

Echo Cliff is a rock outcropping on the eastern side of Panther Mountain. The summit of the mountain is another 300 vertical feet higher than the cliff, but it is covered with trees and offers little view. The cliff is the better destination, a perfect hike if you want little exercise and a big reward.

From the trailhead, follow the blue NYSDEC markers up the wide, well-used path into a hardwood forest. The hike begins on a gentle incline through maple, beech, and birch, but soon becomes more persistent as it passes over a section of slab.

Author on Echo Cliff

At 0.4 mile the trail bends to the right (north) and eases briefly, becoming a smooth, wide but normal footpath, unlike the super-highway below.

It eases again at 0.5 mile, as you cross a small shoulder of the mountain. After passing a square, flat-top boulder on your left, the trail heads upward again, bending to the northeast through scattered rocks and boulders. It climbs along a low cliff, then, as the cliff peters out, the trail turns steep, rough, and rocky. You can glimpse Piseco Lake through the trees on your right

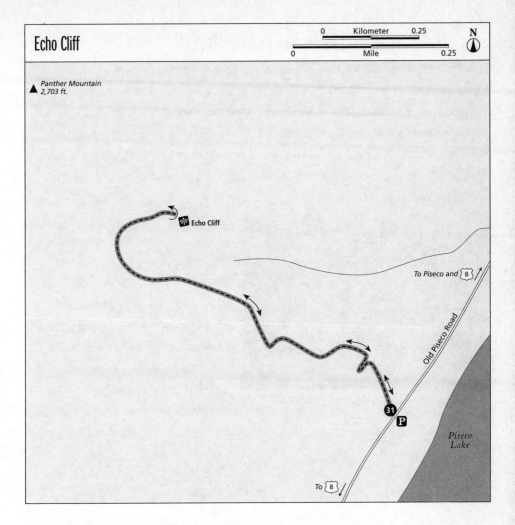

Echo Cliff

Panther Mountain
2,703 ft.

Echo Cliff

To Piseco and 8

Old Piseco Road

31
P

To 8

Piseco
Lake

just before a short scramble up some rock and the exposed roots of a large hemlock. The cliff is just above the hemlock at 0.8 mile.

The view from this lofty perch is an eastern panorama, with Piseco Lake immediately below you with smaller Spy Lake just beyond to the southeast.

Return to the trailhead by the same route.

Miles and Directions

0.0 Begin at the trailhead on the west side of Piseco Lake.

0.4 The route bends to the right, becoming smooth and more like a footpath.

0.5 Cross a small shoulder of the mountain.

0.8 CLIFF! Return by the same route.

1.6 Arrive back at the trailhead.

STATE CAMPGROUNDS IN THE ADIRONDACKS

Throughout the Adirondack Park, ubiquitous brown signs with gold writing point out everything under the State of New York's care, including boat launches, trailheads, beaches, picnic areas . . . and campgrounds. One of the most convenient, enjoyable, and cheapest ways to spend time in the Adirondacks is to stay at a state campground. There are forty-four state campgrounds throughout the park, many located on the pristine lakes and ponds and nearest the trailheads. There are three state campgrounds along the western side of Piseco Lake near the trailhead for Echo Cliff alone!

Ubiquitous State of New York brown sign

State campgrounds vary in size and facilities. Some offer primitive campsites with outhouses and no showers, accessible only by canoe, which can be rented on-site. Others accommodate bus-size RVs and offer showers, drinking water, firewood, and other welcome benefits after a day on the trail.

Most state campgrounds open by mid-May and close by mid-October, though a few are open longer that that. Reservations (permits) are required and fees are charged.

Firewood

Most campsites have a fire pit. If firewood is not available at the campground, you can usually find it nearby from private sources along the road. It's on the honor system. Just grab a bundle and deposit the few requested dollars in the box by the bin.

Do not bring firewood from home! Unless the wood has been treated, you are not allowed to transport firewood over 50 miles from its source in the Adirondack Park. Untreated wood may carry insects or diseases that can destroy an entire forest.

Dogs

If you're planning on bringing your pet, also bring a certificate of rabies vaccination from your veterinarian. Dogs are not allowed at state beaches, picnic areas, or inside buildings, and they must be on a leash, with a maximum length of 6 feet long, if you are walking them outside of your immediate campsite. And remember to clean up after your pooch.

For more information about NYSDEC-operated campgrounds and day-use areas, call (518) 457-2500 or go to www.dec.ny.gov/outdoor/camping.html.

32 Hadley Mountain

A family-friendly hike to a restored fire tower and an expansive 360-deg
includes the High Peaks, the Green Mountains (Vermont), and the Berkshires (Mas-
sachusetts) on a clear day.

Nearest town: Hadley
Total distance: 3.2 miles, out and back
Highest point: 2,650 feet
Vertical gain: 1,500 feet
Approximate hiking time: 4 hours
Difficulty: Moderate

Canine compatibility: Dog-friendly. Dogs
should be on leash around the fire tower. Do
not allow dogs to climb the fire tower!
Map: *USGS Stony Creek Quad* (summit),
Conklingville Quad (trailhead)

Finding the trailhead: At the town hall in the center of Hadley, go 3.0 miles north on Stony
Creek Road (also called Saratoga CR 1). Turn left (northwest) on Hadley Hill Road. Go 4.3 miles,
then turn right (north) on Tower Road (dirt). Go 1.4 miles to the trailhead, which is on the left
(west) side of the road. Trailhead: N43 22.447' / W73 57.048'

The Hike

Located in the Wilcox Lake Wild Forest, a 140,000-acre forest preserve, Hadley
Mountain is the highest point at the southern end of West Mountain, a half-mile-
long ridge. It is a favorite hike in the Saratoga area for the views from its fire tower,
which was placed on the National Register of Historic Places in 2001. While modest
in terms of mileage, it is a persistent climb, which Barbara McMartin, a well-known
Adirondack guidebook author, once described as "one of the most beautiful I have
ever had in the mountains."

From the trailhead, follow the red NYSDEC markers up the broad, rock-strewn
trail. It begins on a moderate slope through a mixed northern forest. Log steps cross
sections of slab to help hold small vestiges of soil on the well-trodden path.

By 0.5 mile the trail becomes predominantly slab as you climb steadily upward.
The slab is smooth underfoot, but use caution, as it can be extremely slick when
wet. As you gain elevation, ironically fewer evergreens grow in the airy, bright forest,
which becomes predominantly birch and maple.

The trail winds around several elongated switchbacks, then resumes its uphill
climb in its original westerly direction. Wild roses and jewelweed bloom beside the
path in early August. At 0.8 mile it reaches a plateau and bends to the right (north).
Though the trees remain tall, your surroundings feel more open and grassy, with
wood asters, black raspberries, and goldenrod coloring the woods around you.

The trail climbs a short, pebbly rise, passing a large boulder with a tree growing
on its top. Minutes later, at 1.3 miles, a yellow arrow points the direction (left) at a
sharp bend in the trail.

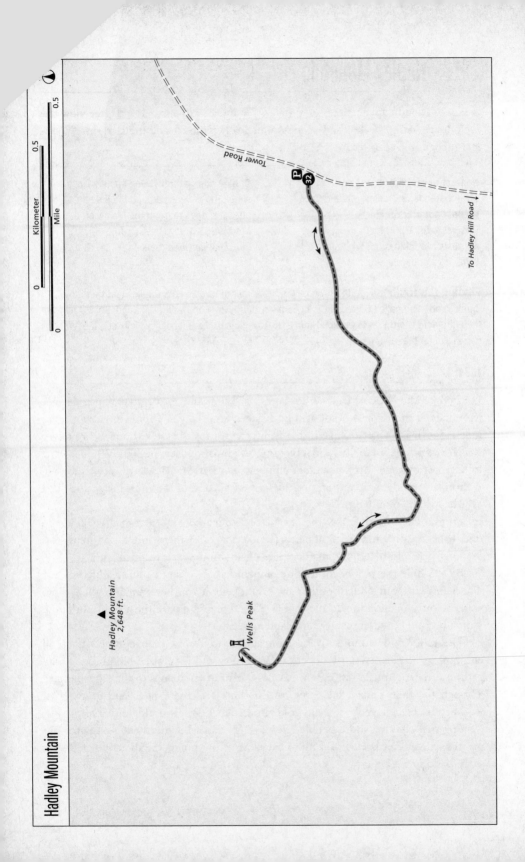

Hadley Mountain

Tower Road

To Hadley Hill Road

P
32

Hadley Mountain
2,648 ft.

Wells Peak

Kilometer

Mile

0   0.5   0.5

The ascent continues on a moderate grade, still in the hardwoods, though they become shorter overhead. After another steep uphill burst, the canopy breaks and you get your first view of Great Sacandaga Lake to the southwest. Great Sacandaga Lake is a 29-mile-long reservoir formed by a dam on the Sacandaga River at its northeast end. In the late nineteenth and early twentieth centuries, the river inundated the Albany area on several occasions, causing extensive damage. The dam has since stemmed the chance of major flood, while creating one of the largest bodies of water within the Adirondack Park.

The trail opens onto ledges that curve around the mountain to the north. You can see Lake George to the northeast extending to the horizon before reentering the trees. The trail climbs easily to the summit

Hikers by fire tower

plateau, passing a spur to the caretaker's cabin and reaching the fire tower just beyond at 1.6 miles.

The original fire tower atop Hadley Mountain was built in 1916 of wood. The steel tower, which stands today, replaced it in 1920. Since 1996 a summit steward has lived in the observer's cabin from July 4th through Labor Day, greeting hikers and answering questions. Hikers receive an "I climbed Hadley Mountain" card, similar to cards that fire-watchers gave out at many of the towers in the Adirondacks when they were still used to detect forest fires. From atop the tower, you can see the High Peaks to the north and the Catskills to the south. The Green Mountains in Vermont lie on the eastern horizon beyond Lake George and Lake Champlain, with the northern tip of the Berkshires to the southeast. The rolling hills of the southern Adirondacks form layers of green and blue to the west.

Return to the trailhead by the same route.

Miles and Directions

- **0.0** Enter the woods on a rock-strewn trail.
- **0.5** Ascend lengths of smooth slab.
- **0.8** Reach a plateau and bend right (north).
- **1.3** Follow the yellow arrow as the trail turns sharply to the left.
- **1.6** FIRE TOWER! Return to the trailhead by the same route.
- **3.2** Arrive back at the trailhead and parking area.

33 Kane Mountain

A short, kid-friendly hike to a restored fire tower and views of the Canada Lake region.

Nearest town: Canada Lake
Total distance: 1.4 miles, out and back
Highest point: 2,180 feet
Vertical gain: 535 feet
Approximate hiking time: 2 hours

Difficulty: Easy
Canine compatibility: Dog-friendly. Dogs should be on leash around the fire tower. Do not allow dogs to climb the fire tower!
Map: USGS Canada Lake Quad

Finding the trailhead: From NY 29A in Canada Lake, turn north on Green Lake Road (dirt). Go 0.6 mile, then bear left at the parking area sign, on a tree to your right. Go 0.1 mile to the trailhead on your left. Parking for hikers is a pullout for 8 to 10 cars opposite the trailhead. Trailhead: N43 10.852' / W74 30.303'

The Hike

Kane Mountain is a small peak on the northwestern side of Green Lake in the Shaker Mountain Wild Forest, a 40,500-acre preserve known for the southern terminus of the Northville–Lake Placid Trail, the "long trail" of the Adirondacks. Though Kane may be a minor peak, it is worth visiting the restored fire tower on its summit for a view of the Catskills to the south, the High Peaks to the north, and the many nearby lakes.

There are three approaches to the mountain, one from the north, one from the south, and a third from the east. The southern route is 0.2 mile shorter, steeper, and without a parking area for hikers. The approach from the north is not clearly marked and crosses a private campground, which charges hikers a fee to pass through. The route described here is from the east. It is slightly longer than the southern route, but it is the most hiker-friendly.

The broad trail departs to the left of the sign-in box, following red NYSDEC markers. It heads northwest at first, climbing steadily on a moderate grade. While some rocks and roots litter the trail, the footing is generally good as you pass through a forest of birch, maple, poplar, and scattered hemlock.

At 0.2 mile the trail bends to the left, heading east. It climbs a couple of short, steep sections that seem easier because of the good footing.

At 0.4 mile you come to a small washout where the trail is worn down to bedrock. The path strays to the right for about 20 yards, where hikers have gone around the washout. It becomes more eroded as you pass through a lawn of ferns beneath the trees, then it arcs left (southwest), continuing to ascend at a moderate rate.

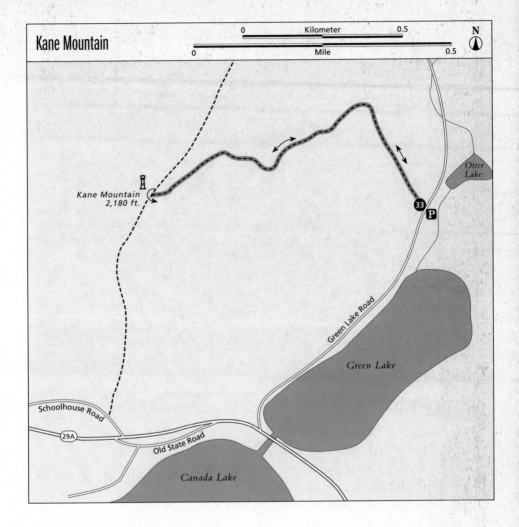

As you traverse a longer length of slab, you sense the top of the hill. At 0.7 miles the trail reaches the summit, passing between the fire tower and the deserted fire-watcher's cabin. Built in 1925, the Kane Mountain fire tower was used for fire detection until 1987, then abandoned. Restored in 1993 by the Canada Lake Protective Association and NYSDEC, it was the second tower, after Goodnow Mountain, to be noted for its historical importance and rejuvenated as a hiking destination in the Adirondack Park. You'll love the breeze on a hot day and the 360-degree view, particularly of sizable Canada Lake to the south. On a windy day, eat lunch on the flat spot just south of the cabin, which is more sheltered than the broad exposed area around base of the tower.

Return by the same route.

Deserted fire-watcher's cabin on Kane Mountain

Miles and Directions

0.0   Take the trail to the left of the sign-in box.

0.2   The trail bends to the left (southwest).

0.4   Climb a small washout where the trail is worn to bedrock.

0.7   FIRE TOWER! Return by the same route.

1.4   Arrive back at the trailhead and parking area.

Central
Adirondacks

T he central Adirondacks are the geographic heart of the Adirondacks. The region is a rough square, bounded by NY 28 and NY 2 between Long Lake Village and North Hudson to the north; US 9 between North Hudson and Lake George Village to the east; the northern quarter of the Wilcox Wild Forest and US 8 to Speculator to the south; and the eastern quarter of the West Canada Lake Wilderness and NY 30 between Blue Mountain Lake and Long Lake Village to the west.

Hiker enjoys view of Indian Lake while climbing Snowy Mountain (Hike 36)

Two U.S. presidents are known to have visited the central Adirondacks. In 1892 Grover Cleveland, no longer in office, visited a famous local guide named Alvah Dunning on the edge of Blue Mountain Lake. In 1901 Theodore Roosevelt was near North Creek when he received word that President William McKinley had died and that he was president of the United States. Among the other famous people to visit area, Thomas Edison used to spend his summers in Blue Mountain Lake, where he wired a local hotel called Prospect House, the first hotel with electricity in the world.

The central Adirondacks offer exceptional hiking for the average person. While the mountains are under the lorded 4,000-foot mark, there are a number of bald summits or fire towers with 360-degree views, which are more accessible than the epic outings in the High Peaks. Though the region was heavily logged, the forests have grown back and are now rich with wildflowers, birds, and animals. Indian Lake lies near the center of the region, but there are dozens of other lakes and ponds, thirty-six in the Siamese Ponds Wilderness alone. Several well-known rivers, including the Hudson and the East Branch Sacandaga Rivers, also flow through the area.

34 Blue Mountain

One of the most popular hikes in the Adirondacks, up a nature trail to a fire tower and a 360-degree view.

Nearest town: Blue Mountain Lake
Total distance: 4.0 miles, out and back
Highest point: 3,750 feet
Vertical gain: 1,537 feet
Approximate hiking time: 4.5 hours

Difficulty: Moderate
Canine compatibility: Dog-friendly. Dogs should be on leash. Do not allow your dog on the fire tower!
Map: *USGS Blue Mountain Quad*

Finding the trailhead: From the junction of NY 28, NY 28N, and NY 30 in the hamlet of Blue Mountain Lake, go 1.4 miles north on NY 28N/NY 30. The trailhead and parking area are on the right (east) side of the road at the top of the hill just beyond the Adirondack Museum. Trailhead: N43 52.475' / W74 25.851'

The Hike

Blue Mountain is one of the most climbed mountains in the Adirondack Park. About 15,000 people ascend to its fire tower along a fourteen-point nature trail each year. If you follow the trail guide available at the sign-in box, over the course of the hike, you get a good sense of the geologic and natural history of the region. Some of the numbered points of the nature trail are included as markers in this trail description.

The route up Blue Mountain (red NYSDEC markers) shares a trailhead with the route to Tirrell Pond (yellow markers). The smooth, flat trail enters the woods, then swings right, just as a smaller footpath from the right joins the main path at a second sign-in box for the nature trail. The path up the mountain begins as a woods road, heading east and climbing gently.

At 0.3 mile the trail passes a "2" on a tree, a marker for the nature trail where a balsam fir grows atop a rock. It crosses a wet area on puncheon steps, then narrows to a footpath, though the path is still obvious and well used.

As you climb through the northern forest, the maples become fewer and the birch and hemlock increase. Painted trillium, hobblebushes, and clintonia bloom beside the trail in early June. The trail flattens as you pass a mature paper birch (#4 on the nature trail), then traverse more lengths of puncheon. At 0.8 mile you cross a pretty stream flowing over some slab (#5), the water from which will eventually end up in the Atlantic Ocean.

Beyond the stream the path gets steeper. Rock steps aid the ascent as the canopy gets thinner above. Then the trail heads downhill briefly, crossing more puncheon, as you pass #7 amidst a stand of paper birch.

After crossing two streamlets the trail climbs again. At 1.2 miles it swings east toward a rise of land, then ascends some rubble and slab. The climb is now more sus-

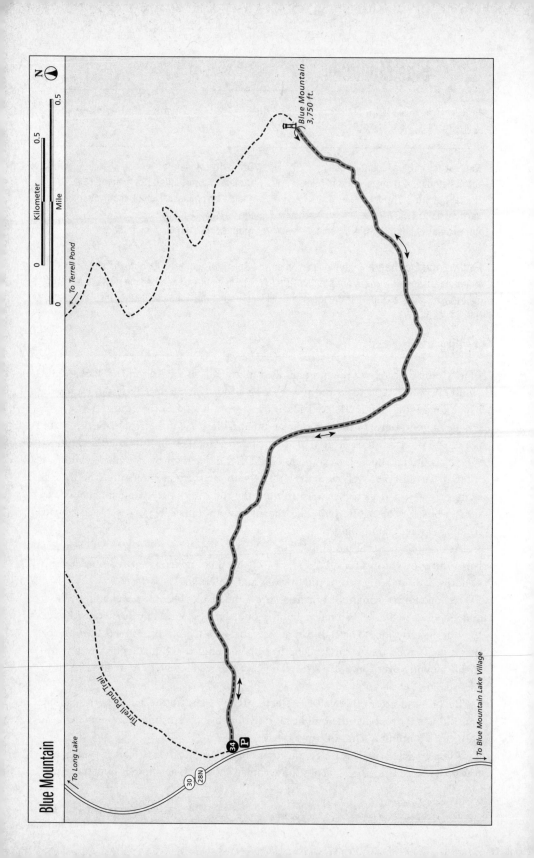

Blue Mountain

To Long Lake

30
28N

Tirrell Pond Trail

P
34

To Blue Mountain Lake Village

To Terrell Pond

Blue Mountain
3,750 ft.

N

Kilometer
0   0.5

Mile
0   0.5

tained—the "real" climb up the mountain—as spruce and other conifers take over the forest mix. The trail is worn to bedrock for most of the steady, steep ascent, which can be slippery if wet.

The grade eases at 1.8 miles (#13) as you near the summit area, winding through stunted evergreens. At 2.0 miles you reach the broad grassy clearing and the fire tower at the top of the mountain. The concrete slabs near the tower are all that remains of the former fire-watcher's cabin.

The view from the tower is an Adirondack favorite, with Blue Mountain Lake and Raquette Lake to the west and the High Peaks on the horizon to the northeast. Snowy and Wakely Mountains, both with fire towers, lie to the south. But more impressive than the peaks is the amount of water all around you. There seems more water than land as you gaze across this region of Adirondacks.

Return to the trailhead by the same route.

Puncheon on the trail up Blue Mountain

Miles and Directions

0.0 From the trailhead, follow the red NYSDEC markers to Blue Mountain.

0.3 Pass a balsam fir tree growing atop a rock (#2 on the nature trail).

0.8 Cross a stream flowing over slab (#5 on the nature trail).

1.2 Swing east and begin the "real" climb.

1.8 The trail eases as you approach the summit plateau.

2.0 FIRE TOWER! Return by the same route.

4.0 Arrive back at the trailhead and parking area.

BALSAM FIR, A USEFUL ADIRONDACK TREE

The balsam fir (*Abies balsamea*) is native to the northeastern United States and is one of the trees most identified with the Adirondacks, perhaps due to its woodsy fragrance. It's impossible to pass through a local gift shop without getting a whiff of balsam from a handmade pillow. Hikers can easily identify the tree from the pleasant aroma it releases as you brush by it along the trail.

Mature balsam firs grow 40 to 60 feet tall, with a narrow crown and scaly bark. Young trees have smooth, gray bark with bubbles of resin that spray when popped. They can grow in a range of moist acidic soils and under the forest canopy.

With its dense short needling and its symmetrical shape, balsam fir is a popular species for Christmas trees and wreaths. Balsam firs have flat needles with a twin stripe on their underside. The needles yield an oil that is used in perfumes and incense. Balsam wood has long fibers, desirable in the manufacture of paper products. Its resin is used as an optical glue and in a local fly repellent called "Save the Baby."

35 Goodnow Mountain

A modest hike along a nature trail to a 60-foot fire tower with breathtaking views of the surrounding mountains, lakes, and ponds.

Nearest town: Newcomb
Total distance: 4.0 miles, out and back
Highest point: 2,664 feet
Vertical gain: 1,035 feet
Approximate hiking time: 4 hours

Difficulty: Moderate
Canine compatibility: Dog-friendly. Dogs should be on leash. Do not allow dogs up the fire tower!
Map: USGS Newcomb Quad

Finding the trailhead: At the junction of NY 30 and NY 28N in Long Lake, travel east on NY 28N toward Newcomb for 11.0 miles. Turn right at the white sign for Goodnow Mountain (not a NYSDEC sign) to find the trailhead and parking area. *Note:* Goodnow Mountain is a day-use area. It is open daily from sunrise to sunset. Trailhead: N43 58.178' / W74 12.864'

The Hike

Named for Sylvester Goodnow, a homesteader who settled at the base of the mountain in the 1820s, Goodnow Mountain is the only hike in this book that is not maintained by the NYSDEC, though the state built the fire tower on its summit. The mountain is located in the Huntington Wildlife Forest, which is owned by the State University of New York (SUNY) College of Environmental Science and Forestry in Syracuse. The forest is a field station for wildlife research and ecology studies. The trail is maintained jointly by SUNY and the Town of Newcomb. Camping, hunting, and plant collecting are not allowed.

Follow the orange markers with black arrows into the woods. As you climb, you also pass by yellow numbered markers that denote stations on the nature trail up the mountain. Look for a brochure inside the sign-in box to help you interpret each point. The trail climbs moderately from the sign-in box up a couple of log ties and then comes almost immediately to a highly constructed wooden staircase with a handrail.

The wide trail bends right (north) and flattens, crossing a wet area. At 0.1 mile it passes over a streamlet on a bog bridge, heads downhill, and crosses another length of puncheon before resuming the climb.

The smooth trail rolls past towering beech, birch, maple, and hemlock. At 0.6 mile the trail turns upward over railroad-tie steps and another bog bridge. Partway up the slope a mature yellow birch grows atop a large rock. Its roots sprawl down the sides of the rock like a giant octopus reaching its tentacles toward the ground.

After passing a bench the climb becomes more persistent but mellows ten minutes later as it bends to the left (south). At 1.4 miles the trail bends left (north), then

Tree roots over rock

ascends up a long length of slab. It traverses a long arcing bog bridge and then comes to the foundation of a cabin. A short spur leads to an old well.

After passing the remains of another old cabin, it crosses a long length of puncheon, then ascends in waves toward the summit. Evergreens take over the forest mix as you sense the elevation gain.

The trail narrows and feels like a long skinny terrace on the side of the mountain. At 1.8 miles you pass another bench, this one with a view of the hills to the southwest. The trail dips off this high shoulder of the mountain, then continues through conifers, climbing moderately. *Note:* Some of the trail markers are now red NYSDEC markers.

After crossing several lengths of slab, you arrive at the fire tower at 2.0 miles. The tower is enclosed, providing welcome protection from the elements and the bugs. The names of the fire-watchers who were stationed here during the tower's working life, from 1922 to 1979, are inscribed on the map inside the high cabin. The circular map helps you navigate around the panorama. Rich Lake is below you to the north, with the Seward and Santanoni Ranges, Algonquin Peak, and Mounts Colden and Marcy in the distance.

Return by the same route.

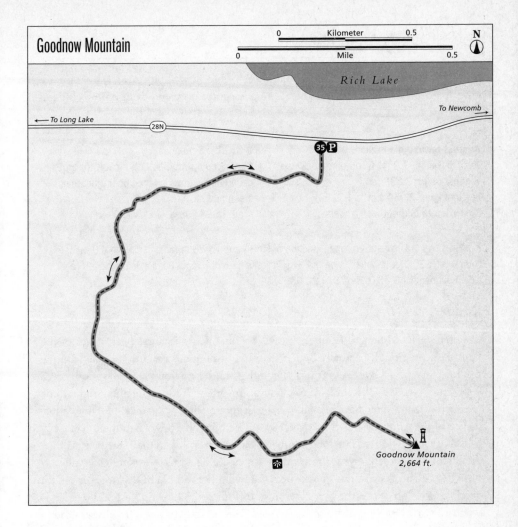

Goodnow Mountain

0   Kilometer   0.5

0   Mile   0.5

N

Rich Lake

To Newcomb

←— *To Long Lake*

28N

35 P

Goodnow Mountain
2,664 ft.

Miles and Directions

0.0   Climb up log ties and a wood staircase just above the sign-in box.

0.1   Cross a streamlet on a bog bridge.

0.6   Climb upward over railroad-tie steps.

1.4   The trail bends left. Pass the remains of two cabins on long stretches of puncheon.

1.8   Pause at a bench with a view to the southwest.

2.0   FIRE TOWER! Return by the same route.

4.0   Arrive back at the trailhead and parking area.

36 Snowy Mountain

A multifaceted hike, with wildlife, wildflowers, a brook, and old-growth trees on the long approach to the mountain, then a steep ascent with views from both a cliff and a fire tower.

Nearest town: Indian Lake
Total distance: 7.2 miles, out and back
Highest point: 3,898 feet
Vertical gain: 2,054 feet
Approximate hiking time: 7 hours

Difficulty: Strenuous
Canine compatibility: Dog-friendly for experienced hiking dogs, as the upper mountain is steep and rocky
Map: USGS Snowy Mountain Quad

Finding the trailhead: From the junction of NY 30 and NY 28 in Indian Lake, go 6.9 miles south on NY 30. The trailhead is on the right (west) side of the road. Parking is on the left (east) side. Trailhead: N43 42.078' / W74 20.089'

The Hike

Originally named Squaw Bonnet, Snowy Mountain is the tallest peak south of the High Peaks region. It's actually higher than two mountains that are included among the forty-six peaks over 4,000 feet. Though #45, Nye Mountain (elevation 3,895 feet), and #46, Couchsachraga Peak (elevation 3,820 feet), made the original cut, measuring techniques have become more accurate since Verplanck Colvin's initial survey of the Adirondacks in the late 1800s. The hike up Snowy Mountain certainly feels like a 4,000-footer. The long approach warms up your legs for a steep climb, then the scramble up a lengthy washout on its upper slope adds interest and challenge.

The trail climbs past the sign-in box, following the red NYSDEC markers, but it quickly levels off above the box on a smooth footpath. The path passes by *big* hardwoods. Try to hug one of these huge trees. Your arms barely reach halfway around their trunks.

The trail rolls along, sometimes heading uphill and sometimes heading downhill, passing a hollow tree at one point on your right. Trillium, clintonia, foam flowers, white baneberry, and violets bloom throughout the woods in early June. At 0.7 mile a length of puncheon leads to a streamlet and then a muddy area, but plenty of well-placed stones help keep your feet dry.

After crossing more puncheon surrounded by jewelweed and passing a number of old blowdowns, Beaver Brook babbles below on your right. The trail dips over a small tributary, then at 1.2 miles it crosses the brook on large stones.

The trail climbs out of the brook hollow up log steps, then resumes its smooth, easy climb. The path dips, then flattens, passing through a hobblebush hedge. At 1.4 miles you cross a small backwater. Look for 4-inch brook trout in the little pond and deer tracks in the mud.

At 1.9 miles the trail comes alongside Beaver Brook, then crosses it. Continue up the gentle slope on left side of the brook. A short time later, at 2.0 miles, the trail crosses the brook again. Stay parallel to the brook, now along its right bank.

The path winds through a confluence of streams that feed the brook. It ascends a half-dozen stone steps, then at 2.4 miles the real climb begins. The trail is not only steep and sustained but noticeably rougher like a dry streambed, and it can be wet after rain.

Soon more evergreens work their way into the forest mix, and you start to see sky through the treetops. By 3.0 miles firs and hemlocks take over, with some white birch scattered throughout the forest

Hiker pausing by backwater on the approach to Snowy Mountain

mix. You can glimpse Indian Lake on your right through the trees.

The trail eases for a moment, then resumes its upward climb. The ascent is moderate at first over a short stretch of slab, then it becomes the steepest of the route as you start up a washed-out slope. The hiking can be wet and tricky as you scramble up the rocks. It feels almost vertical in places. Then, at 3.5 miles you break out atop a cliff with a great view of Indian Lake and layers of mountain to the east. A sign and an arrow point the way to the fire tower.

Above the cliff the walking is easier on a smooth, soft trail through boreal forest. The tower peeks out up above the trees, then, at 3.6 miles, quite suddenly you are there!

It's an awesome view from the restored 50-foot fire tower on the summit, especially of Indian Lake and the Siamese Ponds Wilderness beyond to the southeast. The West Canada Wilderness lies to the southwest. The Blue Ridge Wilderness is to the northwest. Miles of forest surround you, giving a real appreciation of how expansive the backcountry in the central Adirondacks is.

Return by the same route.

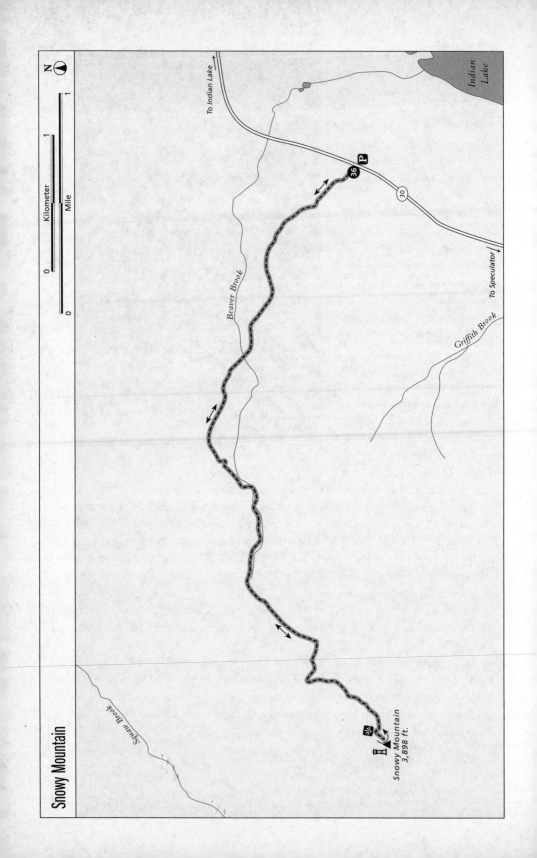

Snowy Mountain

N

Kilometer
0   1

Mile
0   1

To Indian Lake

Beaver Brook

30

36

P

To Speculator

Griffith Brook

Squaw Brook

Snowy Mountain
3,898 ft.

Miles and Directions

0.0 From the trailhead, climb past the sign-in box to smooth, level ground.

0.7 Cross puncheon, then a muddy area on well-placed stones.

1.2 Cross Beaver Brook on large stones.

1.4 Look for small brook trout and deer tracks as you cross a small backwater.

1.9 Recross Beaver Brook, continuing along its right bank.

2.0 Cross the brook again and stay parallel to the brook, now along its right bank.

2.4 Wind through a confluence of streams, then ascend stone steps to begin the "real climb."

3.0 Glimpse Indian Lake to the east through the trees.

3.5 Break out atop a cliff, then follow the sign and arrow toward the summit.

3.6 FIRE TOWER! Return by the same route.

7.2 Arrive back at the trailhead.

37 Vanderwhacker Mountain

A long approach past a couple of beaver ponds, then an ascent to a fire tower and a 360-degree view that includes the High Peaks, Hoffman Notch, and Siamese Ponds wilderness areas.

Nearest town: Newcomb
Total distance: 5.2 miles, out and back
Highest point: 3,389 feet
Vertical gain: 1,679 feet
Approximate hiking time: 5.5 hours

Difficulty: Strenuous
Canine compatibility: Dog-friendly. Dogs should be on leash. Do not allow dogs on the fire tower.
Map: USGS *Vanderwhacker Mountain Quad*

Finding the trailhead: From Newcomb, take NY 28N east for 10.2 miles. At a bridge over the Boreas River, turn right at the sign for Vanderwhacker Mountain (dirt road). Go 2.6 miles past a number of campsites and over old railroad tracks. At the fork bear right, following the arrow and the sign that says TRAIL TO VANDERWHACKER MOUNTAIN FIRE TOWER. The trailhead and parking area is 100 yards up a short hill. From Minerva, travel 8.3 miles north/west on NY 28N. Just after the Boreas River bridge, turn left at the sign for Vanderwhacker Mountain. Trailhead: N43 52.790' / W74 03.532'

The Hike

Vanderwhacker Mountain is the highest point in the 92,000-acre Vanderwhacker Mountain Wild Forest. It is an appealing hike for its mossy streams, wildflowers, and of course, the view from its fire tower. The original wooden fire tower was built in 1911, then replaced in 1918 with the metal one that stands here today. Though decommissioned in 1988, it remains a pleasing destination for hikers.

The route to the tower begins as a woods road. It passes the sign-in box, following red NYSDEC markers and white snowmobile trail markers, as snowmobiles are allowed on public land designated as "wild forest" in the Adirondacks. The road climbs gently to a stream on your left, then narrows to a footpath as it immediately winds away from the stream. It rolls through lush temperate rain forest, heading to the northwest.

At 0.3 mile you come alongside another stream, then cross it before heading up a rise. A few minutes later the trail passes a swamp on your right with an old beaver lodge at the far end.

At 0.6 mile you cross a stream on an old log bridge. The path is wet on the far side, with assorted moose and deer tracks embedded in the mud.

Soon you'll pass another beaver-induced swamp on your left. At 0.9 mile, after crossing another streamlet, look for a sign on a tree pointing uphill to a bridge. Take this higher, narrower route, which is the detour around a particularly muddy stretch.

The path becomes a smooth, wide woods road again, doubling as a snowmo-

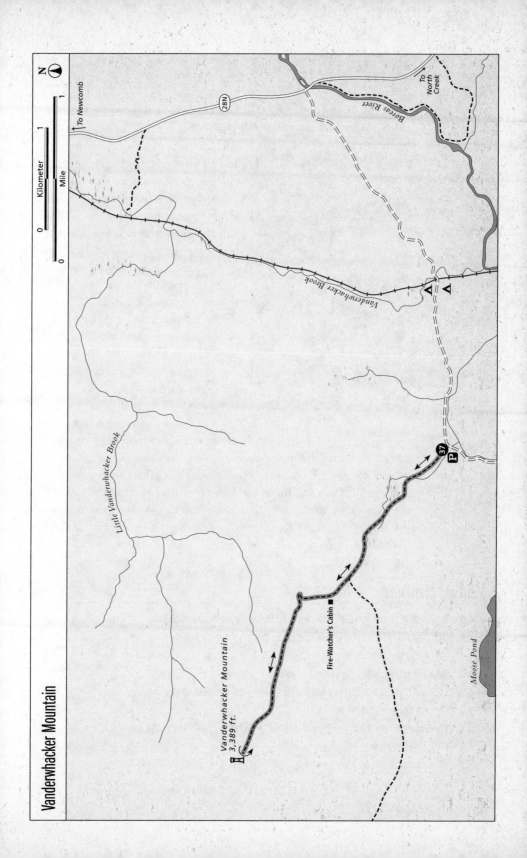

Vanderwhacker Mountain

N

0   Kilometer   1

0   Mile   1

To Newcomb

28N

Boreas River

To North Creek

Vanderwhacker Brook

Little Vanderwhacker Brook

Vanderwhacker Mountain
3,389 ft.

Fire-Watcher's Cabin

37
P

Moose Pond

Author ascends log steps on the trail up Vander-whacker Mountain

bile trail. It bends to the right, heading uphill. After a log water bar and a short rise, you reach the former fire-watcher's cabin at 1.3 miles. The route continues uphill from the left side of the cabin, aided by steps and an elaborate handrail. It's a steep climb but on good footing.

At 1.6 miles the grade moderates as you cross a shoulder of the mountain, then gets steeper again, this time up a rougher, more washed-out section of trail. The roots, rocks, and slab take you into the boreal zone, then the trail smoothes out again.

At 2.1 miles the trail flattens for a moment, then winds up through a long hemlock corridor. The corridor disappears and the canopy opens up as you gain the high ridge of the mountain.

At 2.6 miles you arrive at the fire tower on the summit. The tower is built on a rock knob with an unobstructed view to one side, a nice spot for a picnic. Climb the tower for the best view, which includes the High Peaks region to the north. You can see Hoffman Mountain through Hoffman Notch to the east and Snowy Mountain with its fire tower to the southwest. You can also see a lot of water, including Moose, Beaver, and Split Rock Ponds to the west. On a clear day Lake George shimmers on the horizon to the southeast.

Return by the same route.

Miles and Directions

0.0 Begin on a woods road, double marked for hiking and snowmobiling.

0.3 Come alongside, then cross, a stream before heading up a rise.

0.6 Cross a stream on an old log bridge.

0.9 Take the higher, narrower detour around a muddy area.

1.3 FIRE-WATCHER'S CABIN! Continue uphill from the left side of the cabin.

1.6 Cross a shoulder of the mountain.

2.1 Wind up through a long hemlock corridor to gain the high ridge of the mountain.

2.6 FIRE TOWER! Return by the same route.

5.2 Arrive back at the trailhead and hiker parking area.

38 Wakely Mountain

An uncrowded hike past a beaver pond and then to the top of one of the taller mountains in the region with the tallest fire tower in the Adirondacks.

Nearest town: Indian Lake
Total distance: 5.8 miles, out and back
Highest point: 3,750 feet
Vertical gain: 1,625 feet
Approximate hiking time: 6 hours

Difficulty: Strenuous
Canine compatibility: Dog-friendly. Please keep dogs on leash and off the fire tower.
Map: USGS Wakely Mountain Quad

Finding the trailhead: From the junction of NY 30 and NY 28 in Indian Lake, take NY 30 west for 2.1 miles. Turn left on Cedar River Road at a sharp bend in the road, where there are two signs, one for WAKELY GOLF COURSE and the other, a NYSDEC sign for CEDAR RIVER ENTRANCE, WAKELY MOUNTAIN TRAILHEAD. Go 11.5 miles. The road eventually turns to dirt. Look for the trailhead and parking on the right, though the sign for the trailhead is on the left side of the road. Trailhead: N43 43.897' / W74 28.382'

The Hike

Though the spelling of "Wakely" is slightly different, the mountain was named for William D. Wakeley, an Englishman who extended the road along the Cedar River to Cedar Falls, where he built a dam, a saw-mill, and a hotel. The hike up his namesake peak is two-thirds approach and one-third climb. The nice part of this hike is the lack of crowds, perhaps because it is a longer, bigger peak than nearby Blue Mountain and it's away from the main road.

From the trailhead (red NYSDEC markers), the hike begins on a woods road slightly downhill. Almost immediately you come to a washout and some blowdowns, but a footpath leads you through it and back onto the woods road on the other side.

A stream curves briefly to the right of the road, which then climbs gradually past several clearings. Look for wild raspberries on the right side of the trail in the third clearing.

At 1.0 mile two large rocks form a portal to a footbridge over a stream. Beyond the stream the trail continues smooth and flat,

View from Wakely's fire tower over the fire-watcher's cabin

Wakely Mountain

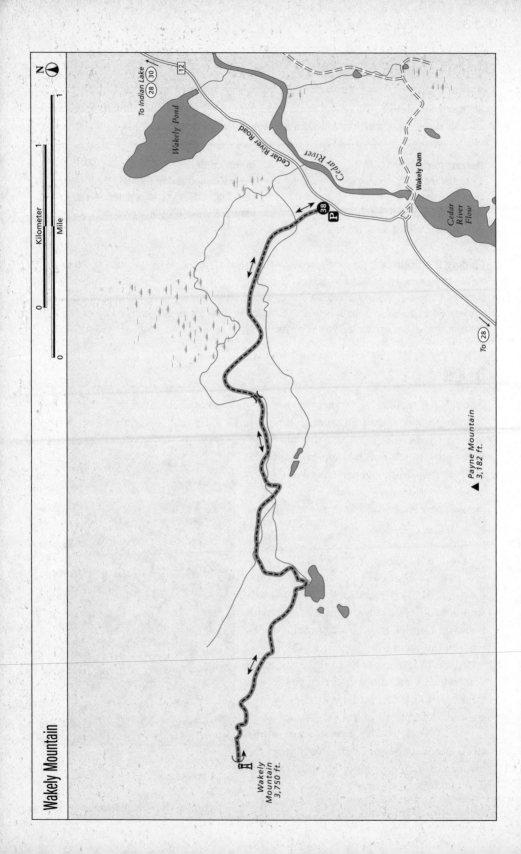

no longer resembling a road, though it is obviously the continuation of it. The path follows the stream, gradually rising above it. In places saplings arch over the trail like a leafy tunnel.

After crossing the streamlet the trail comes to the edge of a sizable beaver pond, where it bends sharply right (northwest) and narrows to a true footpath as the real climb begins. The ascent is steep and direct at first, but soon a flat spot gives a brief reprieve. As you climb, the trail becomes rougher and eroded down to bedrock in places.

At 2.3 miles the trail bends right (northeast) for a short way. You begin to sense the elevation gain as the trees become predominantly conifers. The path winds up the mountain, not exactly through switchbacks but better than a direct ascent.

Beaver-chewed tree

At 2.8 miles the trail bends left onto whitish slab. A break in the trees to the left (southeast) reveals Snowy Mountain on the next ridge and the Cedar River below it. As the trees become shorter and the canopy opens above your head, you pass the spur to a cabin on your right. All that remains is the floor.

The trail curves left, traversing the summit area and reaching the fire tower and fire-watcher's cabin at 2.9 miles. There is a fire pit in the middle of the clearing between the tower and the cabin. The tower is exceptionally tall, about 90 feet high, and considered the highest fire tower in the Adirondacks. It is not maintained like the towers on shorter, more popular routes. There is no mesh on the landings, and a short metal ladder rather than stairs takes you into the tower's cabin. This tower is not for someone who is scared of heights, but it's worth the climb for the view. From the top of the Wakely fire tower, you feel as if you can see farther than from atop other peaks in the region. Snowy Mountain and the Cedar River Flow lie to the southwest. The High Peaks stab the sky to the northeast and Long Lake lies to the east.

Miles and Directions

0.0 Begin on a woods road slightly downhill.

1.0 Pass between two large rocks to cross a footbridge over a stream.

2.0 Turn left, heading uphill at the edge of a beaver pond.

2.3 Sense the elevation gain as the trail bends right (northeast) for a short way.

2.8 The trail bends left onto whitish slab. Check out the view through a break in the trees just before passing the floor of a old cabin.

2.9 FIRE TOWER! Return by the same route.

5.8 Arrive back at the trailhead and parking area.

West-Central Adirondacks

I f you are looking for solitude, you will see few others on the trails in the west-central Adirondacks, though there are many beautiful places to visit. Only a couple of modest mountaintops but a plethora of lovely lakes, rivers, ponds, swamps, and bog lands await those who venture into this peaceful part of the Adirondack Park. The region was heavily logged, then ravaged by fire, but the forests have largely recovered and blanket the region with an array of northern hardwoods and conifers.

Traveling counterclockwise, the west-central Adirondacks extend west from Blue Mountain Lake toward the boundary of the Adirondack Park near Lowville; down the western edge of the park to Hinckley Reservoir; along US 8 to Hoffmeister; then north through the Canada Lake Wilderness along the Cedar River Flow to Blue Mountain Lake. While the hikes in this chapter are not particularly long or challenging, they will take you to four special places, each with a view of water and each lovely in a unique way.

When hiking the west-central Adirondacks, be sure to wear waterproof, breathable footwear as the route may be wet, and bring a generous supply of bug repellent. The hikes described here are particularly appealing from late September through early October, when the leaves are aflame with color, though they are enjoyable any time of the year.

◀ *Lean-to by Middle Settlement Lake*

39 Bald Mountain (Rondaxe)

A kid-friendly hike, even for small children, with a number of cliff-top views en route to a fire tower.

Nearest town: Eagle Bay
Total distance: 2.0 miles, out and back
Highest point: 2,313 feet
Vertical gain: 353 feet
Approximate hiking time: 2 hours

Difficulty: Easy
Canine compatibility: Dog-friendly. Dogs should be on leash. Do not allow dogs to climb the fire tower!
Map: *USGS Eagle Bay Quad*

Finding the trailhead: From the junction of Big Moose Road and NY 28 in Eagle Bay, go 4.6 miles west on NY 28. Turn right at the Bald Mountain Trailhead sign. Go 0.2 mile, then turn left at the Rondaxe Trailhead sign, into the trailhead parking lot. Trailhead: N43 44.732' / W74 54.009'

The Hike

There are sixteen Bald Mountains in New York State. This one is tagged with the suffix "Rondaxe," the name of a lake just to the north. However, the lakes on the other side of the mountain are the main draw on this short hike. Bald Mountain is on the northwestern side of the Fulton Chain of lakes, which begins at Old Forge with First Lake and flows through eight lakes en route to Raquette Lake. The Fulton Chain is a popular canoe route. From Bald Mountain you can see most of the Fulton Chain. It is a classic short mileage/big reward hike, perfect for young children. For a modest effort, you get a number of views along the ledgy climb, then an extraordinary 360-degree view from the fire tower on the summit.

From the trailhead, follow the red NYSDEC markers into a hardwood forest on a broad path. The gentle trail is laced with just enough roots to snag a toe if you're not watching.

At 0.2 mile the trail turns uphill over a length of slab. Stay to the right for the easiest way up the rock, then turn left near the top of the rock to stay on the official trail on top of the ridge, rather than straying into the woods straight ahead.

The trail continues upward over more roots and slab. Soon you can see Fourth Lake through the trees. At a small perch, the trail appears to go left, but bear right up the rock, staying on the ridge.

The trail levels off on slab, passing through shady woods, which cool you on a hot day. At 0.5 mile the canopy breaks above a broader area of bedrock, as the trail passes a lookout. Again the trail looks like it should go right in the woods, but follow the view along the cliff line. Moments later you'll get your first big view of the Fulton Chain.

Just past the overlook, the trail passes over a hump of rock then flattens, winding along the ridgeline. At 0.6 mile it crosses a short, wide bog bridge to another opening on the ledges. Walk farther along the open rock following yellow painted blazes

Hiker departs the summit of Bald Mountain (Rondaxe)

to another view down to the lake and to the mountains at the end of the lake to the east.

The trail continues to traverse the ridge following a rib of rock. At the next long open break in the canopy, you can glimpse the fire tower above the treetops. Bear slightly right away from the edge of the cliff to find the fire tower straight ahead at 1.0 mile.

Built in 1917, Rondaxe Tower was one of 120 fire towers atop peaks in New York in the early twentieth century. Like other fire towers, the original one was built of wood, then later replaced with the steel structure that stands today. The fire-watcher not only looked for forest fires but also recorded all airplanes in the region during World War II. The state retired this tower from active duty in 1990. It reopened in 2005 thanks to efforts by the Friends of Bald Mountain, who maintain it for hikers.

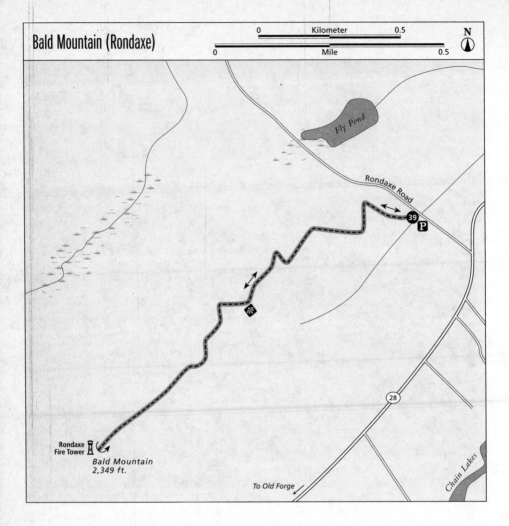

Bald Mountain (Rondaxe)

Fly Pond

Rondaxe Road

39 P

28

Rondaxe
Fire Tower

Bald Mountain
2,349 ft.

To Old Forge

Chain Lakes

The 360-degree view from the top of the tower is pleasing in all directions, but your eyes will be drawn to the panorama from First to Fourth Lakes below. You can also see the ski trails on McCauley Mountain to the west.

Return by the same route.

Miles and Directions

0.0 Begin at the trailhead, following red NYSDEC markers into a hardwood forest.

0.2 Climb a length of slab, then turn left near the top of the slab to stay on the trail.

0.5 See your first view of the Fulton Chain of lakes.

0.6 Cross a short, wide bog bridge to another opening on the ledges.

1.0 FIRE TOWER! Return by the same route.

2.0 Arrive back at the trailhead.

40 Black Bear Mountain

A kid-friendly hike with a fun rock scramble up a rock chimney and a nice view of Seventh Lake from the summit.

Nearest town: Eagle Bay
Total distance: 4.0 miles, out and back
Highest point: 2,454 feet
Vertical gain: 702 feet
Approximate hiking time: 4 hours

Difficulty: Easy
Canine compatibility: Not dog-friendly due to 20-foot rock chimney
Map: USGS Eagle Bay Quad

Finding the trailhead: From the junction of Big Moose Road and NY 28 in Eagle Bay, take NY 28 east 1.1 miles toward Inlet. The trailhead and parking area are on the left (north) side of the road. Trailhead: N43 45.848' / W74 47.632'

The Hike

Located in the Moose River Plains Wild Forest at the northeastern end of Fourth Lake, Black Bear Mountain is appropriately named. If you are observant, you will likely see bear tracks and scat in the clearings beside the lower trail, along with signs of deer and other wildlife. This hike is also appealing for the fun climb up the ledgy upper mountain and the view from the cliff at its summit.

Black Bear Mountain shares its trailhead and parking area with Rocky Mountain. The route up Black Bear Mountain leaves from the right (east) side of the parking lot, following the yellow NYSDEC markers. It crosses an old railroad bed, bending left (north) into the woods. It is a ski trail in the winter, and it is not open to motor vehicles.

From the sign-in box, the smooth path (a woods road) heads into the hardwood forest. At 0.2 mile the woods road seems covered with cobblestones as it begins to climb gently. It becomes extra-broad with logs embedded in places to help stabilize the soil.

After passing a small clearing, the woods road narrows, becoming more like a footpath, but it widens again at the next small clearing. At 0.8 mile, just before reentering the woods, the trail comes to a fork. Bear right (east), heading uphill.

The route becomes a super-trail again. After passing another small clearing, it bends northeast, crossing some slab and becoming flat. Look for signs of deer and bear as you cross a muddy area.

At 1.0 mile you cross a footbridge. Eventually the woods road begins to climb again, heading east. There are more washed-out, eroded spots.

The road narrows to a footpath partway up the slope. After leveling off it continues to wind through the forest, then dips. At 1.6 miles the path swings back to the east, ascending gently. An enormous conifer stands guard beside the trail on your left.

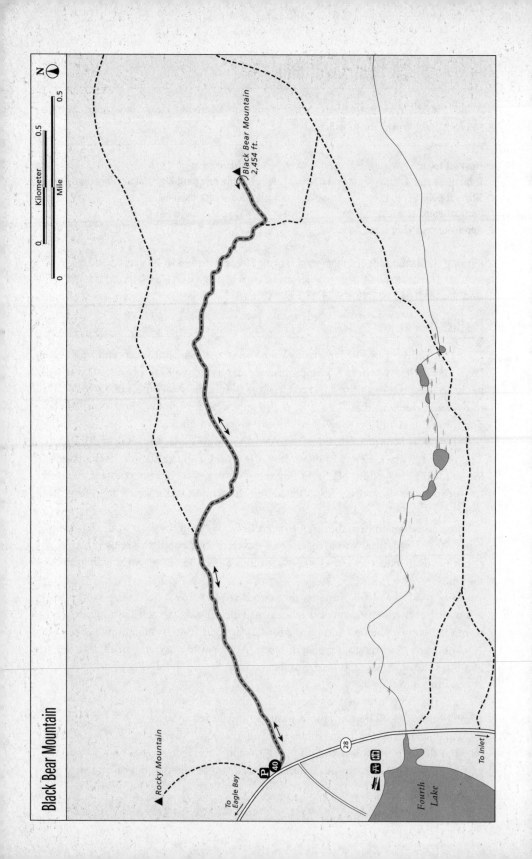

Black Bear Mountain

Rocky Mountain ▲

To
Eagle Bay

P
40

To Inlet

28

Fourth
Lake

▲ Black Bear Mountain
2,454 ft.

N

Kilometer
0   0.5

0   0.5
Mile

Hiker on the summit of Black Bear Mountain

At 1.8 miles you come to the junction with the trail from Seventh Lake. Continue straight, beginning the more aggressive part of the climb. The trail heads up through a jumble of rocks and roots following both blue and yellow markers. The summit looms ahead through the trees.

At 1.9 miles the path is blocked by a 20-foot rock chimney, which is more fun than challenging to climb. Above the ledge the trail angles south, climbing persistently, now following only blue markers. After more slab and ledge, a nice view to the southwest, mainly of nearby hills, opens up, then another view appears behind you of Fourth Lake.

The trail flattens over a length of slab, reaching the summit at 2.0 miles. The top of Black Bear Mountain is an elongated rock plateau with a nice view to the south of Seventh Lake, with Sixth Lake to the southwest beyond a hump of land. In the fall the summit area is ablaze with color, from the maples and from the red berries and colorful leaves of the mountain ash.

Return by the same route.

Miles and Directions

0.0 Follow the broad path (woods road) into the hardwood forest.

0.2 Climb gently on a wide cobblestone-like path.

0.8 Bear right (east) at the fork, heading uphill.

1.0 Cross a footbridge.

1.6 Swing back to the east and ascend gently past an enormous conifer.

1.8 At the junction with the trail from Seventh Lake, continue straight, beginning the more aggressive part of the climb.

1.9 Climb a 20-foot chimney.

2.0 SUMMIT! Return by the same route.

4.0 Arrive back at the trailhead and parking area.

41 Gleasmans Falls

A tranquil trek through airy woods to a gorge that's surprisingly dramatic even during periods of low water.

Nearest town: Crystal Dale	**Approximate hiking time:** 4 hours
Total distance: 5.4 miles, out and back	**Difficulty:** Moderate
Highest point: 1,320 feet	**Canine compatibility:** Dog-friendly
Vertical gain: Under 100 feet	**Map:** USGS Crystal Dale Quad

Finding the trailhead: From Lowville, take Number Four Road east into the Adirondack Park. In Crystal Dale turn right (south) on Erie Canal Road. Go 2.9 miles, then turn left on McPhilmy Road, which turns to dirt. Go 0.7 mile, then turn left on Beach Mill Road (no sign). Go 1.5 miles, then bear left at the fork, continuing on Beach Mill Road. The road narrows to one lane. Go 2.2 miles to the end of the road and the trailhead sign for Beach Millpond.

From Eagle Bay, at the junction of NY 28 and Big Moose Road, turn left (north) on Big Moose Road (CR 1). Big Moose Road becomes Stillwater Road (dirt) just beyond Big Moose. Go 9.0 miles on Stillwater Road to its end. Turn left (southwest) on Number Four Road (no sign). Go 7.8 miles. The road turns back to pavement near Crystal Lake. At the T, turn south on Number Four Road toward Lowville. Go 8.5 miles. Turn left on Erie Canal Road. Go 2.9 miles, then turn left on McPhilmy Road, which turns to dirt. Go 0.7 mile, then turn left on Beach Mill Road (no sign). Go 1.5 miles. Bear left at the fork, continuing on Beach Mill Road. The road narrows to one lane. Go 2.2 miles to the end of the road and the trailhead for Beach Millpond. Trailhead: N43 48.503' / W75 16.569'

The Hike

Located in the Independence River Wild Forest, a 673-acre state forest named for the trout stream that flows through it, Gleasmans Falls is an impressive series of cascades on the Independence River that churns through a long gorge with 30-foot rock walls. The roaring gorge lies in stark contrast to the peaceful northern forest that surrounds it. In late September the many maples seem to glow red, giving warm highlights to the canopy as the sun filters through the foliage. This is a wonderful hike if you are looking for solitude, especially midweek. Many days you'll see more deer tracks than human ones.

From the trailhead, follow signs and the yellow NYSDEC markers toward the Independence River. The trail is wide and smooth, heading downhill to a substantial bridge over Burnt Creek. Bear left off the bridge, passing the sign-in box as you head deeper into the forest.

At 0.6 mile the trail climbs over a low hill, then bends to the southeast.

At 1.1 miles you come to an old, grown-in beaver pond. A bog bridge, then a footbridge aid your passage through the southwestern edge of the swamp. In addition to the beaver lodge in the middle of the swamp, look for deer tracks and signs of other animals.

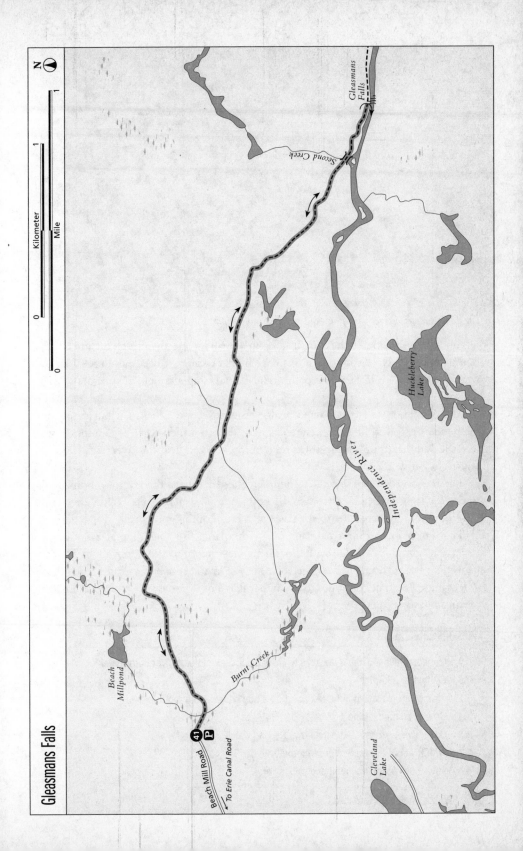

Gleasmans Falls

N

Kilometer
0   1

Mile
0   1

Beach
Millpond

41 P
Beach Mill Road
To Erie Canal Road

Burnt Creek

Independence River

Cleveland
Lake

Huckleberry
Lake

Second Creek

Gleasmans
Falls

The Independence River as it flows out of Gleasmans Falls

At 1.4 miles the trail bends north, goes up a small incline, then levels off and bends back to the east. As it heads down from the height of land, it becomes grassy, like an overgrown lawn. From here, the path undulates, crossing a couple of streamlets at its low spots.

At 2.5 miles a well-constructed bridge crosses Second Creek, a tributary of the Independence River. The creek water is dark due to a high level of tannins. From here, the path heads up a steep, short rock hump. You can hear the river ahead and to your right, but you can't see it yet.

The trail passes a large boulder, then descends sharply to the river. An unmarked spur to the right gives a nice view to the bottom of Gleasmans Falls. Follow the main trail to the southeast, parallel to the river, to the top of the gorge wall.

The trail passes an informal campsite with a large fire ring, then at 2.7 miles it breaks out onto a rock ledge with a dramatic view down to the water, about 30 feet below. The water thunders over the rocks in a dramatic series of cascades, each 5 to 10 feet high. The trail continues to the upper falls, but this is as nice a place as any for a picnic and to enjoy the view.

Miles and Directions

0.0 From the trailhead, head downhill to cross a substantial bridge over Burnt Creek.

0.6 Climb over a low hill.

1.1 Traverse an old grown-in beaver pond on a bog bridge and a footbridge.

1.4 Go over a small incline.

2.5 Cross a well-constructed bridge over Second Creek.

2.7 WATERFALLS! Return by the same route.

5.4 Arrive back at the trailhead and parking area.

ADIRONDACK BEAVERS

Few animals have had as much impact on a region as the beaver (*Castor canadensis*) has on the Adirondacks. Easily identified by its black, flat, scaly tail, the beaver is the largest rodent in the park, and they're widespread. Beavers can be found along most waterways here.

New York's state mammal, the average beaver is about 40 inches long and weighs about 45 pounds. Historically, they were prized for their fur. Trapping beavers was among the first reasons Europeans ventured into the Adirondacks. In the early 1600s fur traders had decimated the beaver populations elsewhere in the state, so they began to venture into this remote region. By 1900 most of the beavers in the Adirondacks had been trapped as well. In 1903 the state legislature appropriated $500 to bring back the beaver. About fifty were released into the Adirondack Park, and they flourished.

Today there are between 50,000 and 75,000 beavers in the Adirondacks. Their dams, lodges, burrows, stumps, and trails leave an unmistakable mark on the landscape. For hikers, these flat-tailed rodents are both a blessing and a curse. They create expansive wetlands that range from open ponds to grassy marshes, which are interesting to observe and break up the monotony of a woodland walk. Yet often they are the cause of flooding, which can lead to problems as minor as damp feet or as serious as an impassable trail.

Swimming beaver

42 Middle Settlement Lake

A forest walk past a large pond to a remote, scenic lake with both a primitive campsite and a lean-to on its northern and western shores.

Nearest town: Thendara
Total distance: 6.0 miles, out and back
Highest point: 1,875 feet
Vertical gain: 254 feet

Approximate hiking time: 5 hours
Difficulty: Moderate
Canine compatibility: Dog-friendly
Map: USGS Thendara Quad

Finding the trailhead: From the junction of NY 28 and Watson Road near the Thendara railroad station, go 2.7 miles west on NY 28. The large paved trailhead parking lot is on the left (southeast) side of the road. The trailhead is on the opposite side of the road, just west of the parking lot. The sign at the trailhead says ACCESS TO STATE LAND. Trailhead: N43 40.615' / W75 03.119'

The Hike

Middle Settlement Lake is located in the middle of the 26,528-acre Ha-de-ron-dah Wilderness, the westernmost wilderness area in the Adirondack Park. Ha-de-ron-dah is another version of the native word "bark eater," from which the name "Adirondack" is derived.

The Ha-de-ron-dah Wilderness is part of a larger 210,000-acre piece of land known as John Brown's Tract. There were two John Browns of historical significance in the Adirondacks: the abolitionist who lived and was eventually buried near Lake Placid, and the millionaire John Brown of Providence, Rhode Island, for whom Brown University is named. In 1798 the latter Brown took over this huge piece of the Adirondacks in an attempt to salvage a deal of his son-in-law's that had gone sour. He put in a rough wagon road, part of which the trail to Middle Settlement Lake follows today, in an attempt to subdivide and sell land to farmers, but the plan failed due to the inhospitable climate and poor soil conditions.

There is a web of trails to the various lakes that speckle the Ha-de-ron-dah Wilderness. You can string together a number of routes of varying lengths, any of which would make a nice backcountry camping trip, especially with kids, since the terrain is generally flat. The hike into Middle Settlement Lake is described here as a day hike, but it can be an overnighter if you would like more time to enjoy the lake.

From the trailhead, a footbridge leads immediately to the sign-in box. Follow the red NYSDEC markers, climbing a couple of rock steps and then a short steep slope through lush ferns. The canopy breaks briefly at the top of the knob as you cross over a stretch of slab. Descend gradually off the other side, heading deeper into the woods.

The trail descends to a footbridge over what one hiker described as a "streamy swamplet," then climbs moderately up another short rise.

Hiker by Middle Settlement Lake

After traversing a couple of mud holes, the path begins a long, gentle descent. At 0.6 mile it comes to a T. The route to the right goes to Middle Branch Lake. Turn left, continuing to the southwest, now following yellow markers.

The trail continues on a flat, sometimes gentle downhill stroll through an upland forest with many maple and beech in the mix. At 0.8 mile you cross another muddy area and climb another small rise. The terrain is so flat here that you notice every nuance of the topography.

At 1.5 miles you reach the junction with the Stony Creek Trail. Turn right (northwest), following blue markers.

The trail narrows, though it is still easy to follow and the footing remains nice. It dips over a grassy, wet spot at the neck of a pond, which is really a backwater of Middle Settlement Creek. It gains a height of land then continues to cut through the forest, heading northwest on a long gentle ascent.

At 2.2 miles the path levels off, then begins a gentle descent. It passes over a length of slab, notable only because most of the footing has been soft dirt to this point.

The trail becomes rougher as it swings left (west), coming to a rock wall. It runs parallel to a small stream at the base of the wall for a short way, arriving at the junction with the Cedar Pond Trail at 2.6 miles. Continue straight ahead (west), following the yellow markers.

The trail winds down among a number of large boulders to the edge of a grassy backwater at the northeast corner of Middle Settlement Lake. Bear right over logs

Middle Settlement Lake

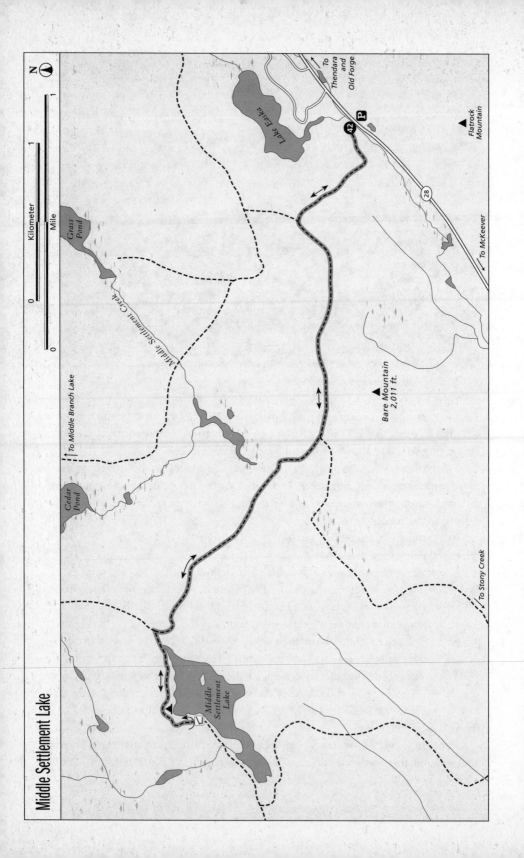

up a rise, following the northern edge of the lake. At 2.8 miles you reach a primitive campsite beside the water. It is a beautiful spot on a broad flat rock, with a fire ring and shaded by tall conifers.

Continue a short way farther along the lake. The trail curls south and soon comes to a lean-to at 3.0 miles. The lean-to sits atop a long rock ledge about 10 feet above the water. Hours quickly melt away in this serene spot, where you feel like the only person in a pristine world.

New York State stocks Middle Settlement Lake with brook trout. There's also largemouth bass and other species in the water. If you are an avid angler, consider carrying a float tube into the lake and casting your line.

Return by the same route.

Miles and Directions

0.0 From the trailhead, cross a footbridge to reach the sign-in box.

0.6 Turn left at the junction with the trail to Middle Branch Lake.

0.8 Cross a muddy area and climb a small rise.

1.5 Turn right at the junction with the Stony Creek Trail.

2.2 Begin a gentle descent, passing over a length of slab.

2.6 Continue straight ahead at the junction with the Cedar Pond Trail.

2.8 CAMPSITE beside the lake! Continue to follow the shore of the lake.

3.0 LEAN-TO! Return by the same route.

6.0 Arrive back at the trailhead and parking area.

Appendix A: For More Information

In case of emergency, dial 911.

Adirondack Mountain Club
Member Services:
814 Goggins Rd.
Lake George, NY 12845
(518) 668-4447
Lodging/Heart Lake Program Center:
Adirondack Loj Road
P.O. Box 867
Lake Placid, NY 12946
(518) 523-3441
www.adk.org

Wood sorel blossom

Adirondack Mountain Reserve-Ausable Club
137 Ausable Rd.
St. Huberts, NY 12943
(518) 576-4411
www.ausableclub.org

Adirondack Trail Improvement Society
P.O. Box 565
Keene Valley, NY 12943
www.atis-web.com

New York State Department of Environmental Conservation
Division of Public Affairs and Education
625 Broadway
Albany, NY 12233
(518) 402-8013
www.dec.ny.gov

NYSDEC Region 5 Office (Adirondack Park)
1115 Route 86
P.O. Box 296
Ray Brook, NY 12977
(518) 897-1200
NYSDEC Campgrounds
(518) 457-2500 for information on day-use areas
www.dec-campgrounds.com
Reserve America
(800) 456-2267 for overnight camping
www.reserveamerica.com

New York State Adirondack Park Agency
1133 Route 86
P.O. Box 99
Ray Brook, NY 12977
www.apa.state.ny.us

Appendix B: Further Reading

There are several hundred books available on Adirondacks natural history, human history, hiking, backpacking, and many other outdoor topics. For hikers and backpackers, the Adirondack Mountain Club publishes a series of "Adirondack Trails" guidebooks, which cover most routes in the six regions of the Adirondack Park (east, north, south, central, west-central, and High Peaks) plus the Northville-Placid Trail.

In addition to the "Adirondack Trails" guidebooks, the following books were helpful in the preparation of this book:

Gange, Jared. *100 Classic Hikes of the Northeast.* Burlington, Vt.: Huntington Graphics, 2005.

McMartin, Barbara. *50 Hikes in the Adirondacks.* Woodstock, Vt.: Backcountry Guides, 2003.

New York Altas & Gazetteer. Yarmouth, Me.: DeLorme, 2008.

Ostertag, Rhonda, and George Ostertag. *Hiking New York.* Guilford, Conn.: FalconGuides, 2002.

Wadsworth, Bruce. *Day Hikes for All Seasons, An Adirondack Sampler.* Lake George, N.Y.: Adirondack Mountain Club, 1996.

Painted trillium

Appendix C: Forty-six over 4,000 Feet

Early surveyors found forty-six peaks in the Adirondacks to be 4,000 feet above sea level or higher. While modern measuring techniques show that four of the original forty-six are actually lower than 4,000 feet, and one—McNaughton Mountain in the Santanoni Range—should be on the list, reaching the top of the original forty-six peaks stands as the requirement for joining the Adirondack Forty-Sixers Club.

In addition to elevation, a peak must be at least 0.75 mile from the nearest higher summit or rise at least 300 vertical feet on all sides in order to qualify as a 4,000-footer. Twenty of the peaks are considered trail-less as they do not have maintained foot-paths, which adds to the challenge. Here is the official list. If the name of a mountain is followed by an asterisk (★), a route up that mountain is described in this book:

1. Mount Marcy★, 5,344
2. Algonquin Peak★, 5,114
3. Mount Haystack, 4,960
4. Mount Skylight, 4,926
5. Whiteface Mountain★, 4,867
6. Dix Mountain, 4,857
7. Gray Peak, 4,840, no trail
8. Iroquois Peak, 4,840, no trail
9. Basin Mountain, 4,827
10. Gothics★, 4,736
11. Mount Colden, 4,714
12. Giant Mountain★, 4,627
13. Nipple Top, 4,620
14. Santanoni Peak, 4,607, no trail
15. Mount Redfield, 4,606, no trail
16. Wright Peak★, 4,580
17. Saddleback Mountain, 4,515
18. Panther Peak, 4,442, no trail
19. Table Top Mountain, 4,427, no trail
20. Rocky Peak Ridge, 4,420
21. Macomb Mountain, 4,405, no trail
22. Armstrong Mountain★, 4,400
23. Hough Peak, 4,400, no trail
24. Seward Mountain, 4,361, no trail
25. Mount Marshall, 4,360, no trail
26. Allen Mountain, 4,340, no trail
27. Big Slide Mountain★, 4,240
28. Esther Mountain, 4,240, no trail
29. Upper Wolfjaw Mountain★, 4,185

Orange Hawkweed, also called Devil's Paintbrush

30. Lower Wolfjaw Mountain★, 4,175
31. Street Mountain, 4,166, no trail
32. Phelps Mountain, 4,161
33. Mount Donaldson, 4,140, no trail
34. Seymour Mountain, 4,120, no trail
35. Sawteeth, 4,100
36. Cascade Mountain★, 4,098
37. South Dix, 4,060
38. Porter Mountain, 4,059
39. Mount Colvin, 4,057
40. Mount Emmons, 4,040, no trail
41. Dial Mountain, 4,020
42. East Dix, 4,012, no trail
43. Blake Peak, 3,960
44. Cliff Mountain, 3,960, no trail
45. Nye Mountain, 3,895, no trail
46. Couchsachraga Peak, 3,820, no trail

Summit elevations recognized by the Adirondack Mountain Club

Bunchberry

Hike Index

Sidebars

About the Author

Born in Saranac Lake, Lisa Densmore has been hiking, paddling, fishing, and skiing in the Adirondacks for over thirty-five years. Though now a resident of New Hampshire, she travels back to the Adirondacks to visit her family, to spend time in the backcountry, and to enjoy her second home on Chateaugay Lake.

Densmore is best known as the Emmy-winning host and field producer of *Wildlife Journal*. She is also a host of *Windows to the Wild* (PBS) and various feature segments on *RSN Outdoors* (RSN). She also works periodically for other networks that cover sports, adventure, and outdoor programming such as the Outdoor Channel, Versus, and ESPN.

When not on camera, Densmore is usually holding one. A passionate nature photographer, her images have appeared in publications such as *Backpacker, Adirondack Life,* and *Adirondack Explorer*. She has an extensive stock-photo file of the Adirondacks. "If you can see it from a hiking trail, I've probably taken a picture of it," she says. To see more of her award-winning images, visit www.DensmoreDesigns.com.

Densmore complements her visual skills with writing. A freelance writer since 1991, she has written hundreds of articles for almost as many magazines, plus five other books: *Ski Faster, Best Hikes with Dogs: New Hampshire & Vermont, Hiking the Green Mountains* (FalconGuides, 2009), *Hiking the White Mountains* (FalconGuides, 2010), and *Backpaker Magazine's Predicting Weather: Predicting, Forecasting & Planning* (Globe Pequot, 2010).